SPENSER STUDIES

IX

BURGESS
PR
2362
.A45
9
1988

EDITORIAL BOARD

Paul Alpers

Judith Anderson

Donald Cheney

Angus Fletcher

Haruhiko Fujii

Thomas M. Greene

A. C. Hamilton

S. K. Heninger, Jr.

A. Kent Hieatt

John Hollander

William B. Hunter, Jr.

Carol V. Kaske

Robert Kellogg

Richard McCoy

James Nohrnberg

Annabel Patterson

Anne Lake Prescott

G. Foster Provost

John Steadman

Humphrey Tonkin

Joseph Anthony Wittreich

EDITORIAL ASSISTANT
James Pervin,
The Graduate Center, CUNY

SPENSER STUDIES
A Renaissance Poetry Annual
IX

EDITED BY

Patrick Cullen AND *Thomas P. Roche, Jr.*

AMS PRESS, INC.
NEW YORK, N.Y.

SPENSER STUDIES:
A RENAISSANCE POETRY ANNUAL

edited by Patrick Cullen and Thomas P. Roche, Jr.

is published annually by AMS Press, Inc. as a forum for Spenser scholarship and criticism and related Renaissance subjects. Manuscripts must be submitted *in duplicate* and be double-spaced, including notes, which should be grouped at the end and should be prepared according to the format used in this journal. All essay-length manuscripts should enclose an abstract of 100–175 words. They will be returned only if sufficient postage is enclosed (overseas contributors should enclose international reply coupons). One copy of each manuscript should be sent to Thomas P. Roche, Jr., Department of English, Princeton University, Princeton, N.J. 08544 and one copy to Patrick Cullen, 300 West 108th Street, Apt. 8 D, New York, N.Y. 10025.

Copyright © 1991 by AMS Press, Inc.
All rights reserved
Manufactured in the United States of America

ISSN 0195-9468
Volume IX, ISBN 0-404-19209-2

Contents

The distinction between pastoral and georgic has not been observed rigorously enough by critics writing on literature that takes the rural world as its subject. This confusion has led to the inaccurate categorization as pastoral of works more accurately described as georgic. If we redefine these two modes as they are understood in Hesiod, Virgil, and Theocritus, we discover that each mode has a vision of the natural world and a corresponding ethic that contrasts with the others'. Pastoral sees the natural world as harmonious with human desire, making possible an ethic of *otium* or leisure conducive to love and art. Georgic, on the other hand, sees the natural world as fraught with potentially destructive forces requiring from humans an ethic of labor, the work that makes civilization and human identity possible. Most works on the rural world put both these modes in a dialectical relationship in which the attractions and strengths of one counterbalance the inadequacies and weaknesses of the other. Spenser's *Shepheardes Calender*, universally categorized as pastoral, uses just such a rural dialectic to develop the various concerns of religion, morality, and art.

The use of the name "E. K." to designate the author of the critical apparatus of *The Shepherdes Calender* can be explained by referring to the practices of self-naming prevalent among sixteenth-century literary scholars. The most favored of these was hellenization of the literal meanings of surnames. If Spenser had chosen to hellenize his own name, then in everyday use as a synonym for "steward," he would probably have translated it as "Edmundus Kedemon," which, abbreviated, would be "E. K." Though such a device would have been obscure to all but his intimate circle, Spenser's correspondence with Harvey reveals several similar transmutations of their names. Contemporary sources reveal that onomastic riddles were highly fashionable in Elizabethan England, at court and in all classes of society. Spenser's use of such a name as his pseudonym clearly alluded to Renaissance editions of the classics, thus affirming his symbolic poetic lineage (like his other pseudonym, "Immerito") and his self-proclaimed position as the new English Virgil.

Increasing awareness that numerological analysis is crucial to an understanding of Spenser's work has led to an extension of this approach to the jointly-published *Amoretti and Epithalamion*. The latter poem, previously considered separately in Hieatt's seminal analysis, is now shown to be integrally related to the former in a complex pattern of pairs, symmetries and symbolic numbers whose significance is here explored in detail. This underlying structure is seen to have influenced—dictated, even—the form of the poems and, arguably, some elements of their content.

After obtaining the raw materials for *Daphnaida* from the *Book of the Duchess*, Spenser imitates the structure of the same work in his own mythopoeic poem, *Muiopotmos*. The poems need to be considered in tandem as different responses by Spenser to his reading of Chaucer. The Ovidian materials in *Muiopotmos* appear in Chaucer's characteristic panel structure. I propose that we read Spenser's poem in the same way we must read Chaucer's—with attention to how the mythic adaptations relate to one another and to the poem as a whole. Changes in Ovidian and Virgilian material identify human envy and presumption as the main themes of *Muiopotmos*. Each of the perplexing first two stanzas corresponds to one of the two Ovid panels. The "mightie ones" are Athena and Arachne, and the "debate" is the weaving contest retold in the poem. Divine and mortal orders of being conflict, invariably to thè disadvantage of the latter. The substitution of "rancour in the harts of mightie men" (line 16) for Virgil's "resentment in the minds of gods" (*Aeneid* I.11) signifies the human application of the poem. Aragnoll is another Arachne, consumed by envy, and Clarion is another Astery, both victims of envy. The themes of human envy and of the folly of imitating the divine are replayed in the story of Clarion. Aragnoll, the new source of envy, slays Clarion, the new imitator. Clarion is doubly doomed because he is a victim of the envy of a malignant power and because he aspires to the divine; here Spenser successfully combines his two Ovidian subjects, Astery and Arachne.

This paper approaches the "chronicle history" canto of *The Faerie Queene* as two alternate genealogies for Queen Elizabeth. By examining contemporary commentaries on the Biblical "begats" and sermon references to the queen's family tree, it identifies Elizabethan methods of constructing and interpreting genealogies. The two uses Spenser's contemporaries had for genealogy were to establish a claim to the throne and to analyze a contemporary figure's character and place in history. These make excellent panagyric sense of *"Briton moniments"* and *"Antiquitie* of *Faerie* lond," freeing a commentator from the burden of distilling a consistent moral and political message from these pages, while still allowing them to be read as praise.

Scholars have suggested that in Book V of *The Faerie Queene* Spenser twice presents the death of Mary Stuart: once when Britomart strikes down Radigund and again when Mercilla allows the execution of Duessa. It seems more likely, however, that the Radigund episode is altogether concerned with the early years of Mary's career, from Queen Elizabeth's aid to the Scottish Protestants in their rebellion against Mary's mother in 1559–60, to Mary's abdication and flight into England in 1567–68 and her subsequent role in the Rebellion of the Northern Earls and the Ridolphi Plot. Thus interpreted, the episode emerges as the first part of a consistent, chronological account of Elizabeth's long struggle with Mary. It serves not just as an illustration for the moral allegory of justice, but also as a major innovation in the genre of the epic: the representation of a living monarch as the subject of heroic myth.

The echoes from contemporary prefatory addresses to the reader that fill Book VI supply a conceptual framework from within which to approach a book remarkable for its diversity of incident. These prefatory allusions and cross-references not only link the Blatant Beast to the figure of the observer critical of what he sees and hears, but act unmistakably to add the concept of "the courteous reader" to the poet's anatomy of courtesy. Focusing on the Priscilla-Aladine episode and the confrontation between Calidore and Colin Clout, it is demonstrated that prefatory definitions of courteous behavior serve alternately to justify the actions of the knight of courtesy and to pin down what he neglects to do when confronted with the vision on Mt. Acidale. Viewed from this perspective, Canto ix emerges not as an expression of despair that conditions essential to the practice of poetry are unavailable but as an effort to set forth a working model for the relationship between audience and piper that appears to the poet most likely to be mutually productive. Such efforts are consistent with Spenser's overall strategy in Book VI: simultaneously to supply the receptive reader with examples of proper and improper ways to respond to the kinds of incidents that comprise the narrative and to drive home to him the potential consequences that adopting unfriendly or prematurely judgmental postures can carry. This strategy of accommodation marks Book VI as an attempt to deal reasonably with the series of critical audiences with whom Spenser has skirmished throughout the epic, an effort abandoned only in the poem's closing stanzas, where he assumes a more confrontational stance amounting to an outright declaration of war.

"My Sheep are Thoughts": Self-Reflexive Pastoral in *The Faerie Queene*, Book VI and the *New Arcadia*
MARGARET P. HANNAY
137

Conscious that direct speech risked the queen's disfavor, Sir Philip Sidney and Edmund Spenser attempted to teach Queen Elizabeth to read their pastoral fictions aright. In the *New Arcadia* and in *The Faerie Queene*, Book VI they mirror the queen's act of reading within the narrative by dramatizing the process of teaching a princess to read a pastoral fiction. In the *New Arcadia* there are three knights who present self-conscious fictions to princesses: Pyrocles, Musidorus, and Amphialus. In Book VI of *The Faerie Queene*, Spenser ignores the tale of the Amazonian Pyrocles entirely, echoes the tale of Musidorus, and incorporates an ironic element from the tale of "the courteous Amphialus" which may help to explain the dubious success of Calidore, the knight of courtesy. As each shepherd/knight wishes to demonstrate his real status to the princess to win her heart, so the poet/courtier wishes to demonstrate his real worth to the queen to win a position at court. For both poets the problem of Right Reading is given urgency by their own experience of envy and resultant slander, embedded in the narrative by Sidney through the Cecropia/Amphialus plot, allegorized by Spenser in the Blatant Beast.

Spenser and the Judgment of Paris
STANLEY STEWART
161

For centuries critics have recognized a link between Spenser and the Judgment of Paris tradition, which was very popular in Elizabethan literature, especially in renditions of Ovid's *Heroides*. In finely nuanced versions of the narrative, Spenser reverses many thematic arrangements well-established in literature and

iconography of the subject, especially as they treated motifs of marriage and
legitimacy. Spenser not only recreates Paris as a father, but as an exile from
pastoral innocence who willfully abandoned the poetic craft as well. Paridell's
claim that he is descended from Oenone would link him with Britomart, whose
ancestry also leads back to the first family of Troy. In Spenser's retelling of the
story, the situation is, compared to that in *Heroides*, morally ambiguous, elim-
inating, for instance, the ethical claims of Ovid's Helen. Spenser handles the
elements of betrayal of craft and wife with masterful subtlety in the *August*
Eclogue and in the Pastorella episode. In the latter instance, the familiar tableau
of the Judgment of Paris—as represented by Cranach, Rubens, Carracci, and
many others—emphasizes Spenser's emerging theme of the poet's need to
transcend insular dependence on a single kind of love and a single kind of song.
The Judgment of Paris is the inciting incident of a Fall—indeed, this is how we
see it in George Peele, Richard Barnfield, Thomas Heywood, John Trussell, and
many others late in Elizabeth's reign—a Fall from pastoral into moral and poetic
error. But where Paris and Colin suffer only the necessary costs of misguided
choice, the true poet transcends their limitations to explore in cosmic scope the
full power of legitimate Love, whose "substance is eterne." He is the uncompromised heir to the region of Mount Ida: Edmund Spenser.

Rereading Mirabella
ANNE SHAVER
209

Attention to the lengthy but generally neglected Mirabella episode of Book VI
of *The Faerie Queene* reveals discomfort with any challenge to accepted hierarchies of class and gender. Surrounded in the Book of Courtesy by numerous
erring women who are rescued, forgiven, and reformed, she alone is not only
punished for her particular discourtesy, but is punished in such a way as to leave
no hope for redemption. Even so, she refuses Prince Arthur's offer of help for
fear of some "greater ill" than the endless penance imposed on her by Cupid.
Tradition suggests this ill to be the dependency in marriage also avoided by
Elizabeth: thus lowborn Mirabella is made to suffer for gender transgressions
unpunishable in a queen.

Spenser and Ireland: A Select Bibliography
WILLY MALEY
225

Spenser's Irish experiences have traditionally been considered as tangential to his
poetics, even to his politics. As the more familiar sources of Spenser criticism
begin to dry up, a turn towards the poet's Irish context suggests itself as one way
of sustaining interest in his work. The purpose of the present survey of material
on Spenser and Ireland is to help bring in from the margins of the literary canon

an aspect of the poet's life hitherto confined to specialist monographs in learned journals, namely the question of his planter status and the manner in which it impinges upon his writings. Taken as a whole, this material allows for a broad contextual view of an author whose Englishness has always been qualified to a certain degree by his close involvement, for the entirety of his literary career, with England's first colony. The bibliography offered here comprises five basic types of evidence: contemporary descriptions of Ireland and the Irish; modern historiography of the period; secondary criticism of Spenser and Ireland; items relating specifically to Munster, the province with which the poet was most intimately associated; and, finally, biographical information on patrons and acquaintances of Spenser active in Elizabeth's viceregal administration.

BRUCE THORNTON

Rural Dialectic:
Pastoral, Georgic,
and *The Shepheardes Calender*

*W*E NO LONGER have the confidence in genre categories' absolute defining power that the Middle Ages had, when the *rota
Vergiliana*—the hierarchy of genres progressing from pastoral to
georgic to epic—signified a totalizing system extending from
tools to social classes.[1] Today we understand genre in more fluid
terms; as Heather Dubrow suggests, an individual work "relates
to generic norms in much the same way actual physical objects
may relate to the color spectrum: no one genre, no one hue
appears in isolation, and none appears in its purest state."[2] Yet
we still find critically and pedagogically useful genre labels'
defining and identifying power, their seeming ability economi-
cally to categorize and interrelate works into a coherent system.
The result, however, is often an oversimplification of a work, a
reduction of its complexity to the sometimes negative connotations of a given genre label.[3] Pastoral's enduring popularity and
appeal have made "pastoral" particularly susceptible to misuse
and distortion, often at the expense of georgic, its sterner older
cousin also concerned with the rural world.[4] But many works
confidently labelled pastoral actually offer not a dominant coherent conception of the rural world we can name pastoral, but
rather a dialectical tension between the pastoral and georgic
visions, a dialogue between them through which the potential
meaning and significance of the rural world emerge.[5] If we shed
our preconceptions and redefine these two visions as they appear
in Hesiod, Theocritus, and Virgil, we will find just such a rural
dialectic, one that also characterizes later rural poetry such as
Edmund Spenser's *Shepheardes Calender*.

In defining the pastoral and georgic visions, two major contrasts emerge: one between the landscapes imagined, another
between the ethics of which each landscape provides the context

1

and rationale. An important characteristic of pastoral is its idealization of the natural world, its assertion of nature's beauty and
harmony with humans.[6] The georgic, on the other hand, sees the
natural world as fraught with potential disorder and destructiveness—an attitude that dominates Greek literature until Theocritus's *Idylls* (c. 275 B.C.), the first works that can be characterized as pastoral.[7] Before Theocritus even beautiful landscapes
evocative of the pastoral *locus amoenus* are consistently the scene
of some destructive encounter with the numinous and elemental
both within humanity and without in nature; often sexuality is
the force emphasized.[8] Thus in the *Homeric Hymn to Demeter*, the
"soft meadow" (*leimōn am' malakon*)[9] filled with a pastoralesque
catalogue of flowers (6–8) yawns open to facilitate the rape of
Persephone by Hades. So too in the *Hymn to Aphrodite*, the
"grassy pastures" (*nomous . . . poiēentas*, 78) and "flowering
pastures" (*nomōn . . . anthemoentōn*, 169) of Mt. Ida are the scene
of Anchises's sexual encounter with Aphrodite; a dangerous
experience, as Anchises realizes when he begs the goddess not to
leave him weak and palsied (187–90). This danger is underscored
by the reference to Tithonus, whom Eos took as husband, gain-
ing him immortality but not perpetual youth (218–38). Likewise
the Calypso episode in the *Odyssey* combines a quasi-pastoral
landscape with a threatening female.[10] Odysseus wants to escape
this paradise, recognizing a potential threat in it and his dangerous relationship with the goddess, as his distrust of her (173–
78) and the references to Orion and Iasion (121–28) emphasize, as
they were other mortals who slept with goddesses and were
destroyed. Again sexuality linked with a beautiful landscape, an
important convention of pastoral, is seen as threatening given the
inherent disorder of the natural world and of human passion.[11]

It is not surprising, then, that Hesiod's *Works and Days* (c. 700
B.C.), the initiator of the georgic, takes the same attitude towards the natural world. In the famous descriptions of winter
and summer[12] the destructiveness of nature dominates; moreover, in the summer description this disorder is linked to female
sexuality:

ἦμος δὲ σκόλυμός τ' ἀνθεῖ καὶ ἠχέτα τέττιξ
δενδρέῳ ἐφεζόμενος λιγυρὴν καταχεύετ' ἀοιδήν
πυκνὸν ὑπὸ πτερύγων θέρεος καματώδεος ὥρῃ,
τῆμος πιόταταί τ' αἶγες καὶ οἶνος ἄριστος,
μαχλόταται δὲ γυναῖκες, ἀφαυρότατοι δέ τοι ἄνδρες

εἰσίν, ἐπεὶ κεφαλὴν καὶ γούνατα Σείριος ἄζει,
αὐαλέος δέ τε χρὼς ὑπό καύματος·

(582–88)

When the thistle blooms and the chirping cicada
sits on trees and pours down shrill song
from frenziedly quivering wings in the toilsome summer,
then goats are fatter than ever and wine is at its best;
women's lust knows no bounds and men are all dried up,
because the dog star parches their heads and knees
and the heat sears their skin.

The flourishing of the natural world—the blooming thistle, the fat goats, the lustful women—does not mean a corresponding flourishing for men; not only is nature not harmonious with man's life, it is "toilsome"; Sirius is destructive to mind (*kephalēn*) and the life-force (*gounata*, "knees"; cf. in Homer where the knees embody the life-force, *Iliad*, 4.314, 5.176, etc.). Likewise Virgil in the *Georgics* (37–30 B.C.) describes the fragility of human order given nature's threats to it. The description of the storm in the first *Georgic*[13] and of the plague in the third (3.441–567) both detail the effects of nature's destructive forces on human civilization:

> non tam creber agens hiemem ruit aequore turbo
> quam multae pecudum pestes. nec singula morbi
> corpora corripiunt, sed tota aestiua repente,
> spemque grcgcmque simul cunctamque ab origine gentem.
> (3.470–73)

> Thicker than squalls
> Swept by a hurricane from off the sea
> Plagues sweep through livestock; and not one by one
> Diseases pick them off, but at a stroke
> A summer's fold, present and future hopes,
> The whole stock, root and branch.

The comparison to a storm at sea links the plague to the general potential destructiveness of nature, a disorder specifically harmful to the order of culture, here the domesticated animals necessary for the survival of the community. But most destructive are the forces also within humans, particularly sexuality. In this description of the effects of sexual heat on cattle, the personification links the bulls' violent behavior to humans:

> carpit enim uiris paulatim uritque uidendo
> femina, nec nemorum patitur meminisse nec herbae
> dulcibus illa quidem inlecebris, et saepe superbos
> cornibus inter se subigit decernere amantis.
>
> (3.215–18)
>
> For a female
> Slowly consumes their strength and burns it up
> With sight of her, and will not let them think
> Of woods or pasture, she with her fetching wiles;
> And often she constrains her proud-horned lovers
> To duel with one another.

Whereas personification in pastoral communicates nature's harmony with humans, in georgic it reveals the natural passions and drives of humans similar to those of beasts and potentially destructive; the two bulls fighting over a heifer in the third *Georgic* will become Aeneas and Turnus plunging their peoples into war over Lavinia. Like the *Odyssey* or the *Homeric Hymns*, the georgic recognizes that nature and humanity are filled with latent disorder arising from the various forces, especially sexuality, that trouble the cosmos.

The reality of these threats to order both internal and external mandates the next major characteristic of georgic, its doctrine of labor, the ethical value of work as the only way to mitigate that potential disorder: "The immortals decreed that man must sweat / to attain virtue" (*tēs d'aretēs hidrōta theoi proparoithen ethēkan / athanatoi*, 289–90), as Hesiod says, and this virtue creates order: "For mortals, order is best, disorder is worst" (*euthēmosynē gar aristē / thnētois anthrōpois, kakothēmosynē de kakistē*, 471–72). And, as in Genesis, labor is the unavoidable contingency of human existence given the decay of the species and the harshness of the natural world that are the heritage of the Iron Age (176–79).[14] We live in a fallen world, and only labor can keep the wolves of hunger and evil from our doors. Virgil's response to the destructiveness of the natural world is similar to Hesiod's, and stems from the same recognition of nature's inherent tendencies to disorder: "So it is: for everything by nature's law / Tends to the worse, slips ever backward, backward" (*sic omnia fatis / in peius ruere ac retro sublapsa referri*, 1.199–200). Thus the glorification of *labor,* the work necessary to overcome the harsh conditions and contingencies of the natural world in order to create and maintain civilization: "Toil mastered everything, relentless toil / And the pressure of pinching poverty" (*labor omnia uicit / improbus et duris urgens in rebus egestas,* 1.145–46). Given the potential disorder of the natural world and of humanity's passions and drives, only relentless struggle and diligence, and the values of hard work and self-control these foster, can create the order and stability that make civilization and ultimately human identity possible.[15]

Pastoral endorses an ethic opposed to georgic's bleak pessimism, but that ethic, like georgic's, is linked to a particular conception of the natural world. We have already mentioned that pastoral asserts a harmony between a beautiful responsive landscape and the humans within it; cf. Theocritus's first *Idyll:*

ΘΥΡΣΙΣ
Ἁδύ τι τὸ ψιθύρισμα καὶ ἁ πίτυς, αἰπόλε, τήνα,
ἁ ποτὶ ταῖς παγαῖοι, μελίσδεται, ἁδὺ δὲ καὶ τύ
συρίσδες . . . .

ΑΙΠΟΛΟΣ
ἅδιον, ὦ ποιμήν, τὸ τεὸν μέλος ἤ τὸ καταχές
τῆν' ἀπὸ τᾶς πέτρας καταλείβεται ὑψόθεν ὕδωρ.

(1–3; 7–8)

Thyrsis
Sweet is the whispered music of yonder pinetree by the springs, goatherd, and sweet too thy piping. . . .

Goatherd
Sweeter, shepherd, falls thy song than yonder stream that tumbles plashing from the rocks.[16]

The music of the pinetree and the stream harmonizes with the music of the singer: *melisdetai,* the word Thyrsis uses to describe the pinetree's song, is etymologically related to *melos,* the word the Goatherd used to describe Thyrsis's song. Virgil in his *Eclogues* (37 B.C.) likewise creates a similar scene of harmonious natural beauty:

Tityre, tu patulae recubans sub tegmine fagi
siluestrem tenui Musam meditaris auena. . . .
tu, Tityre, lentus in umbra

formosam resonare doces Amaryllida siluas.
(1–2; 4–5)

O Tityrus, reclining beneath the shelter of a spreading beech
you practice the woodland muse on slender oaten stalk.
. . . you, Tityrus, relaxed in the shade
teach the woods to echo the beautiful Amaryllis.

The woods reechoing the shepherd's song, like the responsive
waterfall in the first *Idyll*, assert both the landscape's sympathetic
concern for the humans who sing and love in it and its status as
suitable lovely backdrop for these activities.[17] Rather than
threatening and alien, nature now is tamed and subordinated to
the fulfillment of human desire. The paradisiacal elements of the
pastoral landscape—the shade, trees, water, and especially the
catalogue of flowers—emblemize this sympathetic beauty, one
conducive to the ethic of pastoral, that which Tityrus calls *haec
otia* (4), "leisure": the freedom from time, history and the contingencies of the natural world, the leisure to love and sing free from
anxiety and care.[18] In this world the imagination is secure
enough to create its ideal orders in works of art.

These two contrasting ethics and conceptions of the natural
world, however, are not isolated from one another in works we
can label wholly pastoral or georgic; rather they are juxtaposed in
rural poetry, challenging and modifying each other so that the
rural world as a source of imagery can more completely develop
and communicate a work's complex meaning. Thus in the first
Idyll, the harmony and peace of the landscape is challenged by the
reference to Pan (3), the goat-footed god of panic and lust who
evokes a darker more elemental world threatening to humans,
the world the georgic attempts to mediate through *labor*. This
recognition of a potentially destructive natural world is con-
firmed by the debilitating sterile noon hour (15) when piping is
prohibited,[19] and by the reference to Priapus (21), the ithyphallic
fertility god associated with Aphrodite and Dionysus, the goddess of elemental sexuality and the god of the irrational. Moreover, as in georgic, a problematic sexuality links this destructiveness of nature to humanity. The two works of art highlighted in
the poem, the ivywood cup and the elegy for Daphnis, both
focus on a sexuality ultimately destructive. In the Daphnis song,
Daphnis, the inventor of pastoral song,[20] dies in front of a
gloating Aphrodite because he swore a vow of chastity and then

fell in love (85; 95–98). In the description of the cup, the first panel describes two men "long hollow-eyed from love" (38, *kuloidioontes*) being teased by a woman who laughs like Aphrodite (*gelaisa*, 36; *gelaoisa*, 95, 96). The darker side of sexuality links the landscape described in the initial lines, the cup, and the song, and threatens with its chaos the ordering power of the imagination emblemized by the pastoral artist Daphnis and by the harmony between the artist-hersdmen and the landscape. Moreover, the central panel of the cup, depicting a vigorous old man fishing (39–44), evokes the georgic world of labor struggling against a harsh nature: the adjective describing the rocks on which the fisherman stands, *lepras* (40), literally means "leprous." The first *Idyll* balances two visions of human participation in the world: the pastoral ideal of a leisure conducive to the order of art, a leisure sustained by a sympathetic landscape; and the georgic recognition of the necessity for labor to overcome the disorder inherent in humanity and the natural world.

Virgil too balances georgic and pastoral in his first *Eclogue*. Thus opposed to Tityrus is the exile Meliboeus: "We leave the borders and sweet fields of the fatherland. / We are fleeing the fatherland" (*nos patriae finis et dulcia linquimus arva. / nos patriam fugimus*, 3–4). The references to the political reality of the nation (*patria*); to the ploughed fields (*arva*'s literal meaning) that testify to humanity's need to subject a harsh natural world to technology in order to survive; and, in *fugimus*, the reference to the proscriptions of farmland around Mantua by Augustus in order to resettle his soldiers after Philippi in 42 B.C.—all evoke a contingent world subject to time and history, the world Virgil in the first *Georgic* attributed to the will of Jupiter, who imposed these contingencies on humans so that they would leave behind an essentially bestial golden–age sloth and, by overcoming these contingencies, create the civilization that is the essence of humanity's identity (*Georgic* 1. 121–46).

This same juxtaposition can also be seen in georgic literature. Pastoral in Hesiod is muted, perhaps because the harsher contingencies of existence in the late eighth century made an idealization of nature difficult. Yet immediately following Hesiod's description of summer occurs a brief pastoral moment:

ἀλλὰ τότ' ἤδη

εἴη πετραίη τε σκιὴ καὶ Βίβλινος οἶνος

ἐπι δ' αἰθοπα πινέμεν οἶνον
ἐν σκιῇ ἑζόμενον, κεκορημένον ἦτορ ἐδωδῆς,
ἀντίον ἀκρᾶέος Ζεφύρου τρέψαντα πρόσωπα·

(588–89; 592–94)

Then, ah then,
I wish you a shady ledge and your choice wine. . . .
Drink sparkling wine,
sitting in the shade with your appetite sated,
and face Zephyr's breeze as it blows from mountain peaks.

The pastoral motif of sitting in the shade and the cooling breeze
suggests leisure; but in the context of the *Works and Days*, clearly
this ease can only be enjoyed as a reward for the labor endured, a
brief respite in a relentless round of toil, an ideal to be wished for
(note *eiē*, an optative) rather than a reality to depend on. Virgil
too in the *Georgics* calls on pastoral to communicate the peace and
absence of anxiety that can characterize the farmer's life, an *otium*
unproblematic only if it is the result of georgic virtues such as
hard work and simplicity:

> . . . secura quies et nescia fallere uita,
> dives opum uariarum, at latis otia fundis,
> speluncae uiuique lacus, at frigida tempe
> mugitusque boum mollesque sub arbore somni
> non absunt.
>
> (2.467–71)

> Yet peace they have and a life of innocence
> Rich in variety; they have for leisure
> Their ample acres, caverns, living lakes,
> Cool Tempes; cattle low, and sleep is soft
> Under a tree.

This description resembles in some of its details the picture of
Tityrus in *Eclogue* 1 (cf. *otia* with *otia*, 1.6; *mollesque sub arbore
somni* with *recubans sub tegmine fagi*, 1.1). The difference is that
here Virgil uses pastoral *otium* to represent the peace of mind that
results from the virtue of rural hard work preached in the first
Georgic, particularly when rural life is contrasted with the stress
and anxiety and decadence of the complex urban world (*Georgic*
2.461–66; 495–512).[21] Both visions—the negative harsh georgic

one of the first *Georgic* and the more positive "pastoral" of the second—when read together present a complete picture of the values and rewards of *labor*, the physical costs it exacts and the psychological benefits that follow. Nature can be a harmonious context for a leisure conducive to the *vita contemplativa*, but only after labor has created the requisite ordered space.

Whether left in tense juxtaposition, as in the *Idylls* and *Eclogues*, or more coherently linked, as in the *Georgics*, pastoral and georgic provide the axes of a grid on which a poem's meaning can be plotted. Opposing visions of human identity, potential, and achievement can then limit one another, asserting the incompleteness of the fiction, the omissions necessary as it constructs its ideal. From this oscillation results a higher, more complete meaning that recognizes simultaneously the full range of ideal human order, from art to agriculture and ultimately civilization, and the forces of disorder that limit and challenge those orders. Through the dialectic of pastoral and georgic, then, the rural world becomes a powerful complex of imagery capable of developing a meaning rich and dense in implications.

The English poets writing about the rural world found its imagery flexible and expressive in the pastoral and georgic terms of Hesiod, Virgil and Theocritus, and so should not be limited by labels such as pastoral and georgic. A good test case is Spenser's *Shepheardes Calender* (1579), for Spenser is considered one of English literature's best pastoralists, if not the *"prime* Pastoralist *of* England," as Michael Drayton called him; and the *Shepheardes Calender* initiated a vigorous pastoral tradition in the seventeenth century.[22] However, the very title itself, with its obvious evocation of time and the seasons and a natural world hostile to humans, should alert us that Spenser, like Virgil and Theocritus, will call upon the georgic vision as well as the pastoral.[23] All the elements we have identified as characterizing those visions will occur in Spenser: the pastoral idealization of the natural world and its harmony with humans; the pastoral ethic of *otium* predicated on that idealization; the georgic recognition of nature's potential destructiveness, particularly the disorder of sexuality; the ethic of *labor* demanded by such a world; and the use of personification in both visions to link the landscapes to humanity.[24] Analysis of a plaintive, moral, and recreative eclogue reveals that Spenser plays off the pastoral and georgic visions to build his meaning, and so it is a misnomer to call the poem "pastoral."[25]

The "Januarye" eclogue is dominated by a georgic vision of nature's and sexuality's destructiveness developed by a personi fication that links Colin to the harshness of winter's "wastful spight" (2) and the "faynt" and "feeble" sheep (5; cf. also 11). The sterility and disorder of nature is emphasized throughout: "faynting flocke" (11); "barrein ground, whome winters wrath hath wasted" (19); trees "whose shady leaves are lost" (31) and "now are clothd with moss and hoary frost" (33); "dreary ysi-cles" (36); "feeble flocke, whose fleece is rough and rent, / whose knees are weake through fast and evill fare" (44–45). Like Hes-iod's description of winter in the *Works and Days* or Virgil's of the plague in the third *Georgic*, Spenser emphasizes the natural world's hostility to humans and the domesticated nature, such as sheep, that humans need to survive. Moreover, the marked personification throughout the eclogue reinforces this emphasis by asserting humanity's similarity to the natural world, its sub-jection to inner forces and drives such as sexuality: "All as the Sheepe, such was the Shepeheards looke" (7; cf. also 47–48) begins a constant interchange of Colin's and nature's attributes and experiences. The following stanza is typical:

> Such rage as winters, reigneth in my heart,
> My life bloud friezing with unkindly cold:
> Such stormy stoures do breede my balefull smart,
> As if my yeare were wast, and waxen old.
>   (25–28; cf. also 37–42)

Like the natural world, humans are subjected to time, change, and impersonal forces destructive to culture's orders. The hu-man force particularly disordering is, as in Hesiod and Virgil, sexuality: "For pale and wanne he was, (alas the while,) / May seeme he lovd" (8–9). Love, a "balefull smart" (27), a "payne" (13, 18, 54), a "bane" (53), like nature's sterile winter, leaves Colin's "timely buds," his youth of promise and beauty, "wasted" (38), his "blossome" "blowne away, and blasted" (39; cf. also 21–22, 32, 34). The pastoral flowers, emblems of nature's beauty and human love, are here destroyed by the forces of nature inimical to human desire and order, both of art ("so broke his oaten pype," 72) and agriculture (the sheep's "ill governe-ment," 46). In "*Januarye*" the vision of nature and human sexu-ality is georgic, not pastoral.[26]

"Januarye" is dominated by the harsh georgic vision of the natural world; "Februarie" will reinforce that vision and develop

a georgic ethic of labor that is the only valid response to such a
world and that criticizes the pastoral's inauthentic desire for a
timeless leisure. The latter attitude is embodied in the youth
Cuddie, who protests against the harshness of nature, "winters
rage" (1), "bitter blasts" (2), "kene cold" (3): Cuddie's "flowering youth is foe to frost" (31). Once again flowers emblemize the
ideals of youth and beauty; but Cuddie's predicate adjective
"foe" reveals his blindness, for flowers are *victims* of frost, not
the equal adversaries implied by "foe." Cuddie wants a world of
eternal spring, a landscape that can be a beautiful backdrop for
love: "But were they yeares greene, as now bene myne, . . . Tho
wouldest thou learne to caroll of Love" (59, 61). However, as
Thenot responds, such desires ignore both the reality of time and
change that no human can escape, and the labor that a harsh
natural world demands:

> Must not the world wend in his commun course
> From good to badd, and from badde to worse,
> From worse unto that is worst of all,
> And then returne to his former fall?
>
> (11–14)

Given the reality of nature's decline mandated by its fallen status,
humans must accept that reality and tend to the work that
mediates that destructiveness: Thenot

> Ne ever was to Fortune foeman,
>   But gently tooke, that ungently came.
>   And ever my flocke was my chiefe care,
>   Winter or sommer they mought well fare.
>
> (21–24)

He chastises Cuddie for neglecting his task of shepherding and
for believing that spring is eternal: "So loytring live you little
heardgroomes, / Keeping your beastes in the budded broomes: /
And when the shining sunne laugheth once, / You deemen, the
spring is come attonce" (35–38). Thenot criticizes Cuddie not
only for refusing to recognize the reality of change in the natural
world, but also for "loytring" and neglecting his sheep: letting
them eat the "budded broomes" could lead to bloat, a digestive
disorder often ending in death. This sounding of the georgic
theme of labor continues in Thenot's reminder of winter's inev-

iubility. "Then is your careless corage accoied, / Your carefull
heards with cold bene annoied" (48–49). As in Virgil, the necessity of labor, of dedication to one's work and self-denial, is
predicated on a recognition of the unavoidable contingencies of
the natural world.

Both speakers throughout depend on personification to emphasize humanity's subjection to the natural world (e.g., 31, 43–
44, 54–59, et al.). But Cuddie's personification ironically under-
scores Thenot's point: to say his "flowring youth is foe to frost"
is to admit that his youth, like spring's flowers, will ultimately
pass away, and so he validates Thenot's assertion of change and
decay, and the ethic of labor that recognition demands. The fable
of the oak and the briar makes the same point, balancing pastoral
and georgic and ultimately asserting the necessity of georgic's
ethic that recognizes the transience of beauty and the need for
community and interdependence. The description of the oak
emphasizes its subjection to time and a harsh natural world: "But
now the gray mosse marred his rine, / His bared boughes were
beaten with stormes, / His toppe was bald, and wasted with
wormes, / His honor decayed, his braunches sere" (111–114). On
the other hand, the briar is characterized in pastoral terms:

> Yt was embellisht with blossomes fayre,
> And thereto aye wonned to repayre
> The shepheardes daughters, to gather flowres,
> To peinct their girlonds with his colowres.
> And in his small bushes vsed to shrowde
> The sweet nightingale singing so lowde. . . .
>   (118–23; cf. also 129–33)

The flowers, emblems of pastoral beauty and nature's harmony;
the "girlonds," traditional tokens of love; the nightingale, symbol of the artist—all evoke the pastoral world and its representa-
tive activities of singing and loving. But the briar's arrogance and
pride in its beauty (129–32) are misplaced, for that beauty is
subject to change and decay, the contingencies of existence that
give the lie to self-sufficiency and demand the cooperation and
community, the shared technology and culture and labor that
Virgil in the first *Georgic* asserts are the defining characteristics of
humanity (1.121–46).[27] Without that mutual cooperation and
interdependence, humans, like the briar after the sustaining oak
is felled (216–21), are subjected to overwhelming forces of

nature—"blustring Boreas" (226), "byting frost" (231), "watrie
wettc" (232), "heaped snowe" (233)—that ultimately destroy
them. Beauty and love can only flourish when supported by the
values demanded by a precarious existence in an alien world.

Pastoral, however, and its visions of harmony, leisure,
beauty, and art, are powerfully attractive as emblems of human
desire and aspiration. Spenser recognizes this power and in a
recreative eclogue like "Aprill" creates a vision of the pastoral
world of youth and beauty, over which presides an apotheosized
Queen Elizabeth.[28] Again, the catalogue of flowers communicates this harmony and beauty:

> Bring hether the Pincke and purple Cullambine,
>   With Gelliflowres:
> Bring Coronations, and Sops in wine,
>   worne of Paramoures.
> Strowe me the ground with Daffadowndillies,
> And Cowslips, and Kingcups, and loued Lillies:
>   The pretie Pawnce,
>   And the Cheuisaunce,
> Shall match with the fayre flowre Delice.
>   (136–144)

Moreover, personification links the beauty of the flowers to the
beauty of Eliza: "The Redde rose medled with the White yfere, /
In either cheeke depeincten lively chere" (68–69). As well as the
political reconciliation of York and Lancaster, the lines assert for
Eliza a beauty harmonizing with that of the natural world: nature
and humanity are integrated in an ideal pastoral world. And this
world is a timeless one of golden-age peace—"Oliues bene for
peace, / When wars do surcease" (124–25)—when divinities and
humans intermingle—"I see Calliope speede her to the place, /
where my Goddesse shines: / And after her the other muses
trace, / with their Violines" (100–103; cf. also 127–30).[29] The
limitations of an alien nature, the barriers between divine and
human have all disappeared, leaving an ideal sustaining context
for leisure and celebratory dance.

Yet even such a lovely pastoral tableau is subjected to compromise and limitation in both the eclogue and the *Shepheardes
Calender*. In "Aprill" the frame, the dialogue between Thenot
and Hobbinoll, is dominated by the destructive love afflicting
Colin (11–16) and, despite E. K.'s anxious apologetic gloss, by

Hobbinoll's jealousy (10, 23, 28). Thus the innocence of the Hymn to Eliza is challenged by the reality of sexual frustration and loss, the "madding mynd" (25) linked to a predatory nature: "hath some Wolfe thy tender Lambes ytorne?" (2). Within the *Shepheardes Calender* the links between "Aprill" and the lament for Dido in "November," set the Hymn in the broader context of the yearly rhythms of loss and death.[30] The flowers, which in "Aprill" emblemized pastoral beauty and fertility, in "November" now represent the brevity of that beauty doomed to die: "Whence is it, that the flouret of the field doth fade, / And lyeth buryed long in Winters bale: / Yet soone as Spring his mantle doth display, / It floureth fresh, as it should never fayle?" (83–86). The rhythms of natural life, of winter and spring, confirm that the loss georgic accepts limits pastoral's claims of unmitigated peace and fertility. An even more pointed reference to the "Aprill" eclogue makes the same point:

> The water Nymphs, that wont with her to sing and daunce,
> And for her girlond oliue braunches beare,
> Now balefull boughes of Cypres doen aduaunce:
> The Muse, that were wont greene bayes to weare,
> Now bringen bitter Eldre braunches seare,
>   The fatall sisters eke repent,
>   Her vitall threde so soone was spent.
>
>   (143–49)

The links to "Aprill" are close: besides the same general dramatic situation of nymphs and the Muses dancing ("Aprill," 38–40; 109–110), the "And for her girlond oliue braunches beare" recalls "*Chloris*, that is the chiefest Nymph of al, / of Oliue braunches beares a Coronall" ("Aprill," 122–23); "The Muses, that were wont greene bayes to weare" recalls "Bene they not Bay braunches, which they [Muses] do beare?" ("Aprill," 105). The change from Olive to Cypress, Bay to Elder asserts the reality of change in the sublunary natural world, and the limits of the pastoral pleasance and of pastoral praise. Pastoral beauty and harmony and peace are all perhaps necessary fictions, but ultimately salvation in this world and in the next depends on a recognition of our fallen state, of nature's alienation from us, and of an ethic like *labor*, the work of civilization and the work of faith, that alone can mediate and make meaningful the mutability of this world.

I believe the other eclogues of the *Shepheardes Calender* can be read in terms of this dialectic between pastoral and georgic, and that this reading can contain and be reconciled to other critical emphases. Moreover, other works traditionally classified as pastoral or versions of pastoral—"Lycidas," *Upon Appleton House, Windsor Forest, As You Like It*, Keats's Odes, *Adam Bede*[31]—can be analysed in the same terms, and so should not be burdened with the negative or misleading assumptions of a term like "pastoral." At the risk of proliferating terminology, perhaps we need a term like "bucolic" to characterize literature about the rural world, with "pastoral" and "georgic" designating opposing yet complementary modes.[32] At any rate, we should bring to our readings of rural literature a sensitivity to the georgic vision—its steady acceptance of the limitations of human desire, its recognition of the need for a mediating labor that creates civilization and its civilizing orders.

California State University, Fresno

NOTES

1. For discussion and diagram of the Wheel of Virgil see Alastair Fowler, *Kinds of Literature: An Introduction to the Theory of Genres and Modes* (Cambridge, Mass.: Harvard University Press, 1982), pp. 240–41.
2. *Genre* (London and New York: Methuen, 1982), p. 28. For scholarship on genre see Dubrow's bibliography, pp. 119–29. For a more comprehensive and detailed study see Fowler, *Kinds of Literature*.
3. Adrian Marino sees this problem arising from the way we go about relating works to generic categories, thus begging the question: "The most frequent study technique is to select a group of works previously defined as lyrical, epic, dramatic. . . . This *a priori* (though inevitable) approach spoils the whole technique. Instead of proceeding objectively, through inference by *first* identifying the structures we are going to define *a posteriori* as lyrical, epic, dramatic, we only use preconceived notions which we ascribe *a priori* to the structures discussed, which ought to be recognized and named *after* such an examination," "A Definition of Literary Genres," in *Theories of Literary Genres*, ed. Joseph P. Strelka (University Park, Pa. and London: Pennsylvania State University Press, 1978), p. 16.
4. As Addison noted in his "Preface" to Dryden's translation of Virgil's *Georgics* (1697), "[T]he Georgics are a subject which none of the critics have sufficiently taken into their consideration, most of them passing it over in silence, or casting it under the same head with pastoral, a division by no means proper." This confusion still persists in some quarters: John Barrel and John Bull, in *The Penguin Book of English Pastoral Verse* (Harmondsworth, England: Penguin, 1982), p. 297, speak of a "variety of optimistic Pastoral that most often finds expression in the Georgic."

The negative connotations of pastoral resulted from the abundance of formulaic, saccharine nymph-and-shepherd pastorals that flooded England after the Restoration and provoked Samuel Johnson to snort of the genre, "Easy, vulgar, and therefore disgusting." Modern criticism has faulted pastoral for being escapist, an interpretation found in Renato Pogglioli's "The Oaten Flute," in *The Oaten Flute* (Cambridge, Mass.: Harvard University Press, 1975), pp. 1–2; first published *Harvard Library Bulletin*, 11 (1957); a reading given a Freudian formulation in Laurence Lerner's *The Uses of Nostalgia* (New York. Schocken, 1972). Helen Cooper, among others has criticized this mistake of confusing "Pastoral" with "idyllic," in *Pastoral: Mediaeval into Renaissance* (Ipswich, England and Totowa, N.J.: D.S. Brewer and Rowman and Littlefield, 1977), p. 2.

The scholarship on pastoral is prodigious. A useful recent bibliography can be found in Andrew V. Ettin, *Literature and the Pastoral* (New Haven, Conn.: Yale University Press, 1984), pp. 187–96. Also useful is David Halperin, *Before Pastoral: Theocritus and the Ancient Tradition of Bucolic Poetry* (New Haven, Conn.: Yale University Press, 1983), pp. 27–65, for a historical survey and summary of the major definitions and theories of pastoral. For georgic the best general survey is still Marie Loretto Lilly, *The Georgic* (Baltimore, Md.: Johns Hopkins University Press, 1919). More recently cf. Anthony Low, *The Georgic Revolution* (Princeton, N.J.: Princeton University Press, 1985), which focuses on eighteenth-century British georgic literature. For the distinctions between georgic and pastoral see Thomas G. Rosenmeyer, *The Green Cabinet: Theocritus and the European Pastoral Lyric* (Berkeley and Los Angeles, Calif.: University of California Press, 1969), pp. 21–26. More limited in scope but still useful is Annabel Patterson, "Pastoral Versus Georgic: The Politics of Virgilian Quotation," in *Renaissance Genres*, ed. Barbara Kister Lewalski, Harvard English Studies 14 (Cambridge, Mass.: Harvard University Press, 1986), pp. 241–68.

5.   On the way genres tend to interpenetrate cf. Fowler, *Kinds of Literature*, p. 191: "Generic mixtures need not be full-blown hybrids. In fact, it is more usual for one of the genres to be only a modal abstraction with a token repertoire. We shall call such mixture 'modulation.' In modulation, the proportions of the modal ingredient may vary widely, which leads to correspondingly various effects, from overall tones to touches of local color." Also Dubrow, p. 29: "But certain works . . . dazzle and disturb us with a kaleidoscopic array of hues in which it is difficult to discern a dominant one, a single genre whose name we can confidently label the work."

The overlooking of the georgic vision in works assumed to be pastoral has led to a dichotomizing of pastoral into various binary oppositions, one term of which is usually privileged over the other. In modern pastoral criticism this tendency starts with William Empson's assertion that pastoral puts "the complex into the simple," *Some Versions of Pastoral* (1935; rpt. New York: New Directions, 1974), p. 22. Various other oppositions include Frank Kermode's between urban and rural, art and nature, *English Pastoral Poetry* (1952; rpt. New York: Norton, 1972); cf. Paul Alpers, "The Eclogue Tradition and the Nature of Pastoral," *College English* 34, No. 3 (1972), 352–54, for discussion of the "soft" and "hard" views of pastoral, and for his argument that both are viable when the focus of interpretation shifts from the landscape to the human shepherd-singer (355, 357). Cf. also Leo Marx's opposition between "sentimental" and "complex" pastoral, the latter of which recognizes the "counterforce," the reality of time and death challenging the peace of the *locus amoenus*, *The Machine in the Garden* (1964; rpt. New York: Oxford University Press, 1979), p. 25. Peter Lindenbaum posits an "anti-pastoral sentiment" which "expresses the view that in this world of ours man simply has no time for relaxation or even momentary escape from the pressing activity of day-to-day living," *Changing Landscapes: Anti-Pastoral Sentiment in the English Renaissance* (Athens, Ga. and London: University of Georgia Press, 1986), p. 1. Cf. also Ettin, who speaks of a "tension between pastoral and non-pastoral experience," p. 22. My point is that this proliferation of nomenclature and oppositions is unnecessary once one recognizes the presence of georgic and its dialectical relationship to pastoral in literature concerned with the rural world.

6.   For the sympathetic harmony between the landscape and the humans within it see Bernard F. Dick, "Ancient Pastoral and the Pathetic Fallacy," *Classical Literature* 20 (1968), 27–44.

7.   Halperin, pp. 7ff., warns against the distortions that can arise from characterizing Theocritus's poetry in terms of "pastoral" assumptions that were not defined until later.

8.   The alien, culture-threatening quality of the natural world in Greek literature has been usefully analyzed in Charles Segal's "Nature and the World of Man in Greek Literature," *Arion* 2 (1963), 19–53.

9.   *Hymn. Hom. Cer.* 6. Henceforth references parenthetical.

10.   *Od.* V.55–74. Henceforth references parenthetical.

11.   This discomfort with or scorn of even beautiful landscapes continues in later Greek literature. E.g., in the *Hippolytus* of Euripides the pastoralesque meadow that emblemizes to Hippolytus his chastity (73–83) is linked via verbal repetitions to Phaedra's hallucinations during her sexual madness—again, sexuality compromises the integrity of the pleasance. See Charles Segal, "The Tragedy of the *Hippolytus*: The Waters of Ocean and the Untouched Meadow," *Harvard Studies in Classical Philology* 70 (1965), 117–70. Cf. also Socrates's snubbing of the pastoral attractions of the country in *Phaedrus* 230, or Aristotle's contemptuous characterization of shepherds in *Politics* 1256a.

12.   *Op.* 505–535; 582–88. Text of Hesiod that of M. L. West, *Hesiod: Works and Days* (Oxford: Oxford University Press, 1978). Translation from Apostolos N. Anthanassakis, *Hesiod: Theogony, Works and Days, Shield* (Baltimore, Md. and London: Johns Hopkins University Press, 1983). Henceforth references parenthetical.

13.   Text of Virgil that of R. A. B. Mynors, *P. Vergilii Maronis Opera* (Oxford: Oxford University Press, 1969). Translations of the *Georgics* from L.P. Wilkinson, *Virgil: The Georgics* (Harmondsworth, England: Penguin, 1982). Translations of the *Eclogues* are my own. Henceforth references parenthetical.

14.   A distrust of the Golden Age because its leisure and absence of civilization reduce humans to the level of beasts is a persistent theme in ancient primitivism. See Arthur O. Lovejoy and George Boas, *Primitivism and Related Ideas in Antiquity* (Baltimore, Md. and London: Johns Hopkins University Press, 1935). The Romans particularly, with their national values centering on hard work and public service, tended to view the Golden Age negatively, e.g. Lucretius *De Rerum Natura*, V. 925ff or Catullus 64. See Patricia A. Johnstone, *Vergil's Agricultural Golden Age: A Study of the Georgics* (Leiden: E. J. Brill, 1980).

15.   For discussions of the doctrine of *labor* see L. P. Wilkinson, *The Georgics of Virgil* (Cambridge: Cambridge University Press, 1900), pp. 137–41; Gary B Miles, *Virgil's Georgics* (Berkeley and Los Angeles, Calif.: University of California Press, 1980), pp. 81–85.

16.   Text and translation of Theocritus those of A.S.F. Gow, *Theocritus*, 2 vols., 2 ed. (Cambridge, England: Cambridge University Press, 1965). Henceforth references parenthetical.

17.   John Van Sickle's observation concerning Virgilian pastoral, "After the tops of the *locus amoenus* and the Arcadist landscape of the mind, it seems likely to become fashionable to say that Virgil's *Eclogues* are about writing poetry," has become accurate with respect to all pastoral criticism: "Studies of Dialectical Methodology in the Virgilian Tradition," *Modern Language Notes* 85 (1970), p. 884. Georgic also can develop a concern with poetics; cf. Michael C.J. Putnam, *Vergil's Poem of the Earth: A Study of the Georgics* (Princeton, N.J.: Princeton University Press, 1979).

18.   For the philosophical origins of *otium* in Epicureanism cf. Rosenmeyer, pp. 65–97.

19.   Cf. Rosenmeyer, p. 76: the noon hour is "a kind of death which paralyzes nature and imperils its resurgence."

20.   For the origins and status of Daphnis as prototypical pastoral singer cf. Gow, pp. 1–2, and William Berg, *Early Vergil* (London: Athlone Press, 1974).

21.   Cf. Miles, pp. 151ff., for a fuller discussion of this passage.

22.   The dichotomizing of pastoral in order to account for what I am arguing is the georgic vision (above, n. 5), occurs as well in criticism of the *Shepheardes Calender*. Hallet Smith, *Elizabethan Poetry* (Cambridge: Cambridge University Press, 1952), opposes "the contemplative state" free "not only from ambition or greed, but from the vicissitudes of fortune" (p. 8) to "its opposite, a form of ambition which the sixteenth century called most commonly the aspiring mind" (p. 9): "the central meaning of pastoral is the rejection of the aspiring mind" (p. 10). A.C. Hamilton, "The Argument of Spenser's *Shepheardes Calender*," *ELH* 23, No. 3 (1956), opposes a pastoral world of innocence before the Fall with the world of fallen nature: "The simple pastoral life of enjoyable ease must then be rejected for the dedicated life where man does not live according to Nature but seeks escape out of Nature" (175–76): "The argument of the *Shepheardes Calender* is, then, the rejection of the pastoral life for the truly dedicated life in the world" (181). Isabel G. MacCaffrey, "Allegory and Pastoral in *The Shepheardes Calender*." *ELH* 36, No. 1 (1969), elaborates on Hamilton's opposition between an "idyllic version of pastoral" (90) characterized by unfallen innocence and bliss, and a recognition of fallen nature's hostility to a sinning humanity, a hostility which "moves from 'soft' to 'hard' pastoral" (98); "Spenser forces upon us the unwilling recognition that we can never regain Paradise literally" (100), and "nature can be restored to something like its original purity only with the aid of civilization" (106)—a georgic conclusion. Patrick Cullen, *Spenser, Marvell, and the Renaissance Pastoral* (Cambridge, Mass.: Harvard University Press, 1970), identifies a "division within pastoral" whose oppositions he labels "Arcadian" and "Mantuanesque": "Arcadian pastoral . . . takes as the pastoral ideal the *pastor felix* and soft life of *otium*" and locates its characters in "a landscape lush and pleasant but at the same time almost always vulnerable and precarious" (p. 2); "Mantuanesque pastoral takes as its ideal the Judaeo-Christian *pastor bonus*, the shepherd unwaveringly com-

mitted to the flock and to the requirements for eternal salvation, and consequently one largely opposed to the shepherd of worldly felicity" (p. 3). Cullen
expands on C. S. Lewis's "two ways of pastoral," one of "delicate Arcadian
idealization," the other "rough, superficially realistic, full of hard words,
satiric, and much indebted to Mantuan," in *English Literature in the Sixteenth
Century* (Oxford: Oxford University Press, 1954), p. 360. Harry S. Berger,
"Orpheus, Pan and the Poetics of Misogyny: Spenser's Critique of Pastoral
Love and Art," *ELH* 50, No. 1 (1983), identifies a "paradise principle" (27), a
dialectical interaction between an impulse to the "wish-fulfilling fantasy" of a
return to paradise which is the "psychological basis of the pastoral retreat from
life," and an impulse to "bitter rejection of the world that falls short of such a
fantasy" (27). Cf. also David R. Shore, *Spenser and the Poetics of Pastoral*
(Kingston, N.Y. and Montreal: McGill-Queen's University Press, 1985): "The
pastoral ideal is timeless, the eternal song of the unfallen garden, but it becomes
adequate substance for literature only when it is disrupted, however slightly, by
the temporal strains of a harsher song, one which speaks of frustrated love, of
evil or ambition, of time and death" (pp. 11–12). Again, all the oppositions—
contemplative/aspiring mind, prelapsarian innocence/postlapsarian experience, retreat/engagement, fantasy/disillusionment, Arcadian/
Mantuanesque—can be contained and accounted for in a recognition of the
georgic ethic and vision of nature. Moreover, the ethic of labor easily subsumes
the particular order—of art or of priestcraft—that Spenser focuses on.

23.   Cf. Mary Jo Hoffman, *Spenser's Pastoral: The Shepheardes Calender and
"Colin Clout"* (Baltimore, Md.: Johns Hopkins University Press, 1977), pp. 78,
79, who notes the influence on Spenser of visual works such as the *Calendrier de
bergers*, which sets out the farmer's monthly tasks. Cf. also Cooper, p. 160:
"The setting of the *Shepheardes Calender* is the fallen world: the form itself, with
the insistence on the changing season and so on mutability and mortality,
emphasizes that. . . ." An influence closer to home would have been Thomas
Tusser's georgic poem, *A Hundreth Good Pointes of Husbandrie* (London, 1557),
which like the *Shepheardes Calender* is structured by the twelve months.

24.   The pastoral and georgic visions and ethics can be reconciled with E.K.'s
division of the eclogues into Plaintive, Recreative, and Moral. The plaintive are
dominated by but not limited to a georgic recognition of nature's hostility; the
recreative by a pastoral nature sustaining of *otium*; the moral by the georgic ethic
of an ordering *labor*, whether of priestcraft or of poetry, that mediates the
hostility and disorder of the fallen world. Text of Spenser used is *The Works of
Edmund Spenser: A Viarorum Edition*, ed. Edwin Greenlaw et al., *The Minor
Poems*, v. 1 (Baltimore, Md. and London: Johns Hopkins University Press,
1943). Henceforth references by poem line number will be parenthetical.

25.   Fowler, *Kinds of Literature*, has recognized the role of georgic in the
Calender, which "modulat[es] the pastoral eclogue . . . into a very distant
georgic key,: p. 254; I disagree with "very distant." Cf. also Fowler's "The
Beginnings of English Georgic," in Lewalski, p. 113. I am greatly indebted to
Fowler's insights; I am arguing not only for a recognition of the presence of
georgic, but also for, at the very least, its equality with the pastoral vision.

26.   MacCaffrey, p. 98, also characterizes Spenser's depiction of humanity's
place in the natural world in terms compatible with georgic: "Nature is a threat
to man, who must assume with respect to it an attitude of constant vigilance";
cf. also p. 105, and above, n. 22.

27.   For this reading see Shore's discussion, pp. 21, 25. However, working
from the assumption that pastoral juxtaposes urban (complex) and rural (simple), he locates the fable's moral in the "temporal world of urban reality, where
youth and age are necessarily linked by common participation in the social
order" (p. 25). This seems to deny to the rural world any complex social order
requiring mutual cooperation. As Virgil's *Georgics* testify, the farm as well as
the city can provide an image of society that represents the values necessary for
the community's survival.

28.   The naturalizing of historically created political order via pastoral imag-
ery had been before Spenser a vigorous sub-genre since Virgil's fourth *Eclogue*.
For pastoral panegyric addressed to Elizabeth see Cooper, pp. 193–213; Frances
Yates, *Astraea: The Imperial Theme in the Sixteenth Century* (Boston and London:
Routledge and Kegan Paul, 1975), pp. 39–47.

29.   The combination of pastoral and golden-age imagery begins in the fourth
Eclogue, for obvious reasons: both pastoral and the golden-age myth posit ideal
worlds in which humans are freed from necessity and a harsh natural world.
This combination becomes dominant in the Renaissance; cf. Harry Levin, *The
Myth of the Golden Age in the Renaissance* (1969; rpt. Oxford and New York:
Oxford University Press, 1972). pp. 42, 112–38.

30.   Cf. Smith, p. 40: " 'Aprill' and 'November' are in a sense complementary,
and their importance is clearly marked for us by the wealth of metrical invention Spenser lavished upon them."

31.   Fowler, "The Beginnings of English Georgic," p. 113ff., has summarized
the works he feels employs a "georgic modulation." Elsewhere I have analyzed
Adam Bede and Ford Madox Ford's *The Last Post* in these terms. Cf. "A Rural
Singing Match: Pastoral and Georgic in *Adam Bede*," in *Victorian Newsletter*,
No. 74 (Fall 1988), pp. 6–11; "Pastoral or Georgic? Ford Madox Ford's *The Last
Post*," in *English Language Notes*, 26, No. 1 (Sept. 1988), 59–66.

32.   Cf. Halperin's discussion of the ancient distinctions between "bucolic"
and "pastoral," and his historical survey of the fortunes of these terms, pp. 1–
23. He argues that "bucolic" was the accepted designation of rural poetry in
antiquity: "*boukolikos* appears to be a technical literary term—it refers to a
specific type of poetic composition and can be employed as a title—whereas
pastoralis is wholly descriptive, denoting (in particular) a relation to animal
husbandry," p. 10. "Pastoral" as a generic term is late-Classical at the earliest.
Cf. also Fowler, "Beginnings of English Georgic," 108–109, who points out
that conscious imitation of strictly defined genres dominates the eighteenth
century, which is when poems conceived as wholly georgic begin to
proliferate.

LOUIS WALDMAN

Spenser's Pseudonym "E. K." and Humanist Self-Naming

*T*HE ABSENCE of a convincing explanation linking the name "E. K." with the name of Edmund Spenser has stood in the way of complete acceptance of Spenser's authorship of the critical apparatus of *The Shepheardes Calender*. Some attempts have been made to find a connection between the two names, but none has succeeded in framing a convincing historical argument.[1] Yet, it is far from impossible that the initials E. K. were in fact intended to refer to some variation on the name Edmund Spenser. The use of altered forms of personal names was a common and well-respected practice among sixteenth-century humanists. It would come as no surprise if it could be shown that Spenser had chosen to sign the *Shepheardes Calender* gloss with a humanistic variation on his own name, since the poem's *apparatus criticus* was clearly intended to evoke the elaborate scholia with which contemporary humanists framed the works of the classical authors.

A number of ways of forming variants on personal names were popular in the humanist circles of Spenser's time. From the late fifteenth century onwards individuals had begun to use such semi-transparent devices as retrograde spelling, transposition of syllables, and transliteration of names into the Greek alphabet.[2] Yet by far the most important custom was the literal translation of surnames into Greek or Latin.

Although the use of latinized surnames had been common throughout the middle ages, when most public and private business was conducted in that language, the use of hellenized surnames is an innovation that primarily characterizes the sixteenth century.[3] "This translation of names into Greeke or Latine, is still in use among the Germans, for hee whose name is *Ertswert* or Blackland, will be Melancthon; if Newman, *Neander*; if Brooke, *Torrentius*; if Fenne, *Paludanus*, &c. which some amongst us beganne lately to imitate." Thus wrote the historian William Camden in 1605[4]—but the widespread hellenization of surnames quickly fell into disuse just after the end of the sixteenth century.

21

The practice of hellenizing surnames first appeared on a broad scale in the circle of the Aldine Academy in Venice during the last decade of the fifteenth century.[5] Alessandro Bondino, styled by Aldus "artium et medicinae doctor egregius" for his work on the translation of the Organon, translated his surname to Agathemeros, although Zacharias Caliergi, in a letter to Marcus Musurus in 1499, refers to him by the synonymous appellation Euemeros.[6] His fellow Aristotelian Scipio Fortiguerra similarly hellenized his name to Carteromachos.[7] In this milieu charged with excitement over the revival of the ancient world, Greek surnames became the emblems of the learned ideals of humanist scholars, reflecting their commitment to the study of classical texts.

As the ideals of humanism were diffused throughout Europe, the custom of translating surnames travelled with them. In Germany Conrad Celtis, the first Northerner to be honored with the laurel crown for poetry, translated his Greek surname from the German Bickel, or Pickel.[8] His disciple Vincentus Eleutherius took his name from the Silesian city of Freistadt.[9] The sixteenth-century revival of Greek literature was due in large part to the great humanist printers of the North, many of whom issued their editions under hellenized surnames. Thus the Basel publisher Andreas Cratander, whose rediscovery of five lost letters of Cicero secured his place in the heavens of philology, was originally called Hartmann, while Guglielmus Xylander, some of whose redactions were definitive until the eighteenth century, signed his famous 1543 edition of Euclid as Wilhelm Holtzman.[10] Johannes Oporinus, Professor of Greek at Basel, issued his German edition of Vesalius's *De humani corporis fabrica* under his vernacular name Herbst (his father preferring the form Herbster).[11] The Petri family's famous printer's mark, which showed the hand of God striking a hammer upon a huge stone, reflected the practice of hellenization by making a visual pun on the Greek word πέτρος, or "stone" (Plate 1).[12] Another clan of Basel humanists, the Bischoff family, drew this practice into an inspired catena of analogy: playing upon the double meaning of their hellenized name Episcopius, which means both "bishop" and "circumspect," they took as their printer's mark an episcopal crozier and a crane—the bird traditionally known for centuries as the emblem of *circumspectio*—shown in the act of looking over its shoulder (Plate 2).[13] Similar visual puns were also popular in

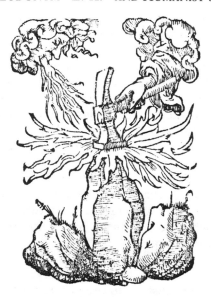

PLATE 1. Printer's mark of the Petri family, mid-16th c. From Petrarca, *Opera omnia quae extant* (Basel, 1554, rpt. Ridgewood, N.J., 1965).

E P I SCOP.

PLATE 2. Printer's mark of the Episcopius family (this version in use 1548–77). From P. Heitz, *Basler Büchermärken bis zum Anfang des 17. Jahrhunderts* (Strassburg, 1895). Rare Books and Manuscripts Division, The New York Public Library, Astor, Lenox and Tilden Foundations.

Spenser's England, having been imported from the continent, according to Camden, in the wake of the Hundred Years' War.

> For whereas a poesie is a speaking picture, and a picture a speechlesse Poesie, they which lackt wit to expresse their conceit in speech, did use to depaint it out (as it were) in pictures, which they called *Rebus*, by a Latine name well fitting their devise. These were so well liked by our English there, and sent hither over the streight of Callice with full saile, were so entertained heere (although they were most ridiculous) by all degrees, by the learned and unlearned, that he was no body that could not hammer out of his name an invention by this wit-craft, and picture it accordingly: whereupon who did not busie his braine to hammer his devise out of this forge."[14]

Apart from such visual/verbal polysemy, the palm for purely linguistic invention must go to the poetic mutations that Wolfgang Schenk (or Schenken) imposed on his long-suffering name. Schenk was an Erfurt humanist who is remembered as the first publisher of books in Greek type outside Italy. On the title page of his *Elementale introductorium in ideoma graecanicum* (1501) he translated his first name into Latin as Lupambulus and his last name into Greek as Oinogoon. Later, not content merely to hellenize the name Schenk (Ger. "cupbearer"), he adopted the identity of Jove's own page, calling himself nothing less than "Lupambulus Ganimedes, *alias* Schenk."[15]

Desiderius Erasmus also combined Latin and Greek names: thus Gerhard, the name given him at baptism, translated into Latin, served as his adopted Christian name, while, translated into Greek, it became his surname.[16] Some humanists would use the Latin and Greek translations of their surnames interchangably, as did Willem van de Voldersgraft, or de Volder, who sometimes called himself Guglielmus Fullonius and at other times Guglielmus Gnapheus.[17]

Many of the humanists with hellenized surnames also made important contributions to the cause of religious reform. Philip Melanchthon was one of these, as we have seen;[18] likewise Johannes Hausschein became Johannes Oecolampadius; Thomas Kirchmeyer, Naogeorgus;[19] and the learned Biblical scholar Theodor Buchmann appropriately used the name Bibliander.[20] As Camden was able to surmise, the name of the German theologian Andreas Osiander was a translation of Heiligmann, though Osiander himself claimed that his father and grandfather had also borne the Greek form.[21] The hellenized names of less well-known figures such as Artophagus, Melander, and Pandocheus fill the pages of the lists of heresiarchs published by the Counter-Reformation Church; and it seems likely that the prevalence of such names among the Protestants contributed to a decline of the practice of hellenization in Catholic Italy, just as it was reaching its greatest popularity in the North.[22]

The first prerequisite, of course, for a hellenizing surname was to know the literal meaning of the name to be translated. Edmund Spenser undoubtedly knew the origin of his family's name, since it was a common term in his day for a butler or steward, the person entrusted with overseeing the expenditures and administration of a household.[23] Camden records that the meaning of the name was still a matter of everyday knowledge in Spenser's time: "Offices have brought new names to divers families, as when *Edward Fitz-Theobald* was made Butler of Ireland, the Earles of Ormond and others descended from them, tooke the name of *Butler*. So the distinct families of the *Constables* in the County of Yorke, are saide to have taken that name, from some of their Ancestours which bare the office of Constables of some Castles. In like manner the *Stewards, Marshalls, Spencers.*"[24]

The various Latin and Greek equivalents for the name Spenser fall along a continuum ranging from the literal and lowly *dispensator* (Gk. δίοπς), which primarily connoted a household steward, to the more prestigious and historically resonant *procurator* (Gk. κηδεμών), which could also refer to the steward of an estate or a community, or, in mercantile usage, to an official factor or agent.[25] *Kedemon* is the closest equivalent to the English office of spencer; and with its greater aura of authority, would likewise have been the most suited to the aims and ambitions of humanist self-naming.[26] Thus the pseudonym E. K. could quite possibly represent the poet's own initials, after recasting the name Edmund Spenser in humanist garb as Edmundus Kedemon.

The possibility that the name E. K. represents a humanistic variation on Spenser's name corroborates the present critical consensus that Spenser issued *The Shepheardes Calender* in a form designed to recall the presentation of classical texts, which at that time were being issued with the complex critical glosses of the humanist editors.[27] The book's visual presentation, which was carefully maintained throughout a number of completely reset editions, wittily alluded to the format of Renaissance editions of Virgil.[28] Just as the pseudonym Immerito evoked the world of continental poetry, Edmundus Kedemon or E. K. recalled contemporary glossers of the classics. If Spenser saw himself as a sort of *Vergilius redivivus*, his addition of the gloss seems to demonstrate that he saw himself also as a new Servius, and the disguises of the "new poet" Immerito and the learned scholiast Edmundus Kedemon would have served to reinforce this symbolic lineage in the eyes of his intimate circle of humanistic literati.[29]

The appropriateness of such a pair of allusive pseudonyms can be seen from the fact that Spenser's circle at the time of *The Shepherdes Calender* revolved around his Cambridge tutor Gabriel Harvey, who was a sophisticated observer of French and Italian Renaissance poetry and an impassioned student of the classics. Further, Harvey's espousal of ancient literary convention was equalled only by his love for the arcane and esoteric.[30]

Harvey's correspondence with Spenser, some of which was published shortly after the appearance of *The Shepherdes Calender*, is full of clever and playful banter on both authors' names—suggesting that they saw the creation of such public enigmas as an important facet of their literary activity. In one of the "Three Proper, and Wittie, Familiar Letters . . . touching the Earthquake in Aprill last, and our English refourmed Versifying," Harvey addressed Spenser (referred to throughout the published correspondence as "Immerito") in a way that makes it appear likely that he was privy to the E. K.-Edmundus Kedemon disguise.[31] In the last of these letters Harvey sent his congratulations on the publication of *The Shepheardes Calender* together with a selection of his own latest efforts in verse. Harvey's first poem bears the title: "A New yeeres Gift to my old friend Maister *George Bilchaunger*."

Harvey's introductory remarks to the poem identify Spenser as the dedicatee of the New Year's gift-poem, thus making it clear that "Maister George Bilchaunger" was Harvey's facetious nickname for Spenser.[32] Here Harvey must have been playing a humorous variation on Spenser's translation of his name to the Greek Kedemon. In the late sixteenth century the use of bills of exchange, corresponding roughly to our modern checking accounts, was already quite familiar in England.[33] A common duty of a procurator or spencer was paying or receiving on bills of exchange for his employer; in fact, one of the chief legal distinctions between a common servant and a spencer in Renaissance

England was that the latter could not be held liable for losses incurred on behalf of his employer in such transactions unless he had been invested with a procuration.[34]

It is equally revealing that this bit of verbal play on Spenser's name is followed by Harvey's praise of Spenser's poetry for its richness in arcane allusion: ". . . *extra iocum*, I like your *Dreames* passingly well: and the rather, bicause they fauour of that singular extraoradinarie veine and inuention, whiche I euer fancied moste . . . aboue the reache, and compasse of a common Schollers capacitie."[35]

There is also the still incompletely explained passage from a draft of an undated letter to Spenser (ca. 1579), in Harvey's *Letter-Book*. There, after rebuking Spenser for covertly publishing a book of Harvey's poems ("Virelayes"), the latter signs himself: "G. H. . . . as affectionate towards your Mastershipp as ever heretofore, conditionallye that neither this palting letter nor that tell tale obligation cum forth in printe. Alias, insteade of the oulde G. H. reade Grandis Hostis, as you redd once in my Greate Ostisses parlour, Grandis Hostis."[36] In other words, the initials G. H. represented Spenser's affectionate friend Gabriel Harvey—but if Spenser should ever publish this letter they would stand for Grandis Hostis ("great enemy").

Alongside the exuberant delight of Spenser and Harvey in transforming their names, we have Camden's testimony to show that such games were also fashionable in the courtly world to which the young poets aspired. Among his sketches of Renaissance onomastics he records the elegant compliment paid to Queen Elizabeth by her courtiers, who busied themselves with translating her name into Greek anagrams.[37] And with evident relish he describes the benefits to be gained from reconstituting disguised names back into English. According to Camden, the puzzling out of a clever pseudonym was considered

a delightful comfort and pleasant motion in honest mindes, in no point yeelding to many vaine pleasures of the body. They will also afford it some commendations in respect of the difficultie (*Difficilia quae pulchra*,) as also it is a whetstone of patience to them that shall practise it. For some have been seene to bite their penne, scratch their head, bend their browes, bite their lips, beate the boord, teare the paper when they were faire for somewhat, and caught nothing heerin.[38]

Camden could well have been referring to the many efforts to make sense of the enigmatic initials E. K., and to explain Spenser's motivation in using them as a literary disguise. But it is clear that, if we seek an explanation in the practices of self-naming that were current among literary humanists of the sixteenth century, Spenser's pseudonym E. K. is hardly as incongruous as it has often seemed. It would indeed have been a whetstone for anyone's patience to discover that E. K. = Edmundus Kedemon = Edmund Spenser, and it is somewhat doubtful that there were few besides Spenser and Harvey who ever penetrated the author's ruse.[39] But it is a puzzle that fits perfectly within the literary practice and popular fancy of Spenser's time, and it also reflects the private interests of Spenser and Harvey in teasing their public with mysterious disguises. By understanding how the pseudonym E. K. functioned as a meaningful counterpart to Spenser's other *nom-de-plume*, Immerito, we are given a new clue to the allusive meaning of the critical apparatus of *The Shepherdes Calender*.

NOTES

1.   The first to do so was the individual calling himself "β" who suggested that the initials E. K. were "intended, not improbably for the poet himself, the initials signifying here Edmund the Kalenderer" ("Menalcas," *Notes and Queries* 5th ser., 6 [1876], p. 365). However, the *Oxford English Dictionary* records no use of the word "calenderer" in the sense "beta" would like to give it, "a maker of calendars" (in actual usage it referred to a method of treating cloth). In 1935 A. D. Kuerstiner proposed the same argument using the Latin version Edmundus Kalendarius ("E. K. is Spenser," *PMLA* 50 [1935], pp. 140–55). Likewise, the Latin "kalendarius" is not cited with this meaning in the *Oxford Latin Dictionary* or in the *Glossarium mediae et infimae latinitatis* of the Abbé Du Cange.

2.   A bronze plaque in Washington bears the retrograde signature of the artist Andrea Ricco, whose works are closely linked to the intellectual milieu of fifteenth-century humanism; C. C. Wilson illustrates it in *Renaissance Small Bronze Sculpture and Associated Decorative Arts at the National Gallery of Art* (Washington, D.C. 1983), pp. 86–87. Antonio di Piero Averlino, an artist whose humanist pretensions led him to adopt the Greek name Filarete, frequently employed the disguise of transposed syllables in his *Treatise on Architecture* (ed. and tr. J. R. Spencer, New Haven, 1965): thus, Onitoan Nolivera Notirenflo = Antonio Averlino Florentino, Iscofrance Notilento = Francesco da Tolentino, etc. Personal names transliterated into Greek are quite common as inscriptions on works of art that have some relation to humanist ideals, particularly on portrait medals—for numerous examples, see G. F. Hill, *A Corpus of Italian Medals of the Renaissance before Cellini* (London, 1930).

3.   Cf. L. R. N. Ashley, "Classical Pseudonyms in Europe at the Time of the Reformation," *Names: Journal of the American Name Society* 14 (1966) pp. 193–96.

4.   *Remains Concerning Britain.* Ed. R. D. Dunn (Toronto/Buffalo/London, 1984), p. 127.

5.   The still invaluable study by A. F. Didot, *Aldus Manuce et l'hellénisme à Venise* (Paris, 1875), contains accounts of many humanists who hellenized their surnames, together with a wealth of documentation on the Aldine circle.

6.   Didot, *Aldus Manuce*, pp. 67–68, 44–47. For a biography of Bondino/ Agathemeros, see *Dizionario biographico degli italiani* (Rome, 1960–) XI, pp. 735–736.

7.   Didot, *Aldus Manuce*, pp. 453-54; cf. the study by A Chiti, *Scipione Fortiguerra, il Carteromacho: Studio biografico con una raccolta di epigrammi, sonnetti, e lettere di lui e a lui dirette*, Florence, 1902.

8.   For a short biography and selections from his work in Latin and English, see F. J. Nichols, *An Anthology of Neo-Latin Poetry* (New Haven, 1979) pp. 436ff., 693ff. See also the entry in the *Allgemeine deutsche Biographie* (Leipzig, 1875–1912) IV, 82ff. (hereafter cited as *AdB*).

9.   Didot, *Aldus Manuce*, pp. 178ff.

10.   For Cratander's life, see *AdB* XLVII, pp. 541–42; P. Heitz, *Basler Büchermärken bis zum Anfang des 17. Jahrhunderts* (Strassburg, 1895), pp. xxiv–xxv. For Xylander's life, see *AdB* XLIV, pp. 582ff.

11.   *AdB* XXIV, pp. 381ff.; Heitz, *Basler Büchermärken*, p. xxxiii; also M. H. Spielmann, *The Iconography of Andreas Vesalius (André Vésale), Anatomist and Physician 1514–1564*, (London, 1925), pp. 124ff.

12.   For biographical information on the Petri family see *AdB* XXV, pp. 520–22; C. W. Heckethorn, *The Printers of Basle in the XV. & XVI. Centuries: Their Biographies, Printed Books and Devices* (London, 1897), pp. 140ff.; Heitz, *Basler Büchermärken*, pp. xxiiff.

13.   The same play on words led, in the 17th and 18th centuries, to the crane's frequent identification with the clergy, who watch vigilantly and circumspectly over the faithful; see H. M. von Erffa, "Grus Vigilans: Bemerkungen zur Emblematik," *Philobiblon* 1 (1957): 301–302. For the various printers of the Episcopus family in Basel, see *AdB* VI, p. 155; Heckethorn, *The Printers of Basle*, pp. 125ff.; Heitz, *Basler Büchermärken*, pp. xxvff.; also *Rechnungsbuch der Froben & Episcopius, Buchdrucker und Buchhändler zu Basel 1557–1564*, ed. R. Wackernagel (Basel, 1881). There appears to have been no relation between the Episcopii of Basel and the Dutch Remonstrant theologian Simon Episcopius (*né* Bischop) who was responsible for systematizing the doctrines of Arminianism (see *AdB* VI, pp. 155–57).

14.   Camden, *Remains*, p. 139.

15.   Didot, *Aldus Manuce*, pp. 588–89.

16.   *AdB* VI, pp. 160ff.

17.   See the entry in *AdB* IX, pp. 279–280; also *Acolastus: A Latin Play of the Sixteenth Century by Guglielmus Gnapheus*, ed. and tr. W. E. D. Atkinson (London, Ontario, 1964).

18.   *AdB* XXI, pp. 268ff.

19.   *AdB* XXIII, pp. 245ff.

20.   *AdB* II, p. 612.

21.   Ashley, "Classical Pseudonyms in Europe," p. 194.

22. See G. H. Putnam, *The Censorship of the Church of Rome and Its Influence upon the Production and Distribution of Literature. A Study of Some of the Prohibitory and Expurgatory Indexes, Together with Some Considerations of the Effects of Protestant Censorship and of Censorship by the State* (New York and London, 1907).

23. *Oxford English Dictionary* IX, p. 573: "*Spencer* . . . Also 4 spensere, 4–5 spenser, 6 *Sc[ottish]*. spensar; 5 spencere . . . One who dispenses or has charge of the provisions of a household; a steward or butler."

24. Camden, *Remains*, p. 123.

25. These shades of meaning sometimes appear to have been more honored in the breach than the observance. While contemporary lexica tend to distinguish between the various administrative terms and titles, in some cases the distinctions are not insisted upon; cf. Ambrogio Calepino, *Dictionarium undecim linguarum* (Basel, 1605? I, p. 434: "*Dispensatio*, f.t. Procuratio, administratio . . . The charge or laying out of money for another, distribution . . . *Dispensator*, m.t., Qui familiae necessaria dispensat, & distribuit: cujusmodi sunt obsonatores, quorum officium est coëmere quae usus domesticus expostulat . . . He that layeth out or distributeth money, a steward.; *Dispenso*, as frequentativum, quod frequentiore in usu est, Dispendo, dispono, procuro . . . Gouverner, dispenser, ou distribuer une chose par raison . . . To lay out money for another, to distribut [sic]."

26. In Imperial Rome the procurators were a somewhat elite group of civil servants and military officials, who were chosen from among the ranks of the *equites*. Their actual duties could vary widely, up to the fiscal administration of an entire province. For the evolution of the office from Augustus to Claudius, see A. N. Sherwin-White, "Procurator Augusti," *Papers of the British School at Rome*, n.s., 2 (1939): 11–26. A prosopography of Roman procurators exists: H. Pflaum, *Les carrières procuratoriennes équestres sous le haut-empire romain*, (Paris, 1960–61). Calepino (*Dictionarium undecim linguarum* I, p. 362) defines the terms procurator and κηδεμών as equivalents. His definition of procurator is also strikingly similar to that he gives for dispensator (see above, n. 25): "Qui absentis negotia gerit . . . A proctour, that seeth to an others affaires. Ulpianus de Procuratoribus & Defensor. I. 1. Procurator est qui aliena negotia mandato domini administrat." Procurator and κηδεμών are also given as equivalents in the *Dictionarium graecum* (Venice: Melchior Sessa and Petrus de Ravanis, 1525), fol. 166 verso; the *Lexicon graecolatinum, seu, Thesaurus linguae graecae* (Venice: Petrus Bosellus, 1560) fol. DDDii verso; and Robert Estienne, *Thesaurus graecae linguae* (Geneva, 1580) II, p. 183a.

27. See, for instance, R. Mallette, "Spenser's Portrait of the Artist in *The Shepheardes Calender* and *Colin Clouts Come Home Again*," *SEL* 19 (1979): 19–41; and M. McCanles, "*The Shepheardes Calender* as Document and Monument," *SEL* 20 (1982): 7–19.

28. R. S. Luborsky, "The Allusive Presentation of *The Shepheardes Calender*," *Spenser Studies* 1 (1980): 29–67.

29. A somewhat similar instance—dealing with scientific rather than literary humanism, is Thomas Heywood's issuing of *Philocothonista, or, The Drunkard, Opened, Dissected and Anatomized* under the name "Tho: Faeni-Lignum" (Hay-Wood)—his pseudonym being a sly barb at the practices of self-naming that set apart the Renaissance scientist from his medieval precursors. The title of the book playfully refers to another innovation of sixteenth-century medicine: the

licit and public practice of human dissection; see A. M. Clark, *Thomas Heywood: Playwright and Miscellanist* (Oxford, 1931), pp. 150–53.

30. The most up-to-date assessment of Harvey is V. F. Stern, *Gabriel Harvey: His Life, Marginalia, and Library* (Oxford and New York, 1979); still valuable are Grosart's "Memorial-Introduction" to his edition of *The Works of Gabriel Harvey* (London, 1884–85) and H. Berli's *Gabriel Harvey. Der Dichterfreund und Kritiker* (Zurich, 1913). A brief but balanced account of him can be found in *The Dictionary of National Biography*, ed. L. Stephen (Oxford, 1885–1900) IX, pp. 83ff.

31. *The Works of Edmund Spenser: A Variorum Edition*, ed. E. Greenlaw, C. G. Osgood, F. M. Padelford, et al. (Baltimore, 1932–49) [hereafter referred to as *Var.*], X, Appendix I [Letter V], pp. 463–77.

32. Cf. his tongue-in-cheek question: "Shall I now sende you a *Ianuarie gift* in *Aprill*: and as it were shewe you a *Christmas Gambowlde* after *Easter*?" (ibid., p. 464).

33. "Bill[8]," *Oxford English Dictionary*, I, 861; cf. G. de Malynes, *Consuetudo, vel, Lex mercatoria, or, The Ancient Law-Merchant* (London, 1686), pp. 269ff.; J. Milnes Holden, *The History of Negotiable Instruments in English Law*, University of London Legal Series, No. 3 (London, 1955), pp. 22ff.; R. de Roover, *L'evolution de la lettre de change, XlVe-XVIIIe siècles*, Affaires et Gens d'Affaires, No. 4 (Paris, 1953).

34. See A. Liset, *Amphithalami, or, The Accomptants Closet, Being an Abridgment of Merchants-Accounts Kept by Debtors and Creditors* (London, 1684), litera B, pp. 23ff.

35. *Var.* X. p. 471.

36. Gabriel Harvey, *Letter-Book*, ed. E. J. L. Scott (London, 1884, repr. New York, 1965), p. 64.

37. Camden, *Remains*, p. 147.

38. Ibid., p. 143.

39. In an article which appeared as this was going to press ("Spenser's 'E. K.' as Edmund Kent (Kenned / of Kent): Kyth (Couth), Kissed, and Kunning-Conning," *English Literary Renaissance* 20 (1990): 374–407), Louise Schleiner proposes that in writing the *Shepheardes Calender* gloss Spenser was attempting to mirror the style of a *specific* humanist: Gabriel Harvey. While her argument in support of this is impressive, I find less convincing her other thesis, namely, that the pseudonym "E. K." represents Spenser in the guise of one "Edmund of Kent."

SHOHACHI FUKUDA

The Numerological Patterning of
Amoretti and Epithalamion

S PENSER'S preoccupation with numerological patterns is a well-established, but in practice often neglected, dimension of his creative genius. Other studies have analyzed the significance of this fundamental element in *Epithalamion* (considered alone) and *The Fairie Queene*.[1] This paper considers the poet's most elaborate mannerist work, the small volume published in 1595 with the title *Amoretti and Epithalamion*, and it is my contention that for purposes of numerological analysis the two poems are interdependent.

As published, the volume contains what appears to be two separate poems: *Amoretti* is a sonnet sequence that tells of the poet's courtship of Elizabeth Boyle, and *Epithalamion* is a marriage song that celebrates his wedding day in June 1594. After *Amoretti* Spenser printed four short poems now usually called anacreontics.[2] The numerological patterning hinted at in the volume, however, seems to indicate that the poet conceived them, not just as two independent poems of love to his second wife, but as a unified whole. Following the hints that Spenser has given, the reader may discover that the volume of *Amoretti and Epithalamion* is carefully designed numerologically.[3] The Italian part of the title suggests that the sonnet sequence is about cupids, conforming with those in the anacreontics and the marriage song; the duplicate sonnets are placed as markers; the last 24 sonnets show a symmetry in which each pair of sonnets, printed on the facing pages, has a corresponding pair; and a similar "pair symmetry" is seen in *Epithalamion*.

I

Amoretti is composed of 89 sonnets, but since sonnets 35 and 83 are identical except for one word, it is often described as a poem of 88 sonnets. A closer look into its structure, however, will reveal that these two sonnets are actually indicators in the array of numbers hidden in this volume. Spenser's first hint is the title he gave to the sequence: "Amoretti" literally means "little loves or cupids." If by cupids the poet means sonnets, the 89 sonnets represent 89 cupids; and since the 4 anacreontics amount to 4 cupids, each being about a cupid, and the 24 stanzas of the Epithalamion amount to 24 cupids, the total number of cupids in the volume is 117. Let us imagine that there is a line of 117 cupids all facing us, or that, better still, arranged on a straight line, they constitute a building. In this array of 117 cupids a special position is given to the 35th and 83rd cupids: each duplicate sonnet is placed at exactly the same distance from the beginning and from the end. 34 cupids come before the 35th sonnet; 34 after the 83rd; and 47 between the two. Alastair Fowler has noted this arrangement of 34/1/47/1 /34,[4] but its symmetry indicates even more than he allows.

The opening and the closing stanzas of the volume are given a special role. The first sonnet addresses the sequence, asking: "Leaves, lines, and rymes, seeke her to please, / whom if you please, I care for other none." The envoy of the marriage song also addresses the song: "Song made in lieu of many ornaments, . . . / Be unto her a goodly ornament, / And for short time an endless moniment." If those two are also taken as markers, there remain 33 cupids before sonnet 35, and 33 after sonnet 83, with 47 in the center, making the following array:

	Amoretti					anacreontics	Epithalamion	
1	2–34	35	36–82	83	84–89	1–4	1–23	24
1	33	1	47	1	6	4	23	1
1	33	1	47	1		33		1

The symmetrical arrangement of this volume may be compared to the structure of Gothic buildings as illustrated in the figure below:

33 cupids	47 cupids	33 cupids

1st	34th	83rd	117th

The proportion of 47 to 33 is 1.42 . . . : 1, which is practically the same as that of the square root of 2 to 1.[5] This is the proportion of the diagonal of a square to its side and, since the same ratio holds infinitely because this proportion of the square root of 2 to 1 is equal to that of 1 to one half the square root of 2, the ratio is traditionally taken to symbolize eternity. In discussing the problem of harmonic proportion in Renaissance architecture Rudolf Wittkower refers to Palladio's general rules of proportion.[6] This Italian architect, following in the footsteps of his predecessors, considers the most beautiful ratios of width to length of rooms and recommends seven shapes of rooms in which the diagonal of the square for the length of the room is given the third place after (1) circular, and (2) square. As Wittkower explains, this is the only irrational number of importance involved in the Renaissance theory of architectural proportion. Another example of Spenser's use of this proportion is seen in the 81 stanzas of *Daphnaida*, which comprise the tale (24 stanzas) and the lament (57 stanzas).[7] The relationship of the whole (81) to the second half (57) is 1.42 . . . : 1, which is extremely close to being the same as the proportion of the square root of 2 to 1. There seems to be little doubt that Spenser was well aware of the rules of proportion observed in his contemporary architecture and that he designed his poetry as the architects did their buildings.

When he designed the volume, Spenser probably had in mind the structure of Dante's *Divina Commedia* with its three books, each made up of 33 cantos. The numbers 3 and 33 are both sacred, as the former connotes the Trinity and the latter is the traditional figure for the number of Christ's years on earth. Spenser's 33, hidden in the form of the volume, is an appropriate number in which to describe stage by stage the progress, or suffering, of his mind in love. Similarly, we notice in 47 a parallel between Christ's suffering and the poet's: 47 is conformable to the 47 days of Lent or 40 days of Christ's temptation in the wilderness and 7 Sundays during that period. Thanks to Dunlop's findings, we already know that the number 47 is firmly established within the sonnet sequence occupying sonnet 22 (Ash Wednesday) through 68 (Easter), and making a symmetry of 21 + 47 + 21.[8]

Of the four markers in the array of 117 cupids, the first and the last ones are, as we have already seen, little more than an address to those that follow and precede. His more specific intention is expressed in the duplicate sonnet. Sonnet 35 reads:

> My hungry eyes through greedy covetize,
>   still to behold the object of their paine:
>   with no contentment can themselves suffize,
>   but having pine and having not complaine.
> For lacking it they cannot lyfe sustayne,
>   and having it they gaze on it the more:
>   in their amazement lyke *Narcissus* vaine
>   whose eyes him starv'd: so plenty makes me poore.
> Yet are mine eyes so filled with the store
>   of that fair sight, that nothing else they brooke,
>   but lothe the things which they did like before,
>   and can no more endure on them to looke.
> All this worlds glory seemeth vayne to me,
>   and all their showes but shadows saving she.[9]

Here Spenser writes that *Amoretti* is to record the fate of "my hungry eyes" that are doomed to keep looking at "that fair sight" "lyke Narcissus vaine". To his eyes the lady is a "proud", "cruel", "stubborne" creature; yet, as in sonnet 34, she is "my *Helice* the lodestar of my lyfe / [that] will shine again, and look on me at last." Placed right after this, the "hungry eyes" sonnet consolidates the state of a lover whose wish, in the sonnet convention, is never fulfilled. This sad, tormented lover is variously depicted, and in sonnet 54 the relation of the lady and the lover is compared to the spectator and the actor "that all the pageants play, / disguysing diversly my troubled wits."[10]

Spenser lived in an age when everything was thought of spatially. In numerological writings the central thought was expressed at the center.[11] In the volume of *Amoretti and Epithalamion* there are three centers. First we should look at sonnet 45 for what the poet intended in the sonnet sequence. The last line of this sonnet is written in Alexandrine, perhaps as an indication of its centrality.[12]

Leave lady in your glasse of christall clene,
   your goodly selfe for evermore to vew:
   and in my self, my inward selfe I meane,
   most lively lyke behold your semblant trew.
Within my hart, though hardly it can shew,
   thing so divine to vew of earthly eye:
   the fayre Idea of your celestiall hew,
   and every part remaines immortally:
And were it not that through your cruelty,
   with sorrow dimmed and deformd it were:
   the goodly ymage of your visnomy,
   clearer then christall would therein appere.
But if your selfe in me ye playne will see,
   remove the cause by which your fayre beames darkned be.

In the 433-line marriage song the central line of 217 tells exactly of what it is all about. It is placed in the twelfth stanza which begins with the poet's direction: "Open the temple gates unto my love." Here are lines 215–17:

> Bring her up to th'high altar that she may,
> The sacred ceremonies there partake,
> The which do endlesse matrimony make . . .

Spenser proclaims here that *Epithalamion* is a song that tells of the "endlesse matrimony" of the poet, as he announces at the center of the central sonnet that *Amoretti* is a series of sonnets that depict in various ways "the fayre Idea" of his lady's "celestiall hew."

At sonnet 59, the center of the whole volume, he does the same thing. It makes a pair with sonnet 58 which has the only headnote in *Amoretti* or elsewhere: *By her that is most assured to her selfe* (here "by" means, in the definition of *OED*, "in the presence of; at the house of"). The italicized headnote belonging to the pair is again an unmistakable sign from the poet to the reader calling attention to its centrality. In tone the first of the pair is negative. It begins by saying "Weake is th'assurance . . ." and goes on to say "Ne none so rich or wise, so strong or fayre, / but fayleth trusting on his owne assurance." In contrast to this soft-spoken lamentation, the second of the pair stands out in its high-spirited pronounce-ment of assurance:

Thrise happie she, that is so well assured
   Unto her selfe and settled so in hart:
   that nether will for better be allured,
   ne feard with worse to any chance to start,
But like a steddy ship doth strongly part
   the raging waves and keepes her course aright·
   ne ought for tempest doth from it depart,
   ne ought for fayrer weathers false delight.
Such selfe assurance need not feare the spight
   of grudging foes, ne favour seeke of friends:
   but in the stay of her owne stedfast might,
   nether to one her selfe nor other bends.
Most happy she that most assured doth rest,
   but he most happy who such one loves best.

The transition from the soft questioning of the concluding lines
of sonnet 58: "Why then doe ye proud fayre, misdeeme so farre, /
that to your selfe ye most assured arre?" to the strong assurance
of the opening lines that follow: "Thrise happie she, that is so
well assured . . ." is sudden, but effective. It is noteworthy that
at this midpoint in the array of 117 cupids Spenser begins his
depiction of the happy union: the miserable man suffering from
unrequited love now becomes the happiest man on earth. In the
concluding couplet Spenser spells out what he wants to achieve
in this book. The praise of the lady ("Most happy she that most
assured doth rest") is followed by a calm statement on his own
happiness: "but he most happy who such one loves best." This is
what he wants to say, and he says it only once. In just one
concluding line of the sonnet placed at the center Spenser makes
perhaps the most important statement of this volume. This is in
accord with the fact that, disregarding the convention that the
sonnet recorded unrequited passion, *Amoretti* tells of the poet's
joy in having found someone to love. Here lies the uniqueness of
Spenser's poetry.

II

We have seen that in the central sonnet Spenser has effected a
change of tone from misery to happiness. In the second half of
the array the poet seems to have incorporated some obvious

patterns of symmetry. If we read the volume as it was first published by William Ponsonby in 1595, sonnet 60 is printed on the left hand page and sonnet 61 on the right-hand page. It is now easy to see these two as a pair: 60 is about the poet himself depicted in the image of "the winged God," and 61 is about the lady portrayed as "My soverayne saynt, the Idoll of my thought." Here he is a tormented lover who has spent one year of courting "in long languishment" (the poet rightly says it here, hinting that he has depicted the pains of love in the first half of his collection). In contrast, his lady is shown in "The glorious image of the makers beautie." This device of writing paired sonnets on the facing pages is used from here to the end of the sonnet sequence.

From here onwards the lady is his sweetheart. The reader sees an upward progress in the relationship variously depicted on the facing pages.[13] The new year comes (62) and he sees the happy shore (63); he kisses her (64) and she is "the gentle birde [that] feels no captivity / within her cage" (65); she is light in the darkness (66) and, finally, his love is granted as grace: "the gentle deer . . . so goodly wonne with her owne will beguyld" (67). Turning the pages from this most elaborate picture of his love, we come to the Easter sonnet (68), in which Christ "having harrowd hell didst bring away / captivity thence captive us to win." This is properly placed in pair with the statement that "Even this verse vowd to eternity, / shall be thereof immortall moniment" (69).

The brevity of life described in the *carpe diem* sonnet (70) is matched with "eternall peace . . . / between the Spyder and the gentle Bee" of the tapestry sonnet (71). Then comes the bliss pair: "my fraile fancy . . . doth bath in blisse" (72) and the poet asks her to "encage" him gently so that he may "sing your name and praises over all" (73). This is followed by the "name" pair: "Ye three Elizabeths for ever live" (74) and "One day I wrote her name on the strand" (75). Spenser's depiction of the lady's beauty culminates in the "bosom" pair: "Fair bosome fraught with vertues richest tresure, / The nest of love, the lodging of delight: / the bower of blisse, the paradice of pleasure" (76) and "Her brest that table was so richly spredd, / my thoughts the guests, which would thereon have fedd" (77).[14]

The transition is unmistakably marked by a sudden change of tone at sonnet 78 which begins with his lamentation: "Lacking my love I go from place to place, / lyke a young fawne that late hath lost the hynd." Like the duplicate sonnet and the central one, this is concluded in the eye image: "Cease then myne eyes, to seek her selfe to see, / and let my thoughts behold her selfe in mee." The facing sonnet talks about "that fayre Spirit" which produces true beauty and ends in a negative tone: "all other fayre lyke flowres untymely fade." In sonnet 80, referring to his unfinished epic, Spenser begs leave to "sing my loves sweet praise" but he has to add: "But let her praises yet be low and meane, / fit for the handmayd of the Faery Queene." Yet this maid is given unreserved praise in sonnet 81 as "the work of harts astonishment." The next pair makes an interesting contrast: 82 is a full description of his joy in loving her. It begins triumphantly with "Joy of my life, full oft for loving you / I bless my lot . . ." and ends calmly celebrating himself and the lady: "Whose lofty argument uplifting me, / shall lift you up unto an high degree." Printed on the right-hand page, the duplicate sonnet (83) takes on an added meaning. Here, "having" at line 6 of sonnet 35 is changed into "seeing." The change makes it clear that, to the same hungry eyes, "the object of theyr payne" is not just "had" as before, but now it is "seen." By this small change, primarily made to indicate that sonnet 83 is not just a repetition of 35, Spenser has achieved considerable effect. In the last three pairs that follow the duplicate sonnet, the tone becomes darker and darker and the poem ends with the image of the poet in darkness and as good as dead.

In the last 24 sonnets of *Amoretti* Spenser has incorporated a scheme of parallel design. The first half records the joy of love and the second half depicts the sorrow of temporary separation before the wedding day. In this frame the first pair (66–67) is contrasted to the last pair (88–89) in such a way that the first sonnet of the pair is contrasted to the first sonnet of the last pair: in 66 the lady is his light ("your light . . . in my darknesse greater doth appeare"), and in 88 the poet wanders "as in darknesse of the night"; in 67 she is "the gentle deare" that returns to the huntsman to be "fyrmely tyde," and in 89 he is "the Culver . . . / [that] Sits mourning for the absence of her mate." A similar parallel is observed between the next pairs (68–69 and 86–87): "Most glorious Lord of lyfe" in 68 is contrasted to "Venemous toung tipt with vile adders sting" in 86; "Even this verse vowd to eternity, / shall be thereof immortall moniment" in 69 is in contrast to "Many long weary days . . . / and many nights" that he has "outworne" in her absence in 87. In the next pairs (70–71 and

84–85), "Fresh spring the herald of loves mighty king" in 70 makes a sharp contrast to "filthy lustfull fyre" in 84; and likewise "all thensforth eternall peace shall see, / betweene the Spyder and the gentle Bee" in 71 to envy of the world in 85.

Between each of the three inner sets of pairs (72–73 and 82–83; 74–75 and 80–81; 76–77 and 78–79) we notice similar contrasts. In 72 "my fraile fancy fed with full delight, / doth bath in blisse," while in 82 "the more your owne mishap I rew, / that are so much by so meane love embased"; in 73 "my hart, that wont on your fayre eye / to feed his fill, flyes backe unto your sight," while in 83 his hungry eyes "with no contentment can themselves suffize." Full praise of his lady in 74 "The third my love, my lives last ornament" becomes in 80 an excuse to "let her praises yet be low and meane, / fit for the handmayd of the Faery Queene"—one should note here the fact that Spenser, remem-

66 now your light in my darkness greater doth appear
67 the gentle deer returned the selfsame way
  68 most glorious Lord of life
  69 this verse vowed to eternity
    70 fresh spring, go to my love
    71 eternal peace between the bee and the spider
      72 my fancy fed with full delight
      73 my heart gently encaged in your bosom
        74 Ye three Elizabeths forever live
        75 my verse your virtues rare eternize
        76 fair bosom
        77 her breast that table was

        78 lacking my love I go like a young fawn
        79 true beauty derived from that fair Spirit
      80 the handmaid of the Faerie Queene
      81 this the work of heart's astonishment
    82 your own mishap I rue
    83 my hungry eyes
  84 let not one spark of lustful fire break out
  85 the world say I do but flatter
86 venomous tongue
87 sorrow still doth seem too long to last
88 I wander as in darkness of the night
89 the culver sits mourning

Figure 1. Contrasting pairs in the last 24 sonnets of *Amoretti*.

bering his public duty to glorify the monarch, placed this ele
ment of prudence in the symmetrical pattern. The strong announcement in 75 that "my verse your vertues rare shall eter-
nize" is contrasted with a calm statement in 81 that "this [is] the
work of harts astonishment." His "sweet thoughts" that rest
"twixt her paps like early fruit in May" in 76 are shown in 78 as
"fancies vayne" that "ydly back returne to me agayne"; and
finally, the beautiful depiction of "a goodly table of pure yvory"
in 77 becomes in 79 a philosophical statement of "that fayre
Spirit, from whom al true / and perfect beauty did at first proceed." Thus, each pair of sonnets from 66 to 77 is contrasted to
one of those from 78 through 89. The symmetrical pattern is
shown in Figure 1.

III

A. Kent Hieatt was the first to see correspondences among the
24 stanzas of *Epithalamion*: he wrote that Spenser intended its 24
stanzas to pair off into the series 1–12 and 13–24.[15] Max A.
Wickert has shown that the marriage song has a strictly symmetrical distribution of stanzas which can be grouped in the proportions: (1) - (3-4-3) - (2) - (3-4-3) - (1).[16] He sees correspondences between stanzas 1 and 24, between 2 and 23, and so on to
the central stanzas, 12 and 13. Alastair Fowler accepts Wickert's
argument as "by far the most accomplished account of the symmetrical structure of the poem," but goes on to point out another
superimposed symmetry which begins at stanza 5 (sunrise),
culminates at stanza 11 (bride crowned) and ends at stanza 17
(sunset).[17]

We may now wonder if Spenser uses the same facing-page
method here as in the last 24 sonnets. If he does, correspondences
are pair-to-pair rather than sonnet-to-sonnet. To find this out we
must look at the original edition which prints one stanza on a
page, beginning with stanza 1 on the right-hand side, and ending
with stanza 24 printed on the left.

The song reaches its climax at stanzas 12 and 13, printed on the
center facing pages: in this correspondence the entrance of the
bride and the sound of the roaring organs are contrasted to the
bride standing and hearing the high priest's blessing in solemn
silence (the singing of *Alleluya* by the angels is inaudible to the

human ear). The bride stands before the altar at the first line of stanza 13, indicating that the poet/bridegroom joins his bride at the beginning of the second half of the symmetry.

Turning the pages, we read "Now al is done" (another Spenserian formula to indicate, as he does at sonnet 78, that the falling action begins here) and find that the stanzas are both addressed to "ye yong men of towne" asking them to "bring home the bride" (14) and to "Ring ye the bels" (15). These are in contrast to stanzas 10 and 11 which both address "ye merchants daughters": stanza 10 portrays the beauty of the bride "Adornd with beautyes grace" and 11 depicts "The inward beauty of her lively spright." In the next pairs the bridal procession (8-9) corresponds to the coming of the night (16-17): the sound of music and "Hymen io Hymen, Hymen" (8) is set against the quiet sunset and the appearance of the bright evening star (16); the bride who walks "lyke some mayden Queene" (9) is in contrast to the bride who lies in bed "In proud humility" (17). These ten stanzas (8-17), placed at the center on ten pages, recount the actions of the wedding from the bridal procession to the wedding feast, and these are the core stanzas of this song. By observing Spenser's symmetrical arrangement here, we note that the two stanzas on facing pages are paired, and that each stanza of this pair is set against one from the corresponding pair.

This method of arrangement is applicable to the rest of the poem. Stanzas 2–7 and 18–23 tell, respectively, of things that occur before the bride leaves for the wedding ceremony and of what happens to the couple after they are united in the marriage bed. In the pairs 6–7 and 18–19, the former marks the beginning of sunshine and festivity while the latter marks the beginning of darkness and silence. "My love is now awake" (6) corresponds to "Now welcome night . . . / Spread thy wing over my love and me" (18). In stanza 7 "let" is repeated five times as in "let this one day be myne," and this is echoed in stanza 19 in the negative form beginning: "Let no lamenting cryes, nor dolefull teares, / Be heard all night."

In the middle pairs of 4–5 and 20–21 the peace and happiness of the morning is contrasted to that of the evening. The bride is so blessed that even the nymphs of Mulla and maids of Diana join in celebration (4) and sons of Venus attend her nuptial bed (20); the sun begins to "shew his glorious hed" signaling to the birds to sing harmoniously (5); and the moon shines to "Encline thy will t'effect our wishfull vow" (21). The opening and the concluding pairs create a contrast between the light festive mood at the beginning and the heavy, solemn tone at the end: Hymen with his torch and young men in "fresh garments" (2) look forward to Juno and the Genius (22); nymphs with gay garlands and fragrant flowers strewn on the ground (3) correspond to the high heavens and the "happy influence" of the stars that rain on the couple (23). The song that begins with an invocation to the muses ends properly with an envoy, an address to the song itself.

In the scheme I have outlined we may imagine a linear array of the form: 1 / 6 / 10 / 6 / 1; or, if we subdivide the ten core stanzas, we obtain: 1 / 6 / 4 / 2 / 4 / 6 / 1. This analysis shows that in either array Spenser has what was, in the thinking of the period, the number of perfection, 10 (in the former the action takes place in 10 central stanzas; in the latter the bride is brought to the church gate in 10 stanzas). This pattern can be illustrated horizontally:

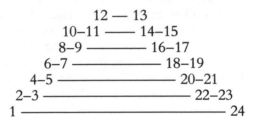

$$
\begin{array}{c}
12 - 13 \\
10\text{--}11 \text{—} 14\text{--}15 \\
8\text{--}9 \text{———} 16\text{--}17 \\
6\text{--}7 \text{—————} 18\text{--}19 \\
4\text{--}5 \text{———————} 20\text{--}21 \\
2\text{--}3 \text{—————————} 22\text{--}23 \\
1 \text{———————————} 24
\end{array}
$$

We now see that in both *Amoretti* and *Epithalamion* Spenser has incorporated a similar form of symmetry representing the number 24. The descending tone of the concluding sonnets of *Amoretti* may trouble the reader. Yet if we assume that Spenser had a structural point of view, the reason is obvious: he wanted the last 24 sonnets to show a symmetry similar to that of the marriage song. Of the sonnet sequence and the marriage song there is no way of knowing which was finished first, but there is no reason to suppose that he wrote them as we have them. I am tempted to assume that, even in compiling his epic, Spenser wrote the core cantos first—the fact that of the seventh book we have only the *Mutabilitie Cantos* (cantos 6 and 7) can be taken as a proof of this practice. It is difficult not to conclude that Spenser began by devising an architectural plan dependent on numerological factors. From the structural point of view it was important for him to print each pair on facing pages and to place them symmetrically. We should assume that to Spenser, as it usually is to any reader, the left page and the right page together meant one unit; we imagine him writing two sonnets or stanzas on a sheet of paper—one on the left and the other on the right—as they would appear to the reader: hence his volume reveals what may be termed the "facing-page pair" system. We may conjecture that, when he decided on the pattern of the last 24 sonnets to match the marriage song, on the left pages (66 and 88) he put down "light versus darkness" and on the right (67 and 89) "deer versus culver"; or alternatively that he first thought of ending the sequence with the image of a faithful bird solitarily awaiting the return of the mate, which then in contrast gave the idea of a hunted deer that returns of her own will.

Between the center of the volume and the last 24 sonnets there remain 6 sonnets, 60–65. These 6 sonnets and 4 poems placed after *Amoretti* give the number of perfection, 10 (also, $6 \times 4 = 24$). The 6 / 24 / 4/ / 24 pattern can be shown thus (c = cupid):

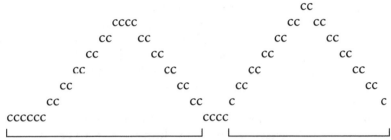

Amoretti 60–89   Epithalamion 1–24

Another important number Spenser has hidden in the volume is 365. In *Epithalamion* it is, as A. Kent Hieatt first discovered,[18] the number of long lines; in *Amoretti*, as Alastair Fowler has noted, it is the number of parts (each sonnet has 3 quatrains and 1 couplet; the anacreontics are in 9 stanzas: $89 \times 4 + 9 = 365$).[19] Thus each has 24 (hours of the wedding day) and 365 (days of the year). Moreover, Spenser has united the two poems numerologically. If we take the 68 short lines as markers, *Epithalamion* is divided in 92 groups of long lines. Now 89 (sonnets) represents, as Fowler explains, 89 days of winter; 93 (89 sonnets + 4 anacreontics) is 93 days of spring, and 92 (groups of *Epithalamion*) shows 92 days of summer from the solstice to the autumnal equinox.[20] Recent research is revealing more elaborate patterns,[21] but here it must suffice to say that in the volume which is written about the happy man "who such one loves best," the numbers of the hours of the day, of the days of the seasons, and of the days of the year were all essential means of making his "endlesse moniment."

From what I have argued it should be clear that Spenser designed his book of love to his second wife with utmost care. His preoccupation with number symbolism is so great that we are tempted to imagine him first putting down numbers from 1 to 117 on sheets of paper and then starting to write. He did not number *Epithalamion*, but he was sure his friends would easily find out that it contained 24 stanzas, representing hours of the wedding day, and that the refrain changed into negative at stanza 17 corresponding to the hours of the day. Perhaps he was less sure that his readers would count, as A. Kent Hieatt did 365 years later,[22] 365 long lines and similar numerologically significant phenomena, but it is hard to imagine Spenser at work without picturing him putting down line numbers 1 to 433 first and then writing, for instance, at line 300: "Now night is come, now soone her disaray," reflecting 16 and a quarter hours of daytime on that day. How many of his own contemporary readers understood what was meant, or what lies hidden in his numerology, is a matter for speculation, but there is no doubt that the poet himself immensely enjoyed making up this elaborate scheme in this volume. We may now conclude that to Spenser what is said is inseparable from where it is said.

I must add that this is not just a numerologically perfect volume. When Spenser wrote this volume he was over forty and had lost his first wife several years earlier. As I have argued elsewhere,[23] if *Daphnaida* is a disguised elegy on the death of his first wife, the joy he records here is genuine; it comes out of the utter misery of Alcyon. The joy of getting a young wife to live with him in a remote countryside home in savage Ireland is the subject of this volume. It seems to me that the extremely elaborate structure reflects the depth of feeling and the quality of emotion he must have devoted to it. As he wrote in his swan song,[24] at the end of his life he was socially still a frustrated man. This sense of injured merit probably prompted him to create the blissful imaginary world as we have it. To see this volume not just as a mannerist masterpiece but as a record of life in his early forties may therefore give us a better understanding of the poet who said of himself, at the center of *Amoretti and Epithalamion*, that "he most happy who such one loves best."

Kumamoto University, Japan

NOTES

1. See A. Kent Hieatt, *Short Time's Endless Monument*: (New York: Columbia University Press, 1960); Alastair Fowler, *Spenser and the Numbers of Time* (London: Routledge and Kegan Paul, 1964).

2. The Ponsonby edition of 1595 has no pagination and one sonnet/stanza is printed on a page; of the anacreontics, the first poem (6 lines) and the second (8 lines) are printed together on a page, the third (8 lines) on the next page, and the fourth (six 10-line stanzas) on the following 6 pages. *Amoretti* is numbered from "SONNET. I" to "SONNET. LXXXIX." while the anacreontics and *Epithalamion* are not.

3. Carol V. Kaske, "Spenser's *Amoretti and Epithalamion* of 1595: Structure, Genre, and Numerology," in *English Literary Renaissance* 8 (1978), pp. 271–95 was first to assert that cruxes of the volume function with a larger, encompassing design. On the ideas of the numerology of the center and of symmetry, the locus classicus is Alastair Fowler, *Triumphal Forms: Structural Patterns in Elizabethan Poetry* (Cambridge: Cambridge University Press, 1970).

4. *Triumphal Forms*, pp. 180–82.

5. For the proportion of $\sqrt{2} : 1$ in the array I am indebted to Mr. Kazuro Korogi, a student in my 1986 Spenser course.

6. Rudolf Wittkower, *Architectural Principles in the Age of Humanism*, (*Studies in the Warburg Institute*, Vol. 19, 1949); fifth ed. (London: Academy Editions, 1988), p. 108. I am particularly indebted to A. Kent Hieatt for drawing my attention to this valuable source.

7. See Shohachi Fukuda, "A Numerological Reading of Spenser's *Daphnaida*," in *Kumamoto Studies in English Language and Literature*, Nos. 29 & 30 (1987), pp. 1–9.

8. Alexander Dunlop, "Calendar Symbolism in the 'Amoretti,'" in *Notes and Queries* 214 (1969), pp. 24–26. Dunlop writes in "The Unity of Spenser's *Amoretti*" in *Silent Poetry: Essays in Numerological Analysis*, ed. Alastair Fowler (London: Routledge, 1970) pp. 153–69 that "the 47 sonnets from xxii through lxviii correspond to the Lenten season for 1594, including Easter and the 6 Sundays before Easter" (155). For commentaries on Dunlop's theory, see A. Kent Hieatt, "A Numerical Key for Spenser's *Amoretti* and Guyon in the House of Mammon," *Yearbook of English Studies* 3 (1973), pp. 14–27; and G. K. Hunter, "'Unity' and Numbers in Spenser's *Amoretti*" in *Yearbook of English Studies* 5 (1975), pp. 39–45.

9. All Spenser references are to the *Variorum Edition* (Baltimore: Johns Hopkins University Press, 1947) with u/v modernized.

10. Louis L. Martz regards sonnet 54 as "perhaps more important than any other individual sonnet for an understanding of the sequence." See 'The *Amoretti* "Most Goodly Temperature"' in *Form and Convention in the Poetry of Edmund Spenser*, ed. Wiliam Nelson (New York: Columbia University Press, 1961), pp. 146–68 at 161.

11. Numerology of the center is fully discussed in *Triumphal Forms*, pp. 62–88.

12. See Shohachi Fukuda and Alexander Lyle, eds., *Edmund Spenser: Selected Poems* (Tokyo: Taishukan, 1983), p. 9 (in Japanese)

13. Steady progress from 62 on has been noted by Hieatt, "A Numerical Key" (n. 8 above) p. 19. Dunlop, "The Drama of *Amoretti*" *Spenser Studies* I (1980), pp. 107–120 writes that "if we count 62 through 89 plus the nine separately spaced anacreontic stanzas plus the twenty-four stanzas of *Epithalamion*, we find that 62 marks precisely the beginning of the second half of the *Amoretti-Epithalamion* volume" (p. 120). James Nohrnberg, *The Analogy of "The Faerie Queene"* (Princeton, N.J.: Princeton University Press, 1970) pp. 68–71 notes pairs of related sonnets: 4–62 (New Year); 23–71 (spider); 33–80 (*FQ*); 17–61 (Angel); 22–68 (Lent-Easter); 19–70 (Amor); 45–88 (Idea). To this list Dunlop ("The Drama of *Amoretti*," p. 120) adds: 39–40 (smile); 33–46 (dereliction); 26–64 (floral blazon). It is interesting to find that these pair sonnets are all symmetrically placed between certain significant sonnets.

14. The 18 sonnets from 60 to 77 can be divided into three units (60–65; 66–71; 72–77), each consisting of three pairs of two sonnets which are matched in theme and printed on the facing pages.

15. *Short Time's Endless Monument*, pp. 16–30; 85–109. For the correspondences between 1 and 13, and 3 and 15, see Hieatt, "The Daughters of Hours: Order in the Stanzas of *Epithalamion*," in *Form and Convention in the Poetry of Edmund Spenser*, pp. 103–121.

16. Max A. Wickert, "Structure and Ceremony in Spenser's *Epithalamion*" in *ELH* 35 (1968), pp. 135–57.

17. *Triumphal Forms*, pp. 104–106. Stanzas 5 and 17 are the only corresponding pair that appears in both Hieatt (94–95) and Fowler (166). Fowler writes: "the first diurnal and nocturnal hours . . . : waking of the bride, matched by bedding of the bride", but in stanza 5 she is still asleep ("why doe ye sleepe thus long, / When meeter were that ye should now awake" 85–86) and we see her awake in stanza 6: "My love is now awake out of her dreams." See also pp. 171–72 for a pattern in which Hymen appears at every 6 stanzas.

18. *Short Time's Endless Monument*, p. 12.

19. *Triumphal Forms*, p. 182.

20. Ibid, p. 181.

21. See Charlotte Thompson, "Love in an Orderly Universe: a Unification of Spenser's *Amoretti*, 'Anacreontics,' and *Epithalamion*," *Viator* 16 (1985), pp. 277–335. Thompson argues that the 89 sonnets represent the 89 days between February 1 and April 30 of the 1594 calendar; that the 41 words in 6 lines of the first poem of the anacreontics represent 41 days between the last date of *Amoretti* and June 11, the wedding day; that the 8 stanzas of the last 3 poems containing a total of 76 lines represent the night hours preceding the wedding day, that the 76 lines represent one hour and 16 minutes or 76 minutes of the eighth unequal hour after midnight at the summer solstice; and that the fact that the last poem contains 60 lines and the last stanza of it contains 60 words may be taken, as Spenser has already hinted in sonnet 87, to suggest dwindling down, or counting down, minutes to seconds of the last time to the day celebrated in the marriage song.

22. *Short Time's Endless Monument*, p. 11.

23. "A Numerological Reading of Spenser's *Daphnaida*," p. 9.

24. See *Prothalamion*, lines 5–9; 140.

JAMES H. MOREY

Spenser's Mythic Adaptations in *Muiopotmos*[1]

*T*HERE ARE multifarious ways of approaching *Muiopotmos*: many read the poem as an aesthetic *jeu d'esprit*—a mock epic concerning a bug. Others read it as a generic experiment on the order of Virgil's *Culex*, and historical allegorical approaches range from Kellogg and Steele's fall of man reading to minute correspondences with contemporary political figures.[2] More recent criticism focuses on iconographical interpretations.[3] The poem is obviously a kind of epyllion—a small epic—if only because of the adaptations of Homer at the beginning and Virgil at the end with some startling adaptations of Ovid in the middle. There is some element of parody of classical literature in these references, and I believe that a promising approach to the poem is to consider Spenser's use of the classical materials, especially of Ovid. Changes in Ovidian and Virgilian materials identify human envy and presumption as the main themes of the poem.

The poem is structured around a series of ekphrases—painted scenes—on the order of a triptych or tapestry. A close structural analogue is Chaucer's early poetry, especially the *Book of the Duchess*, wherein Chaucer adapts the Ovidian myth of Ceyx and Alcyone in a kind of panel structure with the story of the Black Knight.[4] It is universally acknowledged that Chaucer influenced Spenser in *Muiopotmos*, and in 1908 Thomas W. Nadal demonstrated that, in *Daphnaida*, Spenser simply lifted many lines from the *Book of the Duchess*.[5] I wish to build on this evidence and insist on the necessity of considering *Daphnaida* and *Muiopotmos* in tandem as different kinds of responses to Chaucer's poem. First, given the generic and verbal correspondences between *Daphnaida* and the *Book of the Duchess*, it is clear that Spenser simply quarried this work for materials to write an elegy to please a noble widower, as Chaucer had done before him. Second, I propose that Spenser used the same work as a structural model for writing his mythopoeic poem, *Muiopotmos*. Whereas

49

Alcyon's speech and manner are directly patterned on Chaucer's
Black Knight, the Ovidian materials in *Muiopotmos* are structured according to the Chaucerian technique of adapting classical
materials in a panel structure. I propose that we read Spenser's
poem in the same way we must read Chaucer's—with attention
to the mythic adaptations.[6] Changes made by Spenser in his
retelling of Ovid provide significant thematic clues to the poem.

Before I analyze in detail some of these changes, I would like to
respond to the reaction of many critics against Spenser's unre-
mitting gloom in *Daphnaida*, even though I think that gloomi-
ness, even if overdone, is a rather bizarre accusation to make of
an elegy. To cite one example, C. S. Lewis, in an unanaharac-
teristically unperceptive reading, writes the following: "It is a
pity that Spenser was not whisked away from court and England, and back to Ireland and the *Faerie Queene* immediately after
finishing the *Ruins of Time*. Unfortunately he remained to write
Daphnaida, an elegy on the wife of Arthur Gorges. Here, as in
Mother Hubberd, he chose the neo-medieval manner. He resolved
to bring up to date the *Boke of the Duchesse*. Nothing could show
more clearly how imperceptively he read the Chaucer whom he
so revered."[7] I take it that Lewis objects to Spenser's impoverish-
ment of the poem through his exclusion of the Ovidian material,
the hart-hunt frame, and the dream vision. The myths and
frames are missing because Spenser was writing an impassioned
elegy for a close friend—playing games with literary forms was
not his purpose. The poem is a faithful and affecting description
of a blasted spirit; despite Alcyon's excessive grief, the emotions
are sincere.[8] That Spenser was not an imperceptive reader of
Chaucer can be demonstrated by his use of Ovidian materials in
Muiopotmos.

A brief consideration of the printing histories and circumstances of composition of these poems may help to establish their
connectedness and perhaps to establish that Lewis almost got his
wish that *Daphnaida* had not been written. It is important to note
that what Spenser left out in *Daphnaida* he had already recreated
in *Muiopotmos*. Dating the composition of most of Spenser's
poems is extremely problematic, but here several parameters can
be established.[9] The *Complaints* volume, which contains both old
and new work, was registered with the Stationers' Company on
December 29, 1590; its title page bears the date 1591. The separate
title page of *Muiopotmos*, however, within the *Complaints* volume, bears the date 1590, probably indicating that it was pub-

lished before March 25, 1591, when the Elizabethan new year began. Since Lady Douglas Howard, whose death *Daphnaida* elegizes, died in August 1590, and since Spenser dates his dedication "London this first of Ianuarie, 1591," *Daphnaida* was written after *Muiopotmos*. If the date of *Daphnaida*'s dedication is taken to be old style, it conflicts with the dedication to Raleigh of *Colin Clouts Come Home Again* from Kilcolman on December 27, 1591. Thus the dates of both dedications are almost certainly new style; if so, Spenser had less than five months to write the elegy.[10] Spenser apparently wrote his dedication to *Daphnaida* a matter of days after the *Complaints* volume was registered. Any hypothesis here falls apart if one admits, as some critics do, the possibility of a printing error for the dates or of Spenser's deliberately writing the wrong date, but the only two points I wish to make are that *Daphnaida* is subsequent to *Muiopotmos* and that it was written in a short period of time. If an explanation is required for the poem's supposed deficiencies it may well be that it was a rush job, since the time from Lady Douglas's death on August 13 to New Year's Day is less than five months. Being pressed for time, Spenser turns to a well known elegy for a quick composition—a poem he had adapted structurally in *Muiopotmos* some time before. *Daphnaida* is then printed in a form similar to that of the other *Complaints* poems.[11]

Attention may now turn to the artistic uses of the Ovidian materials. What I call the panel structure allows multifaceted perspective and commentary on a poetic event. The technique is analogous to the well known visual effect of the diptych, wherein for example the sacrifice of Isaac flanks the crucifixion of Christ. Chaucer is no more a slavish imitator of his poetic predecessors than is Spenser. Materials are freely adapted to specific thematic ends, as the transformation of the myth of Ceyx and Alcyone in *Book of the Duchess* shows. Chaucer changes details and then makes correspondences within his own poem for thematic effect, and Spenser was surely not oblivious to the technique. There is, of course, no question of direct borrowing from *The Book of the Duchess* to *Muiopotmos* as we find in *Daphnaida*. I argue here for structural and thematic parallels based on the shared technique of building poems out of interconnected panels.

The first Ovid panel and hence the first Spenserian adaptation appears in the metamorphosis of Astery (lines 112–44). Venus is here misled by her maidens into metamorphosing Astery into a butterfly. First of all, this act of transformation is wholly original on Spenser's part, and Venus is exculpated because she is misled—guilt falls not on a wrathful or capricious goddess but on her handmaids. It is also worth pointing out that there are worse things to be turned into than a butterfly. If anything, Venus is the one who is merciful. The myth of Cupid and Psyche has been cited as one of the texts Spenser adapts here, since Venus fears an incipient Psyche in Astery, but I want to point out that this myth is not so much adapted by Spenser as used as a backdrop.[12] It provides a further justification for Venus's actions, and it lends authority to the story by associating it with well known and authoritative Ovidian materials. Spenser here creates his own myth in an original context and for his own purposes.[13]

The second Ovid panel is introduced with a deferral to authority which is typically Chaucerian (lines 257–64):[14]

> The cause why he [Aragnoll] this Flie so maliced,
> Was (as in stories it is written found)
> For that his mother which him bore and bred,
> The most fine fingred workwoman on ground,
> *Arachne*, by his [Clarion's] meanes was vanquished
> Of *Pallas*, and in her owne skill confound,
> When she with her for excellence contended,
> That wrought her shame, and sorrow never ended.

The point is, of course, that it is *not* found written. Spenser, like Chaucer, calls attention to the changes he makes, and the changes made in the Arachne myth are significant. First, that Arachne envies the butterfly in Athena's tapestry implies that she loses the contest. Spenser insists on the loss by changing the order in which the competitors appear. In Ovid, Arachne one-ups Athena by following her and surpassing her work. Spenser reverses the presentations. Athena's tapestry is described after the mortal's, and the goddess laughs last. Spenser changes the order for dramatic effect to ensure that the one who wins comes last, allowing the other to envy the clearly superior effort. Second, Arachne self-transforms into a spider.[15] Neither pity nor malice motivates Athena.[16]

What Spenser chooses to omit from his retelling of Ovid links the story of the butterfly, and by extension that of Clarion, with the theme of envy and human presumption. In Ovid, Athena depicts in her tapestry Neptune's gift of a harbor and her own gift of the olive tree. To make clear the folly of aspiring to the divine, the myth continues:

> Yet to thintent examples olde might make it to be
>   knowne
> To hir [Arachne] that for desire of praise so stoutly helde
>   hir owne,
> What guerdon she shoulde hope to have for hir attempt
>   so madde
> Foure like contentions in the foure last corners she
>   [Athena] did adde.
> The Thracians Heme and Rodope the formost corner
>   hadde:
> Who being sometime mortall folk usurpt to them the
>   name
> Of Jove and Juno, and were turnde to mountaines for the
>   same.[17]

Three other examples of human presumption follow in the other three roundels. Significantly, Spenser has Athena weave the butterfly instead of these four corner roundels.[18] The roundels would be redundant in *Muiopotmos* since the whole poem is about the human envy of the divine. Spenser chooses to provide another perspective on the consequences of such envy with the story of Clarion. The butterfly substitutes for the roundels to make explicit the connections among the fates of the roundel figures, Arachne, and Clarion. That Clarion presumes to rival the gods is abundantly clear:

>   . . . he dar'd to stie
> Up to the clowdes, and thence with pineons light,
> To mount aloft unto the Christall skie,
> To vew the workmanship of heavens hight.
> (lines 42–45)

The pun on Christ is surely intended, and later passages invidiously compare Clarion to classical gods:

> For it [the breastplate] by arte was framed, to endure
> The bit of balefull steele and bitter stownd,
> *No lesse than that,* which *Vulcane* made to sheild . . .

Lastly his shinie wings as silver bright,
Painted with thousand colours, passing farre
All Painters skill, he did about him dight:
Not halfe so manie sundrie colours arre
In *Iris* bowe, ne heavn doth shine so bright . . .

Ne (may it be withouten perill spoken)
The Archer God, the sonne of *Cytheree*,
That joyes on wretched lovers to be wroken,
And heaped spoyles of bleeding harts to see,
Beares in his wings so manie a changefull token.[19]

George Sandys's commentary reinforces the positive interpretation of Athena as opposed to the negative interpretation of Arachne. Whereas Athena's tapestry, particularly the roundels, serves moral instruction, Arachne's tells only of rapes and adulteries. While Athena's border of olive is a "symbol of peace" and "of victory," Arachne's border of ivy is "well suting with the wanton argument and her owne ambition."[20] Sandys comments further that "Minerva teares in peeces what envy could not but commend, because it published the vices of the great ones."[21] That is, envy could not but praise it since it serves envy's purposes so well. Thus according to Sandys and Spenser Arachne is not only the exemplar of envy, she is its agent.[22] Arachne is guilty of presumption in Ovid's and Spenser's versions, but Spenser changes details to exculpate the goddess and to blame Arachne.

If this reading is plausible, the first two stanzas, which have provoked considerable discontent among critics, can be related to the poem as a whole. Each stanza can be specifically applied to one of the Ovid panels. In the first stanza, the "mightie ones" are Athena and Arachne. The "debate" is the weaving contest which is actually retold in the poem (lines 1–8):[23]

I sing of deadly dolorous debate
Stir'd up through wrathfull *Nemesis* despight,
Betwixt two mightie ones of great estate,
Drawne into armes, and proofe of mortall fight,
Through prowd ambition, and hartswelling hate
Whilest neither could the others greater might
And sdeignfull scorne endure; that from small jarre
Their wraths at length broke into open warre.

To resume my Chaucer parallel, this stanza foreshadows the principal Ovid panel—the weaving contest of Athena and Arachne. Both characters can be described as mighty—Athena without question and Arachne by virtue of her skill ("The most fine fingred workwoman on ground" [line 260]).

In stanza two (lines 9–16), the results of that debate give rise to a curse which reduplicates itself:

> The roote whereof and tragicall effect,
> Vouchsafe, O thou the mournfulst Muse of nyne,
> That wontst the tragick stage for to direct,
> In funerall complaints and waylfull tyne,
> Reveale to me, and all the meanes detect,
> Through which sad *Clarion* did at last declyne
> To lowest wretchednes; And is there then
> Such rancour in the harts of mightie men?·

This stanza corresponds to the first Ovid panel, the metamorphosis of Astery. It is one of the "meanes" by which the main story of Clarion is generated, since it provides another perspective on why the tragedy occurred. More important, the Astery story really does describe the "roote" of the "tragicall effect," which is itself a kind of inherited Oedipal curse.

The changes made in the Ovidian material highlight thematic concerns of Spenser's story of the butterfly. Aragnoll is another Arachne, consumed by envy, and Clarion is another Astery, since both are victims of envy. These changes make it clear that this is a poem about human envy and the consequences thereof. The debate is between Arachne and Athena, or between the mortal and the divine. This reading has the advantage of relating one order of beings to another: humans (whether in original or metamorphosed bodies) to divinities.[24] Spenser, with his typical bias toward aristocracy, favors the divine.[25] His bias is clearly indicated by his exculpation of both goddesses. The themes of human infirmity and of the folly of aspiring to the divine are parodically replayed in the story of Clarion. Aragnoll, the new source of envy, slays Clarion, the new imitator of the divine. Clarion is doubly doomed because he is a victim of the envy of a malignant power and because he aspires to the divine; with this character Spenser successfully combines his two Ovidian subjects, Astery and Arachne.

Line 16, the last line in the problematic first two stanzas, can also be accounted for: "And is there then / Such rancour in the harts of mightie men?" The answer is yes, and the "men" appear in the poem as the jealous handmaids, Arachne and Aragnoll (the son of Arachne—see line 259), who through their "rancour" instigate the tragedy of the poem and by extension the tragedy in the world brought about by envy. "Mightie" is used not only mock-heroically to describe power but also ironically to indicate how widespread the consequences of their actions are. The scenes progress bathetically from a goddess and nymphs, to a goddess and a mortal, to two bugs. But I do not want to lose sight of the essentially human application of the poem, an application highlighted by Spenser's substitution of line 16 for Virgil's "Can such resentment hold the minds of gods?" (*Aeneid* I.11).[26] Aragnoll and Clarion are merely the latest victims in the cycle of human presumption and back-stabbing. Doubtless Aragnoll is more evil than Clarion, but both are postlapsarian.

The cycle began, of course, in Eden. Original sin, of which envy is just one manifestation, is after all the Christian version of the Oedipal curse. In this poem Spenser comments on how the sin of envy continues to work its way through the world even as it works its way through his own poetry. The *Mutabilitie Cantos*, and *Faerie Queene* V.xii, where the hags Envy and Detraction, with the Blatant Beast, slander Artegall, are just two of the more prominent loci where envy threatens to bring down good fame. Artegall, it is worth mentioning, like Clarion and almost any other Spenserian hero, is not wholly blameless.[27] If an allegorical or theological reading were called for in *Muiopotmos*, it would be that the poem reveals how the sin of envy leads to human sin in gardens. In this respect I come close to Kellogg and Steele's reading of the fall of man but, I think, with significant differences. This poem concerns fallen, not falling, man, and the only Satan in the poem is the baseness of human passions.

Texas Tech University

NOTES

1.   A version of this paper was originally delivered at "Spenser at Kalamazoo," session 253, May 6, 1989. I wish to thank Carol V. Kaske of Cornell University for her comments and suggestions on earlier drafts.

2.   See the introduction to the poem in Robert Kellogg and Oliver Steele's edition of selected poetry (New York: Odyssey, 1965) 526. For allegorical readings see the *Variorum*, ed. E. A. Greenlaw, et. al., 11 vols. (Baltimore:

Johns Hopkins University Press, 1923–49) vol. 7, part 2, appendix V, pp. 599–608; and Franklin E. Court, "The Theme and Structure of Spenser's *Muiopotmos*," *SEL* 10 (1970), 1–15. Court summarizes allegorical interpretations as well as generic classifications (1–3).

3. See Andrew D. Weiner, "Spenser's *Muiopotmos* and the Fates of Butterflies and Men," *JEGP* 84 (1985), 203–20 and Judith Dundas, "*Muiopotmos*: A World of Art, *YES* 5 (1975), 30–38.

4. Compare the reading of Ronald B. Bond, "*Invidia* and the Allegory of Spenser's *Muiopotmos*," *ESC* 2 (1976), 144–55, who also sees the poem as a "triptych" which demonstrates the "aetiology of envy" (146). Though I agree with his thematic identifications, the influence of Chaucer is not addressed.

5. Thomas W. Nadal, "Spenser's *Daphnaida*, and Chaucer's *Book of the Duchess*," *PMLA* 23 (1908), 646–61 and "Spenser's *Muiopotmos* in Relation to Chaucer's *Sir Thopas* and the *Nun's Priest's Tale*," *PMLA* 25 (1910), 640–56. See also Judith H. Anderson, "Nat worth a boterflye": *Muiopotmos* and *The Nun's Priest's Tale*," *JMRS* 1 (1971), 89–106 and Duncan Harris and Nancy L. Steffen, "The Other Side of the Garden: An Interpretive Comparison of Chaucer's *Book of the Duchess* and Spenser's *Daphnaida*," *JMRS* 8 (1978), 17–36.

6. For a study of this Chaucerian technique see Robert M. Jordan, *Chaucer and the Shape of Creation* (Cambridge, Mass.: Harvard University Press, 1967): "The typical Chaucerian narrative is literally 'built' of inert, self-contained parts, collocated in accordance with the additive, reduplicative principles which characterize the Gothic edifice" (p. xi). I here wish to emphasize the idea of "parts" which "reduplicate."

7. *English Literature in the Sixteenth Century Excluding Drama* (Oxford: Clarendon Press, 1954), p. 369.

8. William A. Oram, in "*Daphnaida* and Spenser's Later Poetry," *SSt* II (1981), 141–58, writes that "the governing strategy of the *Book of the Duchess* is to confront sorrow with the reminder of its opposite. Elegy mixes with love-vision and together they insist that the world is more complex than any single version of it might suggest. It is just this balance of perspectives which Spenser's elegy seems conspicuously to destroy" (142). I agree, but what Spenser seems to destroy in *Daphnaida* he recreates in *Muiopotmos*. The poems need to be considered in tandem.

9. See Oliver F. Emerson, "Spenser, Lady Carey, and the *Complaints* Volume," *PMLA* 32 (1917), 306–312.

10. The *Variorum* critics (vol. 7, part 1, pages 435–438) almost unanimously agree that the *Daphnaida* date must be new style. William Nelson favors this conclusion in *The Poetry of Edmund Spenser: A Study* (New York: Columbia University Press, 1963), p. 316, note 7.

11. See Emerson, 312.

12. See Reed Smith, "The Metamorphoses in *Muiopotmos*," *MLN* 28 (1913), 82–85 and Don Cameron Allen, *Image and Meaning: Metaphoric Traditions in Renaissance Poetry* (Baltimore: Johns Hopkins University Press, 1968), 29. Allen's reading of the butterfly as the "rational soul" (i.e., "psyche," p. 29) has become almost standard.

13. Smith finds no source for the Astery metamorphosis; Charles W. Lemmi cites a passage in Lactantius's commentary on Statius, *Thebaid*, IV.226. While the passages describe similar circumstances (though here Cupid transforms the

nymph into a dove) I can find no rationale for Lemmi's also citing the Cupid and Psyche myth as an influence nor for the allegorical interpretation he goes on to deliver; "Astery's Transformation in *Muiopotmos*," *PMLA* 50 (1935), 913–14.

14.   All references to the poem are to Ronald Bond's edition in *The Yale Edition of the Shorter Poems of Edmund Spenser*, gen. ed. William A. Oram (New Haven & London: Yale University Press, 1989) 412–30. In *Book of the Duchess*, compare the insomniac's telling (lines 57–61) of how "This boke ne spak but of such thinges, / Of quenes lives and of kinges, / And many other thinges smale. / Amonge al this I fond a tale / That me thoughte a wonder thing" (*The Riverside Chaucer*, gen. ed. Larry D. Benson, 3rd ed. [Boston: Houghton Mifflin, 1987]). It would be a strange book indeed that told the myth of Ceyx and Alcyone in the form that Chaucer goes on to record.

15.   Allen's statement that Athena "effects this metamorphosis [of Astery]" (p. 25) is a misreading of the poem and his transposition of lines in stanza two (p. 23) is a violation of it.

16.   See lines 337–52. Cf. the negative depictions of spiders at the entrance to the Cave of Mammon (*Faerie Queene* II.vii.28) and at Acrasia's bower (II.xii.77). Spiders (not specifically identified with Arachne) appear in *Amoretti* 23 and 71. Both sonnets comment on the cunning and deceitfulness of the spider. Bond ("*Invidia* and the Allegory of Spenser's *Muiopotmos*" [147–48]) cites iconographic examples which link spiders to envy.

17.   *Ovid's Metamorphoses, the Arthur Golding Translation, 1567*, ed. John Frederick Nims (New York: Macmillan, 1965) p. 139, Book VI, lines 101–107. The other examples are: a pygmy woman turned to a crane for vying with Juno's beauty; Antigone, guilty of the same offense and changed to a stork; and Myrrha, daughter of Cinyras and mother of Adonis by him, turned to stone for refusing to honor Venus.

18.   "Rounds" is George Sandys's term; *Ovid's Metamorphosis Englished, Mythologized, and Represented in Figures*, ed. Karl K. Hulley and Stanley T. Vandersall (Lincoln: University of Nebraska Press, 1970), 267, line 85. Robert A. Brinkley, "Spenser's *Muiopotmos* and the Politics of Metamorphosis," *ELH* 48 (1981), 668–76, discusses this omission by Spenser (670) in a very interesting reading which links Elizabethan court politics with Ovidian and Virgilian poetic modes.

19.   Lines 61–63, 89–93, 97–101, emphases added. These are just some of the comparisons of Clarion to divine figures: the uneasiness expressed by the aside in line 97 highlights the danger of such presumption. Court (8) points out the same comparisons of Clarion to the pagan gods, but he does not put the comparisons in the context of the Ovidian roundels.

20.   Sandys's commentary on Book VI, pages 289, 291. Anderson (p. 105, note 28) suggests that "The border of Arachne's tapestry, formed solely of ivy leaves, perhaps suggests the merely natural order to which her vision is bound." She understates: the ivy illustrates Arachne's sinfulness. The border is also not "solely" of ivy. See line 298.

21.   Sandys's commentary, p. 291. I find Franklin Court's reading that "Both Ovid and Spenser, it seems to me, are firmly on the side of Arachne; she does what few mortals dare—she challenges divinity" (13) utterly untenable. The whole point of the poem is that *too many* mortals have so dared—an act of daring which tragically repeats itself.

22.   The description of the hag Envy (*Faerie Queene* V.xii.32) recalls how Arachne "did . . . inly fret, and felly burne, / And all her blood to poysonous rancor turne" (lines 343–44).

23.   Compare the cogent reading of William Wells, 'To Make a Milde Construction': The Significance of the Opening Stanzas of *Muiopotmos*," *SP* 42 (1945), 544–54, where he also suggests Athena and Arachne (548) while rejecting allegorical readings. Perhaps after over 40 years of speculation critics should admit he was right, though I do not agree with all of his correspondences.

24.   Here I disagree with Nelson's relation of different orders of beings: in his reading Aragnoll is to Clarion as Olympus is to mankind (72). There is, however, nothing godlike about Aragnoll.

25.   Cf. Carol V. Kaske, "Spenser's Pluralistic Universe: The View from the Mount of Contemplation (*F.Q.* I.x)," in *Contemporary Thought on Edmund Spenser*, ed. Richard C. Frushell and Bernard J. Vondersmith (Carbondale & Edwardsville: Southern Illinois University Press, 1975), 121–149: "there are certain values which seem from their repetitions in all Spenser's works to be built into his very nature . . . above all the intrinsic value and lastingness of earthly fame, but also the innate superiority of the aristocracy . . ." (146).

26.   Allen Mandelbaum's translation, *The Aeneid of Virgil* (Bantam, 1961), 1.

27.   See, for example, *Faerie Queene* V.vi.1 and V.xi.41.

MARGARET CHRISTIAN

"The ground of Storie": Genealogy in *The Faerie Queene*

*T*HE HIGH point of the visit to Alma's castle, at least for Arthur and Guyon, is the visit to Eumnestes's room, where they read the books which give II.x. its familiar designation, the "chronicle history" canto. Many readers of Spenser have contrasted the work Arthur reads, "*Briton moniments*," in its recital of historical defeats as well as victories, with the unbroken success and succession of "*Antiquitie of Faerie* lond."[1] But Spenser himself does not draw our attention to this contrast; nor does Arthur, "rauisht with delight" (x.69), share our reaction to the document which has left later readers so disappointed and perplexed. Others have pointed out the thematic importance of the chronicles as illustrations of the need for "temperance" or "prudence" in a ruler or on a national level,[2] though a skeptic might be tempted to ask why Spenser, seldom backward in stating his theme, omitted to use such words in the passage itself. We can, however, consider II.x. from another reference point, one Spenser does suggest.

We may regard *moniments* and *Antiquitie* as genealogies. Spenser, in II.x.1, invokes aid in undertaking a "haughtie enterprise"—to recount "the famous auncestries / Of my most dreaded Soueraigne." This formulation recurs in III.iii.4, introducing another passage of "chronicle history," Britomart's consultation with Merlin:

> Begin, O *Clio*, and recount from hence
> My glorious Soueraines goodly auncestrie,
> Till that by dew degrees and long protense,
> Thou haue it lastly brought unto her Excellence.

The same suggestion of a restricted account of the lineage of rulers, rather than a more general history, is implicit in Spenser's summary of what Arthur has read: "the royall Ofspring of his natiue land" (II.x.69)[3] But before considering what insights a "genealogical reading" of II.x. might yield, it would be well to establish some of the methods and meanings associated with tracing a family tree in the sixteenth century.

Genealogy and history need not be mutually exclusive. Indeed, Elizabethans saw in genealogy a most useful tool for establishing the meaning of history, whether national or personal. In classical mythology, in Bible stories, and in current events, a person's lineage defined not only his physical origins, but also his character and spirit.

No family in England was more conscious of its heritage and history than the Tudors, especially early in their rule, when a respectable family tree helped validate their claim to the throne. Even as late as Elizabeth's reign, those who would flatter her made a point of invoking the memory of her royal predecessors. But the fascination the Elizabethans felt for genealogy, though no doubt related to the royalty's and nobility's preoccupation with lineage and title, was far from being a merely political, social, or materialistic concern. In remembering their ancestors, the Elizabethans were continuing the practice of Biblical heroes and patriarchs; for many chapters of the Bible are given over to genealogies of the Old Testament worthies and of Christ. Thus, two useful parallels to Spenser's "chronicle history" canto, should we wish to view it from a genealogical standpoint, are Biblical genealogies and, because of the Biblical provenance of this species of praise, sermon references to the queen's family tree.

Biblical chapters of "begats" were especially dear to Hugh Broughton and his fellow Hebrew scholars, who considered these genealogies an important key to the meaning of scripture. Roger Cotton, a draper and an admirer of Broughton, explains their importance in his *Direction to the waters of lyfe* under the heading "The Genealogies are the ground of Storie":

> And I pray you, what part of the Bible is there, that doth not thereof consist? be not men the grounde and cause of all the matter there? And how can we knowe the matter as we ought, vnlesse we know the men of whom the matter speaketh? As for example, if the holy Ghost say, *Sheba* and *Seba* shall bryng gyftes, or *Nebaroh* and *Kedar* shall come and serue: how can we know rightly what is meant hereby, vnlesse we know the people of whom the holy Ghost doth speake, and also the cause why they were estranged from

the Lord, & now should come agayne? Or if the Lorde do tell you, how that he wyll subdue the *Canaanites, Iebusites, Gergesites*, and the rest of those nations, to geue vnto *Israel* their possessions: must you not of necessitie (if you wyll know the cause cleerely) understande what these people are, and of whom they come, and also vpon what former prophesie & promises these matters do depende? . . . For when as the holy Ghost doth tell you of blessednesse to befall *Sem*, and his posteritie: and lyke wyse the contrary vnto *Canaan* and his posteritie: and also of a reuersion of *Sems* blessednes to befal *Iapheth* in the ende, and his posteritie, and also how *Canaan* and his posteritie shall be seruantes vnto both them and theirs: how is it possible, I say, for you to vnderstand any thing with iudgement, vnlesse you be able in some good sort to distinguish of these Families? . . . Or agayne, if the holy Ghost do tell you of *Moab, Ammon, Edom*, and diuers mo with them, to be ioyned in league against the people of God: must you not of necessitie also (yf you wyl knowe the cause cleerely herein) vnderstande of what rootes those wicked branches do also proceede: and likewyse how, and for what cause they became such rotten ones as they were: and also how, and for what cause the other, the *Israelites* became the people of God, and of whom they also come? Yes in deede must you, . . . because without the knowledge of these thinges, you are neyther able to heare or reade the worde of God with vnderstanding. Therefore in the name of God take heede, that you be not so perswaded by them, to beleeue that the Genealogies in the holy Scriptures be endles, or vnprofitable, or superfluous: for if you so thinke, then do you nothing els, but take away from the Scripture, and so the curse of God wyll come vpon you, euen to your vtter damnation.[4]

Men constitute the matter of Scripture; genealogies explain the men by documenting their fathers. With the fathers' names before us, we can recall, in turn, their deeds, and interpret their children's character and fate, for the children embody and experience the results of their forefathers' choices, whether for good or ill. The founder of a nation determines, for Cotton, the national destiny: the Jews were called and blessed through Abraham, and the descendents of Ham were cursed.

The most notable examples of important and useful genealogies are those of Christ, found in Matthew 1 and Luke 3. Of these Broughton writes,

> The holy *Genealogie of Iesus Christ* (may not be reckoned in the number of those prophane ones, which *S. Paul* condemneth in I. Tim. 1. 4. for it) doth not consist in a vaine repetition of Names, (as many doe thinke) neither is the knowledge thereof superfluous, (as some doe affirme;) But verily (if it be rightly vnderstood) it is of exceeding great vse and consequence; not onely to prooue *Christ* to be the promised Seede, (which is a weightie poynt;) But also it serueth as a speciall guide, to direct vs in the true vnderstanding of all the *Holy Storie*: . . . all the *Holy Storie* dependeth vpon [our *Lords line of Fathers*], and from it, as from a Fountaine, doth branch it selfe into a most pleasant varietie of all Gods holy proceedings, in the wonderfull preseruation of his Church, and in the fearefull ouerthrow of all the enemies thereof.[5]

These gospel genealogies serve two ends: "to prooue *Christ* to be the promised Seede," and "to direct vs in the true vnderstanding" of Christ and his story. And as such important documents, the construction of a properly revealing genealogy is a task requiring careful judgment.

Matthew's and Luke's judgments conflict on this point. Luke, in his concern to establish Christ's common humanity with both Jews and Gentiles, traces Jesus' biological heritage all the way back to Adam, whereas Matthew, demonstrating Christ's kingly lineage to Jewish readers, begins with Abraham. The two gospels agree in the catalogue which extends from Abraham to David. Then they follow almost completely different lines from King David to Joseph, the husband of Mary. The two accounts diverge through almost twenty generations, as Matthew follows the line of the kings of Judah, from Solomon to Jehoiachin, and Luke follows the line of Solomon's brother Nathan, from whom, Broughton says, Christ actually descended. The two branches converge at the point where, during the Babylonian captivity, Jehoiachin died without issue and a son of Nathan's line, Salathiel, succeeded to the throne of Judah (although the exile made the succession an academic, rather than political, problem). Salathiel's grandson Zerubbabel was ancestor to both

Mary and Joseph. Zerubbabel had two sons, and, according to Broughton, Matthew derives Joseph's ancestry from the elder, to whom the theoretical crown should have passed, while Luke follows the younger son's line to Joseph's father-in-law and thus to Mary, Jesus' mother. The discrepancies between the two accounts, then, result from Matthew's decision to follow Christ's "Kingly" rather than "naturall" line, and his apparent paternal, rather than actual maternal, heritage. Luke, on the other hand, documents Christ's physical forebears rather than his credentials for the kingship of Judah. This confusing circumstance provided Broughton with the occasion to enlarge upon the different purposes and methods of genealogizing.

At least two kinds of genealogies are possible, and one, the kingly line, can "prooue *Christ* to be the promised Seede." Thus, even though Christ was not the biological offspring of the kings in this list, it can still contribute to an understanding of his identity and work, since it endorses him as "King of the Jews." While the "Kingly" line can be used to buttress a claim to the throne, so the "naturall" line had its uses as well. This type of genealogy was useful for the analysis of individual characters. Broughton moralizes Luke's bare list of names to show how it enhances an understanding of Christ's character and work. To this end, he supplies the original meaning of each Hebrew name, for "vve should not be as Parrets, to regard the bare sond of name, but to knovv vvhat the notation told."[6] Thus David is glossed "Beloued," Nashon (fifth in descent from Judah the patriarch) is glossed "Experimenter. He had experience of the Promise, from Egypt"—that is, he was of the generation of the Exodus—and Joash, whose grandmother slaughtered as many of her descendents as she could find, in order to have the crown for herself, is glossed "Desperate: and so he had bin, but for Iehoiadah, that saued him from Athalih."[7]

Beyond simply supplying the meaning of each name, however, Broughton reminds his readers of the character and deeds of many of Christ's ancestors, showing how Christ "honoured all his true Fathers [that is, those who were actually his physical forebears] with the gift of fayth." [8] Abraham

hath no vvorkes to reioice in before God. For his request vnto Sara to hazard her Chastity vvas a fault; . . . an egregious trespas, a gross fault, an exceding sin; bred from great mistrust in God; & the cause of Israels sorovv & fall in

Egypt. So he hath not to rejoice before God: Therfore he
vvas not iustified by vvorkes before God . . . but by faith he
vvas iustified.[9]

Thus the mention of Abraham's name in the list of Christ's
forebears holds a spiritual lesson pointing forward to the need for
Christ.

The appearance of Pharez, the son of a Gentile woman, in
Christ's genealogy should remind us of two spiritual truths.
First, Gentiles can participate in salvation as well as Jews. "God
was in disposing counsel hovv Messias should come of Thamar;
of Thamar, a Chananean: of Thamar, Iudas daughter in lavv: of
Thamar, by Iudah."[10] Tamar gave birth to twins, and the eagerness Pharez showed in shoving past his brother, whose hand had
already appeared, to be born first, reveals a godly disposition all
believers should emulate. "Again Phares striving to be borne
before Zara, (vvho first stredched out his hand) hath his name
[glossed "a breach-maker" in *Our Lord his line of Fathers*] of
violence, shevving at his byrth that he vvold lay strong hand
vpon the Kingdome of heauen; & is a patren for all, as Iacob, to
striue for the Kingdome from yong yeres."[11] David, the paragon
of the kings of Judah, had experiences which not only prefigure
Christ's excellences but also typify the need for Christ's forgive-
ness and grace:

> He, vvhile he vvas afflicted, vvas godly; at rest, he fell; in
> Vriah, & Bathseba; To be an example for all that shall
> beleue. . . . And Bathseba the adulteress rarely Godly in
> the end, is a grandmother of Christ; celebrated in the psalme
> of repertance [sic] .51. & [wrote] pro.31 & all prophetes are
> in the Kingdome of heauen. Lu.13.[12]

A study of Christ's genealogy, according to Broughton, reveals
the Lord as the answer to all his ancestors' yearnings and shortcomings, the fulfilment of their expectations. Only by reviewing
their faith and their faults can we appreciate the significance of
Jesus' perfections. By looking to the personal history of genealogy, we can rightly value and interpret an individual.

At least two kinds of genealogies are therefore possible, and
even that which lists men unrelated to Christ still contributes to
an understanding of his identity and work. Broughton insists
that Christ's natural line of fathers included only good men: "he

honoured all his true Fathers with the gift of fayth, being the roote of goodnes, whom we are to follow in the honouring of our Parents, and can not goe before him."[13] In Christ's family tree, there was thus a happy coincidence between his "naturall line" and what we might term his "spiritual line." Many of the kings of Judah, memorialized in Christ's "Kingly line," are "most wicked folke," and to suggest that such could be Christ's physical ancestors is "attributing folly vnto the Eternal wisdome of God, to bring the most holy, of the most wicked."[14] Indeed, Matthew spares us some of the embarrassment of this suggestion in the course of recording Christ's "Kingly line" by omitting several of the most notorious. "*Achaziah, Ioaz,* and *Amaziah*" appear on Broughton's table with the note, "These bad 3. and worse *Iehoiakim,* which were kild for euill ruling, *S. Matthevv* omitteth."[15] Apparently the omission of the least exemplary branches of the family tree does not compromise the value of a genealogy. Indeed, such a judicious omission testifies to the discretion of the chronicler. Including such names would only suggest avenues of interpretation which must be fruitless, even misleading.

The explication of Biblical genealogies, however sublime a science, was mostly pursued in learned treatises. Whether too lofty, too occult, or too dull, it found little currency in popular preaching. But the confidence expressed by Cotton and Broughton in the spiritual value of such studies emerged in a different context when preachers treated Queen Elizabeth's fore-bears. Knowing her lineage, her ancestors' qualities and deeds, led to a more accurate appraisal of the queen herself. Preachers who developed the queen's genealogy tended to allow them-selves as much latitude as the gospel genealogists did: those connections that would be spiritually misleading or simply em-barrassing were suppressed, as Matthew ignores the more igno-minious among the kings of Judah. Thus, Mary Tudor never appeared in such catalogues of Elizabeth's natural, kingly, or spiritual kin. Bishop Curteys, in a 1573 sermon, stressed the spiritual resemblance between Elizabeth and her father and brother, while he ignored her sister altogether. Henry VIII was God's "noble Moses," who "brought hys people of England out of the Egipt of error, blindnesse, and superstition." Among other benefits, Henry, like Moses, delivered the word of God to the people in their own language, but he failed to lead them all the way to the promised land. "Josua his sonne," that is, Edward VI,

led the people into Canaan, "and with the blast of [God's] worde
and the shout of his Ministers, hurled downe the walles of
Jericho," ending idol-worship.[16] With this spiritual heritage,
which preceded and explained her, Elizabeth could not help but
be a "gratious Debora, by whome God brought down Jabin, and
Cusan, and caused his Church of Englande to prosper in health,
wealthe, peace, pollicie, learning, religion, and many good gifts
and graces."[17] She recapitulated in her reign the deeds of these
worthy forebears, rescuing her people once more out of the
slavery of Catholicism and settling them in the promised land of
Protestantism. Thus could a knowledge of Elizabeth's heritage
enrich an appreciation of her character and achievements.

As queen, the embodiment of the state as well as a private
individual, Elizabeth could lay claim not only to the Tudor
family tree, but to the spiritual bloodlines of the throne of
England as well, just as Matthew's genealogy of Christ includes,
according to Hugh Broughton, "Kinges that vvere not fathers to
Christ."[18] Since her role as head of state, not her genetic make-
up, was the issue, she could even count the best of Biblical
princes as her forebears in her person as a godly ruler. Hence, the
invocation of her ancestors in the sermons often included her
pre-Norman, Norman, and Plantagenet antecedents as well as
her own immediate family: her grandfather, father, and brother.
A catalogue of this sort from the second Queen's Day sermon by
Archbishop Sandys traced the family resemblances which defined and described Elizabeth.

> *England* liked well, and took it for no small blessing of
> God, when *Henry* the first, *Henry* the second, *Edward* the
> first, *Edward* the third, *Edward* the fourth, *Henrie* the fifth,
> *Henrie* the sixt, *Henrie* the seuenth, *Henrie* the eighth, and
> *Edward* the sixth, bare rule ouer it. But did God euer bless
> the throne of any man as he hath done the roial seat of his
> anointed at this day? Hath the like euer beene heard of in any
> nation to that which in ours is seen? Our *Debora* hath
> mightily repressed the rebel *Iaben*: our *Iudith* hath beheaded
> *Holophernes*, the sworne enemy of Christianity, our *Hester*
> hath hanged vp that *Haman*, which sought to bring both vs,
> and our Children into miserable seruitude. And if we may
> compare with the Ancients of *Israel*, *Moses* was not more
> mild, nor *Samuel* more iust, nor *Dauid* more faithful, nor
> *Salomon* more peaceful, nor *Iehosaphat* more ready to assist

his Neighbours, nor *Ezekias* more carefull for Gods cause, nor *Iozias* more zealous to restore sincere religion: If, ye make the comparison betweene her owne predecessors, neither was *Henry* the first better learned, nor *Henrie* the second more easy to forgiue and put vp iniuries, nor *Edward* the first more chast, nor *Edward* the third more loth to accept of forren dominion, being offered, nor *Edward* the fourth more iust in yeelding all men their owne, nor *Henry* the fift more happy, nor *Henry* the sixth more holy, nor *Henry* the seuenth more prudent, nor *Henry* the eight more valiant in quelling the Pope, nor *Edward* the sixth more sincerely affected towards the Gospell of Christ.[19]

These comparisons approximate to a genealogy in that Sandys selected the queen's spiritual, as well as physical and legal, kin, and invoked their reputations for the qualities he mentioned, in order to show their relationship to Elizabeth. Such a recital not only placed the queen within a chronological sequence, but also located her on a spiritual map, showing her as the heir of all these men and women. This genealogy was the ground of Elizabeth's "Storie" in that the actions and characters of which it reminded listeners could help them to understand and appreciate the queen. Perhaps a rehearsal of some of the parallels will help clarify Sandys's method.

Deborah, for instance, was a respected peacetime judge and military leader; indeed, the general Barak declined to face the Canaanites in battle unless Deborah shared his command. Elizabeth's preparations and reliance on God in the face of the Spanish threat were comparable, and Sandys may also have had in mind the revolt of the Low Countries and their request for Elizabeth's aid against Spain. Another redoubtable woman, Judith, used her beauty and resourcefulness to deceive and behead Holofernes, a general of the Assyrian king Nebuchadnezzar, who had subjugated Judah. Elizabeth likewise used both persuasion and force to extirpate Catholicism from England: the comparison emphasizes the combination of tact and resolution required of the queen, as well as the selflessness of her personal risk, to preserve England's independence and Protestantism during those dangerous early years of her reign.

Elizabeth was the heir of several great kings of Judah as well. Jehosaphat, for example, the king of Judah in the days of the wicked Ahab and the prophet Elijah, remained true to the Lord and demonstrated his neighborly spirit by accompanying Ahab in a campaign against the enemy at Ramoth Gilead. This eagerness to assist neighboring Israel, commendable in itself, met with failure, and Ahab was killed. The quality of Jehosaphat which Sandys sees in Queen Elizabeth led her to aid the Low Countries and the Protestant Scots, although what she represented as aid to her sister queen Mary Stuart brought danger upon herself and her kingdom, and ended in Mary's death, as Jehosaphat's efforts exposed him to danger and could not prevent Ahab's death. Two other kings Elizabeth resembled were Hezekiah and Josiah, both remembered for their restoration of true religion after a period of idolatry.

Sandys carefully stipulated Elizabeth's likeness to her kingly English ancestors. She resembled Henry I, the Norman ruler who was reputed to know Greek, understood Latin, spoke English easily, and had such a remarkable taste for books that he was known as "the clerk." Elizabeth inherited his predilection for learning, even surpassing him as a linguist. Henry II, renowned for his forgiving nature, pardoned his sons for their unsuccessful rebellion against him, offering amnesty and reconciliation rather than exacting punishment. With few exceptions, Elizabeth handled her rebellious nobles with similar forebearance after the Northern Rebellion, and forgave Mary Stuart time and again for her plots and intrigues against her.

Edward I's chastity was celebrated, not because he remained a virgin like his spiritual heir Queen Elizabeth, but because of his deep attachment to his first wife, who bore him thirteen children, and whom he mourned throughout his second marriage until his own death, seventeen years after hers. Elizabeth lavished the same chaste devotion on England. Edward III, when only a teenager, balked at offering the required homage to the French king in return for his French holdings, first obtaining legal opinions that such service did not prejudice his own claims to the French crown. A lover of war, he sought to expand his territory in France and into Scotland. Similarly, Elizabeth began her reign by establishing her independence from Spain: a delicate task when the Spanish king had lately been her brother-in-law and maintained a household in England as its uncrowned king. Though she lacked her progenitor's taste for war, she executed the ruler of Scotland, brought its council under her influence, and ensured the realization of Edward III's ambition of adding Scotland to the dominions of the English crown. Edward IV's ingratiating manners and eagerness to conciliate the nobles after his chaotic contest with Henry VI led to his relaxing the traditional policy of enriching the royal treasury through zealous legal proceedings and levying heavy fines against his wealthier peers; this shift could be euphemized as justice "in yeelding all men their owne." Perhaps in Elizabeth's case the reference is to her discontinuing Mary Tudor's unpopular efforts to trace monastic holdings and wealth and return them to their original orders. In any case, Elizabeth's nobility felt her to be less demanding an overlord in terms of grants and taxes than many of her predecessors, and noted, if they did not celebrate, her frugality.

While Elizabeth did not resemble Henry V in conquering France, she was as fortunate in the outcome of her contest with Spain. Moreover, she was happy in her people's love and respect, just as he was. Her speech at Tilbury, expressing her solidarity with and commitment to her men-at-arms, recalled the sentiments of Henry's speech before the battle of Agincourt, in which he assured his troops that his own efforts would be so wholehearted that none should pay ransom for him. Henry VI, considered a martyr and a saint, was remembered for his scrupulous tithing, his hair-shirts, his regular attendance at divine service, and his graces at table. Though Queen Elizabeth resembled him in none of these particulars, except in hearing service regularly, she was celebrated as a narrowly-escaped martyr in Foxe's *Actes and Monuments*, sermons, and the popular imagination.

Henry VII's prudence was manifested not only in his cultivation of unity at home after the Wars of the Roses, but also in his diplomatic successes abroad—his alliances with Spain and Scotland in particular, the latter of which ultimately led to the union of Scotland and England under James I. Elizabeth's prudent handling of the divisive religious issues of the time, marrying Protestant theology with Catholic ritual in her settlement, bore out her resemblance to her grandfather, as did her cautious approach to foreign affairs. Like her father, Henry VIII, she insisted on the English Church's independence from the bishop of Rome, and if she did not, as her brother Edward did, read ten chapters of the Bible daily, she consciously imitated him in reissuing his prayer book and book of homilies. Listeners could trace the spiritual resemblance between Elizabeth and her predecessors, both Biblical and English, and gain a better appreciation of her character in the light of these comparisons. Any potentially embarrassing reference to less exemplary rulers Henry IV, Richard III, Mary Tudor—was avoided.

The form of Sandys' compliment is worth considering, for it was patterned after a gospel genealogy in certain particulars. Of Luke's list, Broughton says, "The vvhole number is disposed in order fit for memorie Ten to the flod: ending the old vvorld; ten to Abraham heyre of the nevv vvorld."[20] Sandys imitates Luke's pattern by listing ten Biblical "ancestors" of Queen Elizabeth, all of whom figure in the Old Testament, and ten kingly ancestors, all of the period following the Conquest and well within Britain's Christian era. Such an admirable and varied assortment of qualities and deeds represented by twice ten worthy names helped the auditor to distinguish the queen's spiritual forbears, and thus to appreciate her own achievements and character.

So how does II.x. look in the light of these roughly contemporary sermons and treatises? As an accurate physical genealogy for Elizabeth, or even for Arthur, *Briton moniments* is disappointing. Arthur cannot trace his "naturall line," to use Broughton's phrase, through all these kings directly back to Brut, where the chronicle proper begins, because both Dunwallo's and Coyll's dynasties intervene between the last representatives of Brut's direct line, Ferrex and Porrex, and the second Constantine, founder of Arthur's house. Thus, the greater portion of *Briton moniments* is analogous to the first chapter of Matthew, which traces Christ's ancestry through Solomon, though Solomon was not his physical ancestor: it shows the "Kingly line," the version of the genealogy that validates Arthur's, and Queen Elizabeth's, claim to Brut's crown. The wording of II.x.4 seems to emphasize this "kingly" notion of lineage. While Elizabeth derives her name, realm, and race from Prince Arthur, her rule—"that royall mace, / Which now thou bear'st"—descends to her not only from Arthur, but from other "mightie kings and conquerours in warre," including some who are her "fathers and great Grandfathers" by convention and kingly succession, rather than by birth.

The Elizabethan notion of various allowable types of genealogizing, among them tracing the kingly and the natural lines, helps resolve one problem posed by the material in II.x.: the appearance therein of what Broughton refers to as "most wicked folke." Why should Spenser include them in what we must assume to be a complimentary gesture to the queen? Hugh Broughton insists that all of Christ's physical forebears had "the gift of fayth, being the roote of goodnes," and explains the presence of "most wicked folke" in Matthew's table by identifying them as kingly, rather than natural, ancestors of Christ. Similarly, there is nothing to embarrass Queen Elizabeth in her physical ancestors as they descend from Constantine II and Artegal. The unnatural ambition of Ferrex and Porrex, the adultery of Locrine, the usurpation of Octavius, do not compromise the value of *Briton moniments* as compliment, because these are not Elizabeth's fathers, and their moral and political lapses do not reflect on her. Indeed, the contrast of their wickedness throws her humility, chastity, and worthiness in greater relief, and shows England's need of her redemptive virtue, just as the wickedness of the kings of Judah and the occasional lapses of David and Abraham are recalled to us to heighten our appreciation of Christ's sinlessness and demonstrate the Jews' need for a Saviour. The natural line, followed from Constantine II to Uther, and then from Artegal to Cadwallader, includes no one who discredits the queen morally or politically, though some ancestors suffer reverses for which they are not responsible. For instance, Cadwallin martyrs the Saxon "good king *Oswald*" out of pity for "his peoples ill" and to avenge the "vassalage" to which the Britons have been subjected, and is thus not morally reprehensible. Vortipore, Artegal's grandson, is crossed by "froward fortune"; Cadwallader will lose his crown to the Saxons. These failures, however, are not those of wicked men, and in Cadwallader's case part of a Providential design.

Briton moniments, taken together with Merlin's prophecy, provides the queen with a "Kingly line" which extends back to Brut and Aeneas, and a "naturall line" from Constantine II to Cadwallader. Guyon's book, "*Antiquitie of Faerie* lond," provides a complementary genealogy which reveals a different aspect of her character and deeds, much as Luke's list of Christ's ancestors complements Matthew's. Matthew's table, directed to a Jewish audience, traces Christ's line from Abraham, founder of the Jewish race, much as *Briton moniments* traces Elizabeth's line from Brut, founder of the British race. Luke begins with Adam, Broughton says, to emphasize Christ's common link with all humanity,[21] and the "*Antiquitie of Faerie* lond" likewise goes back to a myth of origins. The *Antiquitie* also presents the queen and her immediate antecedents in much greater detail. While Merlin speaks of her only as "a royall virgin," Guyon reads of her grandfather, uncle, and father, and is given two names for

her, Gloriana and Tanaquill. The myth of origins and the unmistakable portrait of three generations of Tudors are elements
which this genealogy shares with the "naturall line" that Luke
traces for Christ.

Most critics emphasize the idealized nature of the Faery chron-
icle, and note its omission of Edward VI's and Mary's reigns.[22]
Fewer note the problematic realism inherent in the inclusion of
Henry VII's elder son Arthur:

> After all these *Elficleos* did rayne,
>   The wise *Elficleos* in great Maiestie,
>   Who mightily that scepter did sustayne,
>   And with rich spoiles and famous victorie,
>   Did high aduaunce the crowne of *Faery*:
>   He left two sonnes, of which faire *Elferon*
>   The eldest brother did vntimely dy;
>   Whose emptie place the mightie *Oberon*
> Doubly supplide, in spousall, and dominion.
>   (x.75)

Oberon had an elder brother—that is, he was not born to rule, as
the other Faery emperors inevitably seem to be. His brother
Elferon "did vntimely dy," another shadow on the ideal heritage
of Faery. But why introduce, in an ostensibly positive way, the
detail of Oberon's marriage to his brother's widow, when the
lady referred to was not Elizabeth's mother and the previous
marriage was later cited as grounds for annulment? Certainly it is
a peculiar notion of idealizing, to select of all possible family
details the most potentially embarrassing to Elizabeth. But these
are details uniquely apt to make readers recognize this as the
"naturall line" of Elizabeth, and to see in them a further reflec-
tion of the ideal.

Spenser probably includes Elferon, the older brother, because
of the historical older brother's name, "by way of salute to the
dynastic myth of descent from Arthur," in Cain's words.[23] The
detail of Oberon's marriage to his brother's widow emphasizes
how completely he filled Elferon's "emptie place," and thus
reminds us that the Arthurian mantle has passed to Henry, and
through him, to Queen Elizabeth. Indeed, Spenser's formulation
was probably constructed to remind readers of an Old Testament dynastic expedient: a childless widow would be encouraged to marry her deceased husband's closest male relative in

order to produce an heir, who would then inherit her first husband's title and property. Such an arrangement yielded at least two important links in David's, and thus Christ's, ancestral chain: Tamar conceived twin boys after seducing her father-in-law, the patriarch Judah, who had failed to provide her with another husband when her first one died; and Ruth became David's great-grandmother after Boaz, a cousin of her deceased husband, agreed to redeem his dead kinsman's wife and lands. Tamar and Ruth are two of only three women Matthew mentioned in his list of Christ's forebears; except for Fay, the mother of the race, Arthur's and Henry's wife is the only woman the *Antiquity* even alludes to until it arrives at Tanaquill. If Spenser, in this genealogical context, meant to remind his readers of this Biblical practice, he intended Gloriana to be regarded in some sense as the child not only of Henry/Oberon but also of Arthur/Elferon. Thus, in her Faerie type, Elizabeth is doubly associated with Arthur: as bride as well as daughter. What initially looks like an awkward concession to realism, an irrelevant reminder of Henry's unlucky first marriage, is transmuted by the genealogical context into a heraldic compliment.

The Elfin chronicles, like *Briton moniments*, prefixes a different type of genealogy to a "naturall" one. Though two stanzas idealize the Tudors, earlier emperors, Elfin, Elfinan, Elfiline, and the others, do not seem intended for historical Tudor or British rulers. Isabel Rathborne identified the "historical" figures which Spenser allegorized here, and saw Elfin as Osiris/Bacchus; Elfinan as Hercules Libicus, founder of, among other cities, Heracleopolis (a name which, Rathborne points out, bears a striking resemblance to the name Cleopolis, the city Elfinan founded), and Elfinor as Brutus.[24] Though other critics have been more cautious in assigning names, many agree with Rathborne that Spenser's intention was to claim Elizabeth's spiritual descent from the great kings of the earth—a descent which need not have been physical in order to be important, as we saw with reference to sermon genealogies of Elizabeth. In any case, their historical identity should be less important than how the Elfin emperors' heritage reflected on the current queen. One possible analysis follows.

Elizabeth, the spiritual heir to Elfin, whom Spenser describes as ruling America and India, was destined to command an empire of similar extent. This is the kind of ambition we would expect Spenser, an enthusiastic supporter of English imperial-

ism, to applaud, Elizabeth does not especially seem to resemble
"*Elinan*, who layd / *Cleopolis* foundation first of all," if we think
of literal building, but the heir would only need to restore what
the ancestor established—perhaps the honor and integrity, that
is, the "fame," of the English nation, after Mary's troubled
reign. This interpretation seems more plausible when we return
to the next line, and observe its concern with defenses: "But
Elfiline enclosd it with a golden wall." The security and strength
in which Elizabeth maintained England's territory was hailed by
poets and people alike. Elfinell, "who ouercame / The wicked
Gobbelines in bloudy field," set Elizabeth the example she followed in decisively defeating the Spaniards in 1588—a spiritual as
well as a military victory, we may infer from the epithet "wicked
Gobbelines," a moral judgment on a supernatural race. The crys-
tal temple of Panthea for which Elfant is remembered may well
prefigure the English Church, which Elizabeth restored to its
apostolic purity of doctrine. Elfar killed "two brethren gyants,"
"The one of which had two heads, th'other three": a heroic
personal victory over monstrosities which Elizabeth duplicated
not in its fabulous character, but in a no less astonishing triumph
over the obstacles of her own sex, religious controversy, and
international doubts over the legality of her claim, in order to
become an effective ruler. Elfinor, the learned builder and magi-
cian, "built by art vpon the glassy See / A bridge of bras." He
passed on to Elizabeth his skill and wisdom, which she used, as
he did, to overcome the isolating effect of the sea and extend her
realm's influence: to Ireland, to the Netherlands, to the New
World. In Sandys's sermon, Queen Elizabeth was likened to each
British ruler in a particular quality. Similarly, each pre-Tudor
Elfin emperor is distinguished by a great deed which can be seen
as his legacy to Gloriana, and which she, in her historical person
as Elizabeth, repeated and renewed, thus demonstrating her
spiritual heritage.

This reading of the Elfin *Antiquities*, treating it as the same sort
of selective genealogy which appears in Sandys's sermon, may
not identify in every case the deeds and qualities of Elizabeth
which Spenser intended, but I believe that it fairly represents an
Elizabethan approach to genealogy: analyzing the acts and characters of the fathers in order to place those of the child in perspective; tracing the lineaments of the fathers in the child's face. Even
what Cain calls "the historically murky and morally perplexing
British chronicle"[25] makes excellent panagyric sense when read

as "the ground of [Elizabeth's] Storie"—the succession it traces validates her title to the throne, and its "most wicked" characters and actions, like those appearing in Matthew's genealogy of Christ, help readers appreciate their own queen the more. Approaching these passages as genealogies frees a commentator from the burden of distilling a consistent moral and political message from them, while still allowing them to be read as praise.

The Elizabethan interest in genealogy not only manifested itself as the family pride of the nobility, but also characterized the contemporary approach to Bible study and accounted for a major strain in contemporary praise of the queen. The fact that genealogy was thought to offer a key to character and spiritual kinship also can help to explain the prominence Spenser awards the tables of ancestry in *The Faerie Queene*. Biblical commentators and Elizabethan preachers agreed with Spenser in seeing spiritual rather than biological kinship as the qualifying criterion for inclusion in such a list, and thus supplied the queen with a heritage which, for the preachers, even embraced Biblical elements. Spenser, with a similar concern for capturing her essential nature more completely, provided the queen with ancestors from prehistory and from invention.

Penn State University / Allentown

NOTES

1. Michael O'Connell, in *Mirror and Veil: The Historical Dimension of Spenser's Allegory* (Chapel Hill: University of North Carolina Press, 1977), 72–87, believes that Spenser is mainly concerned to "evoke [a] consciousness of history in the reader" by using "patterns that show the complexity, conflict, and uncertainty of human endeavour" as opposed to the "conscious and poetic idealization" of the Faery chronicle: a juxtaposition of an earthly with a heavenly version of history. Thomas P. Roche, Jr., in *The Kindly Flame: A Study of the Third and Fourth Books of Spenser's "Faerie Queene"* (Princeton: Princeton University Press, 1964), 33–50, sees the contrast between the two chronicles in somewhat different terms: the British chronicle records the history of an individual nation within the Providential scheme of history, while the Elfin chronicle gives the "story of every civilization," the "expanding cycle of human glory." Thomas H. Cain, in *Praise in "The Faerie Queene"* (Lincoln: University of Nebraska Press, 1978), 115–19, insists on the contrast between the two chronicles, but relates them by pointing out that Elizabeth "reflects [glory and significance] back on the historically murky and morally perplexing British chronicle from which her line emerges." He finds that the British chronicle

points in at least three interpretive directions; for instance, toward "the absence of moral design in history," toward "a sense of repeating pattern in history that somewhat imitates design," or even toward a foreshadowing of Elizabeth in queens and heroines that, "by typology, intimate[s] escape" from the meaningless succession of events it records. Harry M. Berger, *The Allegorical Temper: Vision and Reality in Book II of Spenser's* "Faerie Queene" (New Haven: Yale University Press, 1957), 101–13, sees the chronicles as straightforwardly didactic, teaching the need for a proper heir, the importance of the law and of the consent of the governed, and the urgency of vigilance against domestic and foreign threats. Though these themes inform both the British and the Faery chronicles, in the second, he notes, everything succeeds. In this the two chronicles offer a contrast: the earthly chronicle is a beginning and a warning, while the Elfin chronicle, stretching "forth to heaven's height," is a consummation. On the other hand, Angus Fletcher, *The Prophetic Moment: An Essay on Spenser* (Chicago: University of Chicago Press, 1971), 180–186, emphasizes, not the contrast between the chronicles, but their complementary nature: "the doubling of the two chronicles provides a stereoscopic vision of the two time-systems out of which Faerieland makes its legendary and prophetic momentousness." Similarly, Jacqueline T. Miller, in "The Status of Faeryland: Spenser's 'Vniust possession,'" *Spenser Studies* 5 (1984), 31–44, agrees that Faery history is not unmarred by usurpation and violence, pointing to its origins and to the fate of Elf's patron Prometheus. This "act of creation" "insists that Faeryland is ultimately part of the actual world where these ideals cannot be permanently possessed"—and thus those who see an absolute contrast between Faeryland and British history are mistaken.

2.   Among critics concerned to demonstrate the relevance of Canto x to the rest of Book Two, Ruth Pryor, "Spenser's Temperance and the Chronicles of England," *Neuphilologische Mitteilungen* 81 (1979), 161–168, considers this material a national analogy illustrating personal intemperance, while Jerry Leath Mills, "Prudence, History, and the Prince in *The Faerie Queene*, Book II," *Huntington Library Quarterly* 41 (1978), 83–101, shows the didactic value of chronicle history by using the principle of deferred retribution, with God "visiting of the iniquities of the fathers upon the children unto the third and fourth generations." Thus, Arthur learns that a ruler's intemperance leads to "chaos, regression, and sterility." Brenda Thaon, "Spenser's British and Elfin Chronicles: A Reassessment," *Spenser and the Middle Ages*, ed. David A. Richardson (Cleveland: Cleveland State University, 1977), 96–130, sees an imagistic link between the chronicle history and the book as a whole: the water and flood metaphors dramatize the issues of pride, ambition, and intemperance, revealing, among other things, that the Elfin dynasty was not the succession of ideal emperors critics have thought—Elfinell, the famous bridge-builder, was ambitious and proud. Joan Warchol Rossi, "*Briton moniments*: Spenser's Definition of Temperance in History," *English Literary Renaissance* 15 (Winter 1985), 42–58, argues that both chronicles manifest the importance of the active virtue of temperance throughout history's three distinct phases: "sworde," law, and "gouernement."

3.   As Rossi observes, at many points the chronicle is "compress[ed]" and "rush[es] literally from ruler to ruler" (p. 57). Graham Hough, *A Preface to "The Faerie Queene"* (New York: Norton, 1962), 128–29, calls these passages

genealogies: "So Queen Elizabeth is furnished with two genealogies, one supposedly historic, through the British kings, and one purely in the fairy line."

4. Roger Cotton, *A direction to the waters of lyfe* (London, 1590), C1-1v.
5. Hugh Broughton, *The holy Genealogie of Jesus Christ* (London, n.d.), Preface.
6. Broughton, *Our Lordes Famile* (Amsterdam, 1608), D2v.
7. Broughton, *Our Lord his line of fathers* (London, 1595).
8. *The holy Genealogie*, ¶ 2.
9. *Our Lordes Famile*, C2v.
10. Ibid., D1.
11. Ibid., D1-1v.
12. Ibid., D3.
13. *The holy Genealogie*, ¶ 2.
14. *Our Lordes Famile*, E1.
15. *The holy Genealogie*, ¶ 2.
16. Richard Curteys, *A Sermon preached before the Queenes Maiestie. . . . at Grenewiche, the 14. day of Marche. 1573.* (London, 1586), D1.
17. Ibid., Dlv.
18. *Our Lordes Famile*, D3.
19. Edwin Sandys, "A Sermon preached in the same place, and vpon the same occasion, with the former." In *Sermons of the most Reuerend Father in God, Edwin Archbishop of Yorke, Primat and Metropolitaine of England* (London, 1616), 34–34v.
20. *Our Lordes Famile*, A1v.
21. lbid., B3v.
22. See Berger, pp. 112–13; Fowler, pp. 180–86; Cain, p. 115; and O'Connell, p. 80.
23. Ibid.
24. Isabel E. Rathborne, *The Meaning of Spenser's Faeryland* (New York: Columbia University Press, 1937), 108–124.
25. P. 116.

DONALD V. STUMP

The Two Deaths of Mary Stuart: Historical Allegory in Spenser's Book of Justice

S CHOLARS SEEM to have reached a consensus on Spenser's treatment of Mary Queen of Scots in Book V of *The Faerie Queene*. The prevailing view is that she is represented twice: first as Radigund in Cantos iv–vii and then again as Duessa in Cantos ix–x.[1] This is, I think, a useful insight. As it has usually been presented, however, the theory leads to at least one embarrassment: it requires Mary to die twice, once when Britomart cleaves her helmet in Canto vii and again when Mercilla sends her to be executed after Canto ix. It seems bizarre that Spenser should present the death of Mary in some detail and then, only two cantos later, circle back to the same event all over again. The problem is further compounded by major discrepancies between the two accounts. In Canto vii the character representing Queen Elizabeth is seeking revenge and strikes furiously:

> The wrothful Britonesse
> Stayd not, till she came to her selfe againe,
> But in revenge both of her loves distresse,
> And her late vile reproch, though vaunted vaine,
> And also of her wound, which sore did paine,
> She with one stroke both head and helmet cleft.
>
> (vii.34)[2]

In Canto ix, however, the character who stands for Elizabeth is not furious but full of pity. Although she permits the execution to take place, she acts reluctantly, and her reasons have nothing to do with love-rivalry, reproaches, or wounds, but with her divine role as a just and merciful ruler:

But she, whose Princely breast was touched nere
With piteous ruth of her so wretched plight,
Though plaine she saw by all, that she did heare,
That she of death was guiltie found by right,
Yet would not let just vengeance on her light;
But rather let in stead thereof to fall
Few perling drops from her faire lampes of light . . .
(ix.50)

The discrepancies between the two accounts have never been satisfactorily explained. The best attempt has come from Thomas Cain, who suggests that Mercilla's course of action represents what Elizabeth actually did and Britomart's behavior represents what Elizabeth ought to have done. Cain writes, "Britomart acts with clearheaded correctness, while Mercilla bungles and temporizes."[3] This interpretation is ingenious, but it also raises difficulties, for Mercilla is so thoroughly idealized in Cantos ix–x that it is hard to believe she is acting in direct opposition to Spenser's own views.[4]

The failure of critics to reconcile the two accounts is related to a second difficulty: the vagueness of current historical interpretations of the Radigund episode. Although scholars have supplied very full accounts of the relationship between the trial of Duessa and that of Mary Stuart, they have not examined in comparable detail the earlier material on the Amazons. No one has looked into the historical background of Artegall's rescue of Terpine, his skirmishes with Radigund in the city gate and in the lists, his subsequent imprisonment and dealings with Clarinda, or Britomart's battle to save him. In short, scholars have treated the episode as a historical allegory without demonstrating that its incidents are historical.

Of course, it is conceivable that most of the incidents are not historical. Spenser may have alluded to Mary only in the death of Radigund. Yet it is hard to think of a reason that he should be so erratic, writing all but the final moments of an episode without any topical reference and then suddenly calling to mind the most notorious and dramatic execution of his era. Since he was writing about the virtue of justice, one would expect him to have taken primary interest in the crimes committed and the just response to them, not in the bare fact of an execution.

In light of the difficulties raised by current interpretations, it seems worthwhile to reexamine the entire episode. I begin with the simplest hypothesis that seems plausible to me: that Spenser saw in the career of Mary Stuart an illustration of key principles of justice; that he set out to weave into his allegory an account of her injustices and the trial to which they led; and that he worked in more or less chronological order. What incidents in Mary's life, then, would have been most pertinent to his aims? What were the main phases in her relations with the English? How do these relate to the allegory of Mary's trial and execution in the later episode at the Palace of Mercilla? To find answers to these questions, we must step back for a moment to review Mary's career.

I

From the point of view of an Englishman loyal to Queen Elizabeth, Mary's first injustice was committed in 1558. After the death of Mary Tudor, Henry II of France claimed the crown of England for his teenage daughter-in-law, Mary Stuart, and this claim led to serious legal, diplomatic, and military struggles with Elizabeth. Although Mary actually wore the English royal insignia only briefly, she never formally renounced her right to it, and until her execution in 1587, she was repeatedly involved in schemes to gain the crown.

The first phase of Mary's struggle with the English began in earnest in 1559. In August, her mother, Mary of Guise—who was acting as Regent of Scotland during Mary's minority—brought in French troops to suppress a rebellion among the Scottish Protestants. The ostensible purpose of this move was to restore civil order, but the English feared that it was part of a long-range plot to supplant Elizabeth by a French invasion from the North. Consequently, in the winter of 1559–60, Elizabeth ordered an invasion of Scotland. By the following summer she had driven Mary's troops back to France and installed a Protestant government in Edinburgh. At about the same time, Mary's husband, Francis II, died and the young queen left France to take up active rule in Scotland.

The second phase of Elizabeth's struggle with Mary occupied the period 1560–68. It was not a time of military confrontation but of personal diplomacy, which was conducted with outward appearances of amity. Elizabeth tried to lure Mary into marrying an Englishman who could be trusted to look after Elizabeth's interests, and Mary responded by choosing one who could not· Lord Darnley. When the marriage went sour and the Scottish lords assassinated Darnley, Mary was implicated and her support began to wane. In 1567 she was forced to resign her crown, and in the following year she fled into England.

With her exile began the third phase of her quarrel with Elizabeth. For the first time she met the English face to face. In the autumn following her arrival, they tried her before a special commission for her part in the Darnley affair and for her conduct as the Scottish queen. At the same time, she became involved in various schemes to woo the English aristocracy to her side. She entertained many prominent lords and gentlemen and pursued a plan to marry the most highly titled peer in the realm, the Duke of Norfolk. He went along with the scheme, and in 1569 several Catholic lords in northern England rose in rebellion against Elizabeth, hoping to place Norfolk and Mary on the throne. Elizabeth responded dramatically, crushing the rebellion, depriving Mary of the means to regain power in Scotland, and placing her under indefinite house arrest.

The final phase of Mary's struggle lasted from 1571 until her death and consisted largely of a series of plots to assassinate Elizabeth. For the last of these, the Babington plot, Mary was tried and executed.

With this summary of the main events of Mary's career in mind, we may begin to perceive the outlines of Spenser's allegory. The Radigund episode follows the same course as the first three phases in Elizabeth's struggle with Mary. First, Artegall intervenes to save Sir Terpine, who is about to be hung by Amazons, just as Elizabeth intervened to save the Scottish protestants from the French. The Amazons represent the women who held sway in France and Scotland in this period: Mary Stuart, Mary of Guise, and Catherine de Medici. After a full-scale battle corresponding with the English invasion of Scotland in the winter of 1560, Artegall and Radigund begin a second phase of the struggle by exchanging gifts and emissaries and engaging in private combat in the lists. This matches well the period from 1560–68 when Anglo-Scottish relations were outwardly amicable and Elizabeth was dueling privately with Mary over the all-important marriage issue. Then comes the moment when Artegall has Radigund in his power, removes her helmet to kill her, and unexpectedly yields to her instead. This incident parallels the early days of Mary's captivity in England, when the English aristocracy first beheld her face to face, sought to try her for murder, and, at least in the case of Norfolk and the Northern Earls, fell under her power instead. After Radigund has mastered Artegall, she falls in love with him and makes amorous approaches, just as Mary courted Norfolk from 1568 to 1571. At this point Artegall's first love, Britomart, defeats Radigund decisively, ending her rule of the Amazons and releasing Artegall. Leaving aside for the moment the fact that Radigund dies and Mary lived on, this stage in the allegory corresponds well with the third phase of Elizabeth's struggle with the Queen of Scots. In 1569–71, Elizabeth suppressed the rebellion of Mary's most powerful supporters in England, ended forever her power as a queen, and established a Protestant government in Scotland that became England's closest ally.

Laid out in this fashion, the correspondences between the Radigund episode and the career of Mary Stuart are promising. Yet questions remain. How detailed is the allegory? Are there, for example, specific events corresponding to each skirmish between Artegall and the Amazons? Are there historical counterparts for characters such as Sir Terpine, Clarinda, and the mysterious Bellodant? Is there any reason for Spenser to portray the first three phases of Mary's career in the character of Radigund, and then to switch in the last phase to portray Elizabeth's rival as Duessa? And finally, what are we to make of the problem with which we began, the two deaths of Mary? To answer these questions, and to reveal the extraordinary richness of Spenser's allegory of Mary Stuart, we need to examine the episode in more detail.[5]

II

Artegall first encounters the Amazons in Canto iv when he discovers them attempting to hang Sir Terpine. As he draws near the gallows, the women begin to threaten him as well, and he is forced to employ his servant Talus to disperse them. Afterwards, the grateful Terpine tells the story of their Queen—how she had fallen in love with a knight named Bellodant and, when he rejected her, had turned her bitterness against all men, particularly the Knights of Maidenhead. In response to a challenge from Terpine, who had fought and overpowered him, giving him two choices: to exchange his armor for "womens weedes" and do domestic chores, or else to be hanged. Terpine stoutly chose the latter. Once Artegall has heard this story, he resolves to avenge the Knights of Maidenhead and, with Terpine by his side, fights a pitched battle in the gates of Radigone in which he rescues Terpine a second time and forces the Amazons to call a cease-fire.

The beginning of Radigund's vendetta against the Knights of Maidenhead has a clear analogue in the experience of Mary Stuart. She, too, lost the first love of her heart, the sickly boy-king Francis II, and with this loss came a stinging personal rejection that did indeed turn her toward a course of open struggle with Elizabeth and her court (the Knights of Maidenhead). From her girlhood, when Mary was first betrothed to the young Dauphin, she had set her heart on being Queen of France, and when he died in 1560, she failed to win the support of the de Medici faction at court. Consequently, she was forced to make a tearful and humiliating retreat to Scotland.[6] Once there, she seems to have consoled herself for the loss of France by turning her attention toward England. Thus, as Spenser's allegory suggests, the jilting of the young queen by the French made her rivalry with Elizabeth a major preoccupation. This interpretation is supported by the name of Radigund's lover. "Bellodant" means "one who makes war," and from the death of Henry VIII until the conflict with Spain began to brew in the 1570's England's chief military opponent was France. The two nations engaged in open hostilities in Scotland and France in 1548–49, in France in 1557–58 and 1562–63, in Scotland in 1560, and again in the Netherlands in 1572.

Several details of the incident with Sir Terpine confirm the view that it refers to events in the same period. When Mary of Guise sought to suppress the Protestant rebellion of 1559–60, her daughter, Mary Stuart, was not in Scotland but in France, and her absence may account for the fact that Radigund is not with the Amazons when Artegall first encounters them. His rescue of Sir Terpine also has a precise analogue in Elizabeth's intervention on behalf of the Scottish faction known as the Lords of the Congregation. During the rebellion of 1559, Elizabeth cultivated close ties with the leaders of this group, most notably with Mary's illegitimate half-brother, James Stewart. If Spenser meant Terpine to represent a particular person, it was probably

Lord James. The knight's name means "thrice sorrowful," and Stewart did indeed suffer three major defeats that are represented in Spenser's allegory.

The first calamity for Lord James came in late summer of 1559. From May through July, Stewart's rebels managed to control most of Fife and to occupy Edinburgh, but their volunteers soon lost their will to fight, and the Lords of the Congregation were forced to call a truce with the Regent and disperse. In July, on the death of Henry II, Mary Stuart became Queen Consort of France, and this emboldened her mother to bring in French reenforcements in August and September. Thoroughly out-manned and outmaneuvered, the Protestants then appealed to Queen Elizabeth for help. They received it in two forms: money to provision and pay their troops, and diplomatic aid to spirit the son of one of their most powerful potential allies, Châtelherault, out of France so that his father could safely join the rebellion. With money and Châtelherault, the Protestants were able in October to regain control of Edinburgh.[7]

These incidents are portrayed in Artegall's initial intervention to save Terpine. Like the English government in this period, Artegall hesitates to become directly involved; he regards it as "shame on womankinde / His mighty hand to shend" (V.iv.24). Yet, just as England was forced to reconsider its neutrality when French forces began to swarm into Scotland and occupied the strategic fortress at Leith, so Artegall is forced to defend himself against the sudden hostility of the Amazons. He sends Talus, his executive arm, to help disperse the crowd.

The second defeat and rescue of Terpine corresponds with the events of November 1559 through January 1560. In November, after a disastrous attempt to overrun the French garrison at Leith, the Protestants were again forced to withdraw from Edinburgh. By January, most of their strongholds in Fife had been retaken by the French, and the Protestants' plight was desperate. Elizabeth could not afford to remain on the sidelines any longer, and in January 1560 she sent Admiral Winter with a contingent of the English fleet into the Firth of Forth. Although Winter denied any military involvement—claiming instead that he was in search of pirates—he nonetheless managed to distract the French troops until Elizabeth could arrange a more forceful strategy. In February her representatives concluded the Treaty of Berwick, in which Elizabeth promised to defend the Lords of the Congregation, and in March an English army invaded Scotland under the command of Lord William Grey, the father of Spenser's friend Arthur Grey. The English directed their attack against the French stronghold at Leith, but after a number of bloody French forays, in one of which Arthur Grey was wounded, the troops were forced to settle in for a prolonged siege. In June, Mary of Guise died, leaving Mary Stewart without the means to prosecute the war from a distance. Consequently, in July 1560, France hastily concluded the Treaty of Edinburgh, which required that all foreign forces leave Scotland and that Mary Stuart cease wearing the English royal insignia. For a time, the Lords of the Congregation were finally in control. They assembled a Parliament, renounced the authority of the Pope, abolished the Mass, and adopted a Protestant confession of faith.[8]

Against this historical background, certain details of Spenser's allegory take on special meaning. For example, the hostilities take place in the gateway to the city and involve a preliminary verbal exchange between Artegall and the porter, surely because Leith is the "sea-gate" that controls access to Edinburgh from the Firth of Forth, and English diplomats protested loudly against the French presence there.[9] After the first day of fighting, Radigund's women separate the chief combatants and cast their troops "far asunder," probably because the end of the brief war of 1560 saw the English withdraw over their northern border and the French return to the Continent. Once Artegall has drawn back from Radigone, he leaves his servant Talus near the city "to keepe a nightly watch for dread of treachery" (iv.46). This I take to be a reference to the English forces left in Berwick after the Treaty of Edinburgh to keep an eye on the Scottish border.

III

The second day of Artegall's battle and his subsequent period of subjection to Radigund represent the next phase in Anglo-Scottish relations: the period of mingled enmity and rapprochement from 1560 to 1568. Spenser signals a change in the allegory by having Radigund propose a "single fight" with Artegall, which is not to take place on the open battlefield, as before, but in lists that are "closed fast, to barre the rout" (v.5). At the outset, there is an elaborate show of courtesy between the two combatants, Radigund sending "wine and juncates" with her messenger

Clarinda, and Artegall responding with "curt'sies meete" and "gifts and things of deare delight" (iv.49, 51). Such civilities also characterized relations between Elizabeth and Mary in the early 1560s, when Scottish ambassadors were warmly greeted in London and returned with sisterly letters and tokens of affection from Elizabeth to their mistress. The man responsible for Mary's relations with England was William Maitland of Lethington, a man of whom I shall say more when we come to the sections on Clarinda later in the episode. He was committed, above all else, to promoting an alliance between Scotland and England. In September 1561 he brought Mary's first amiable overtures to the English court, and in early 1562 he became the prime mover in negotiations to arrange a personal meeting between the two monarchs.[10]

Under the surface of amity, however, a serious struggle for power was in progress. As Radigund suggests in setting the conditions for the tournament, the outcome of the battle was to decide who governed the British Isles. She says of Artegall, "if I vanquishe him, he shall obay / My law, and ever to my lore be bound, / And so will I, if me he vanquish may" (iv.49). The relevance of this compact to Mary is obvious. Although her agents had negotiated the Treaty of Edinburgh, she had never ratified the document and had therefore retained her right to claim the titles and insignia of the Queen of England. In the decade after 1560, her negotiations with England came to turn on this point, for Elizabeth interpreted her adversary's refusal as a sign that Mary still intended to supplant her.[11] Of course, the terms of Radigund's challenge also apply to Elizabeth, for Henry VIII and Protector Somerset had recently made war on Scotland to enforce a claim of suzerainty over that country,[12] and though Elizabeth did not openly assert her father's claim, she was certainly eager to extend her power. She particularly wanted to control Mary's policy toward the Protestant Lords at home and toward the Catholic opposition abroad.

To this end, Elizabeth made a bold but curious proposal that deeply offended Mary and began their struggle in earnest: she put forward her own favorite, Robert Dudley, as a prospective match for Mary. Obviously, Dudley was too low in station for a queen, but Elizabeth thought to overcome this objection by advancing him to the Earldom of Leicester. The advantage of the plan was that, even if Mary ultimately refused, the marriage negotiations would set back the day when she turned to Catholic princes on the Continent for a husband. And if Mary accepted, Leicester would help to draw the realms into a firm alliance.

That the private combat between Artegall and Radigund is an allegory of marriage negotiations is suggested in Radigund's attire and in the language of love used to describe the joust. The Amazon enters the lists dressed, not in the gear of battle, but in the delicate fashions of a coquette. She wears a light dress of "sattin white as milke," probably because Mary was fond of white and had become so well known for splendid gowns in this color that, for a time, she was called "the lily of France."[13] Over Radigund's white dress, with its associations of purity, there is a quilting of "purple silke" (v.2), with suggestions of royalty but also, perhaps, of amorous passion. The latter connotation is reinforced in Spenser's statement that her dress was "short tucked for light motion / Up to her ham" (v.2). There may also be amorous overtones in the way she first approaches Artegall, "as if she had intended / Out of his breast the very heart have rended" (v.6). Not even the exposed "ham" and her "light motion" can win Artegall's heart, however, for the poet tells us that he "from that first flaw him selfe right well defended" (v.6). Once again, the point is historically accurate, for Leicester never succumbed to Mary's attractions or to the lure of a Scottish crown. Although publicly he "gan fiercely her pursew," privately he was cool to the entire scheme.[14]

In the stanzas that follow, the poet continues the allegory of marriage negotiations by incorporating a series of double-entendres:

> Like as a Smith that to his cunning feat
> The stubborne mettall seeketh to subdew,
> Soone as he feeles it mollifide with heat,
> With his great yron sledge doth strongly on it beat.

> So did Sir *Artegall* upon her lay,
>   As if she had an yron andvile beene,
>   That flakes of fire, bright as the sunny ray,
>   Out of her steely armes were flashing seene,
>   That all on fire ye would her surely weene.
>   But with her shield so well her selfe she warded,
>   From the dread daunger of his weapon keene,
>   That all that while her life she safely garded . . .
>   (v. 7–8)

In light of the earlier descriptions of Radigund's attire, Spenser's repeated references to heat carry inevitable overtones. The key point is that, although Radigund seemed at first to be "mollifide with heat" and "all on fire," she was never really so. She was all along guarding herself from "the dread daunger of his weapon keene." The point is historically apt, for, although Mary was outwardly receptive to the idea of marriage with Leicester, she was inwardly offended by the very idea of marrying a commoner of Elizabeth's choosing, and set herself resolutely against the match.

Artegall then shears away half of Radigund's shield, leaving her "naked" on one side. She counters by striking his thigh and letting forth "purple blood," and he responds by shattering the other half of her shield and removing her helmet in order to slay her. It is tempting to associate the wound to Artegall's thigh with the act in which Mary's enemies insisted that she had shed the purple blood of English royalty: the murder of Darnley, who was high in the English line of succession.[15] More certain, however, is the historical significance in the destruction of Radigund's last defences and the removal of her golden helmet. After the murder of Darnley, Mary made the mistake of marrying James Bothwell, the chief agent in the plot to assassinate the King. The Scots were outraged and rose in rebellion, driving Bothwell from the country and imprisoning Mary in Loch Leven Castle. There, in the summer of 1567, James Stuart demanded that she resign her crown to her infant son and, upon her compliance, assumed control of Scotland as the new Regent.[16] This train of events is neatly represented in the the removal of Radigund's golden helmet, which is linked by the adjective "sunshynie" with the traditional symbolism of royalty.

IV

The removal of Radigund's helmet is, of course, a turning point in the action, for the sight of the Queen's beauty arouses pity in Artegall. After beholding her face for the first time, he cannot bring himself to harm her and casts aside the sword of justice. At this point, she revives and attacks him ruthlessly, constraining him to accept the subservience and the women's chores that Terpine had previously refused. In consequence,

Terpine suffers the third sorrow suggested by his name: Radigund puts him to death. Then a new period of wooing begins, brought on when Radigund unexpectedly falls in love with Artegall. Without understanding her motives, he agrees to sue for her favor in order to gain his freedom. Clarinda then comes to the fore again as a deceitful intermediary, seeming to act on behalf of Radigund but lying to her and to Artegall out of a newly conceived infatuation with the knight.

In these events the career of Mary Stuart continues to govern the action. In 1568, she escaped from Loch Leven, gathered a small army, and after a disastrous encounter with the superior forces of Lord James, fled over the southern border. When the English first beheld her, they were, like Artegall, moved to pity. She and her small band of adherents arrived in a state of exhaustion, without funds, baggage, or even clean linen. In Spenser's words, she was "voide of ornament, / But bath'd in bloud and sweat" (v.12). Although Elizabeth retained her under house arrest until she could be cleared of the Darnley murder, the English queen was genuinely appalled at Mary's destitute state. She undertook the maintenance of Mary's household and laid plans for her restoration as Queen of Scotland. More significant for the allegory, however, is the pity shown by Elizabeth's subjects. Important officials soon began to pay their respects, won by Mary's charm, or perhaps by the possibility that she might one day be their queen.

Not the slowest of those who courted Mary was Elizabeth's own Earl of Leicester. As Master of the Queen's Horse, he had reason to be in contact with the Scottish queen, for he was placed in charge of her stable.[17] It was not long before rumors began to circulate that he had revived the old scheme to marry her—though this time the plotting was more dangerous because it was done behind Elizabeth's back. Apparently, he did not encourage such rumors himself, but he was eager to ingratiate himself with Mary and sent her several costly gifts, including gold and silver boxes containing prized antidotes for poison and a piece of what was sold to him as the horn of a unicorn.[18] Of course, we cannot know how much Spenser knew of Leicester's life in the 1560s, but he may have heard scraps of the story while he was employed at Leicester House in 1579–80. In any case, there is an amusing parallel between the demeaning chores performed by Artegall in Radigone and Leicester's subservience to the Queen of Scots.

A more dangerous development in the English courtship of Mary was the scheme conceived in November 1568 to marry her to the Duke of Norfolk. In his ambition, Leicester so far forgot himself that, urged on by the Spanish ambassador, he became a prime mover in the plot. Other members of Elizabeth's council, including Cecil, knew of it too and gave it at least the sanction of their silence.[19] It may be that Leicester and the others hoped that Elizabeth would welcome the arrangement. After all, she herself had once suggested Norfolk as a match for Mary in the early 1560s, and the points that recommended him then had not changed: he was a Protestant of rank and considerable power, and he could be expected to look after English interests in Scotland. All the same, the plan was self-serving and encouraged a dangerous division of loyalties. Leicester and the others tacitly admitted as much by keeping it secret for nearly a year.

The scheme was all the more unsavory because, when Norfolk first began to pursue it in earnest, he was the chief English commissioner in Mary's trial for the murder of Darnley, and Leicester later served on the same judicial panel. The proceedings took place in York and Westminster in the fall and early winter of 1568–69 and concluded without arriving at a judgment against the Scottish Queen, even though letters extremely damaging to her had been introduced in evidence. In fairness to Norfolk and Leicester, it should be added that Elizabeth herself intervened to dissuade the commission from rendering a judgment. Yet the marriage negotiations certainly compromised the proceedings and opened them to charges of partiality.[20]

To Spenser it must have seemed that Norfolk, Leicester, and the other commissioners had relinquished their just responsibility to condemn Mary for the murder of Darnley and, by their foolish subservience, had set the stage for the most disastrous act in the entire drama of Mary's imprisonment in England: the Rebellion of the Northern Earls, which took place in the following year. The poet gives numerous suggestions of his opinion, but the most obvious is that, upon seeing Radigund's countenance, Artegall throws away his sword, which here and elsewhere in Book V symbolizes retributive justice. The Amazon then awakens and resumes her former cruelty and "greedy vengeance," just as Mary did after her trial. Immediately after the commission decided not to render a judgment, she sent out secret messages urging her allies in England and Spain to provide troops to release her. In Scotland her supporters responded with renewed violence against the government of James Stewart, and in England the powerful Earl of Northumberland began to plot with the Spanish ambassador to overthrow the English queen.[21]

The ceremony in which Radigund breaks Artegall's sword and takes him as her vassal is, then, an apt (if exaggerated) representation of Mary's effect on a key segment of the English nobility. As Cecil noted at the time, Mary's "cunning and sugared entertainment of all men" was surprisingly successful. Spenser makes the same point in describing Artegall's first impression as he enters Radigund's chamber to begin his servitude: he beholds there "Many brave knights, whose names right well he knew" (v.22). England's failure to render judgment against Mary at the end of her trial in 1568 had left the nation vulnerable, and it is a nice irony that, in portraying this period of Mary's imprisonment, Spenser suggests that it was Artegall—the character representing the English—who was beaten and in bondage.

The first consequence of Artegall's failure to bring justice upon Radigund is the death of Terpine. This has its historical analogue in the assassination of James Stewart in January 1570, less than a year after Mary had begun to stir up the Scottish Catholics against him. He was gunned down by an assassin hired by the Hamiltons, one of the Catholic families most loyal to Mary, and she personally granted the murderer a pension for the deed.[22]

A second consequence is that Radigund unexpectedly falls in love with Artegall. This infatuation probably refers to Mary's own overtures to Norfolk, which were revealed during his later trial for treason in January 1572. In the period from 1569 to 1571, Mary corresponded with Norfolk in openly amorous terms. When, for instance, she presented him with a pillow that she had embroidered, and he responded with a costly diamond, she pledged to wear it at her neck "until I give it again to the owner of it and me both."[23] Other details of the allegory also suggest Mary's involvement with Norfolk. Radigund employs her emissary Clarinda to communicate with Artegall, and for this purpose she must supply a ring to bring Clarinda past a prison guard, Eumenias. Similarly, Mary had to devise ways for William Maitland and others to convey messages past her warder, the Earl of Shrewsbury.[24]

Finally, the role of the double-dealing emissary Clarinda in the love negotiations corresponds neatly with Maitland's activities during this period. While he was serving as one of the Scottish

commissioners at Mary's trial in 1568, he played an extraordinary game of diplomatic deceit. Like Clarinda, who unexpectedly
falls in love with Artegall, Maitland seems to have been motivated by a personal desire to arrange an alliance with England.
Moreover, like Clarinda, he played a key role both as a match-
maker and as an obstacle to the very match he was supposed to be
arranging. It was Maitland who first approached the Duke of
Norfolk with the idea of a marriage with the Queen of Scots.
Yet, as one of the Scottish commissioners, Maitland also did
something that helped to drive the English away from Mary, and
thereby made the Norfolk scheme all the more difficult to support. During the trial he actually helped to make the case against
Mary, bearing witness to the authenticity of the incriminating
letters to Bothwell that turned the English commissioners
against her. Throughout this double-dealing, he was also sending Mary messages, assuring her of his loyalty and warning her
in advance that damaging evidence would be presented at the
trial.[25]

Against this background, Spenser's description of the duplicity of Clarinda is very much to the point:

> Ne ever did deceiptfull *Clarin* find
> In her false hart, his bondage to unbind;
> But rather how she mote him faster tye.
> Therefore unto her mistresse most unkind
> She daily told, her love he did defye,
> And him she told, her Dame his freedome did denye.
>
> (v.56)

Maitland certainly did intend to keep those involved in the
Norfolk scheme in "bondage" to Mary, but he also exploited
Mary's fears of rejection, and all the while he was pursuing his
own private aim: an alliance with England.

V

In the autumn of 1569, the secret scheming involving Mary
came at last into the open. Elizabeth heard the full extent of
Norfolk's involvement, and within a few weeks the Duke was
imprisoned in the Tower and the Catholic Lords Northumber-

land and Westmoreland took arms in the North. After months of legal and diplomatic maneuvering, Elizabeth was finally forced to take military measures against the Marian Catholics in England and Scotland. Her initial deliberations and her ultimate victory are portrayed in Cantos vi and vii. From Talus Britomart learns of Artegall's surrender, and though she is deeply jealous, she nonetheless sets out to release him. After episodes at the House of Dolon and Isis Church (which, because they are tangential to the story of the Amazons, cannot occupy us here), she meets Radigund in battle, beheads her, releases Artegall, and restores male supremacy in the city of Radigone.

Even before she hears Talus's news, Britomart's first reaction is to fear that Artegall has found "some new love" or that his foe Grantorto has entrapped him, and this concern has an important basis in fact. Before Elizabeth had hard evidence of a conspiracy, she was shrewd enough to perceive that something was awry with Norfolk and Mary, and she was also deeply concerned about Philip II, whom Spenser allegorizes in Grantorto. In 1569, tensions were running high between England and Spain, and war seemed imminent. Moreover, the Spanish ambassador was at the heart of the treasonous plotting that Northumberland and his friends carried out behind the more honorable maneuvering of Leicester and Norfolk. It was widely—and correctly—rumored that, if the English Catholics had risen in force against their queen, the Spanish would have backed them using Alva's forces in the Netherlands. [26]

Britomart's next reaction, after hearing Talus's report that Artegall is in prison, is also important in the historical allegory, for it reveals one of Spenser's purposes in writing this section of the poem: to exonerate Leicester and his cabal. In judging Artegall's actions, the main question that Britomart considers is "whether he did woo, or whether he were woo'd" (vi.15). Talus's reply—that Artegall was "not the while in state to woo" because he was in "thraldome"—is more to the point than may at first appear. It was not the English but Mary's supporters, particularly Maitland, who had initiated the marriage talks, and Leicester and his faction seem to have played along mainly in order to stay in Mary's good graces. Of course, in light of the disastrous consequences of this maneuvering, Spenser could not very well let Leicester's error in judgment pass without condemnation. He could, however, paint it out as entirely human and understandable by citing the example of other men from the past who had been beguiled by women. This excuse, though flimsy, may well have been adequate to the occasion, for, like Britomart, Elizabeth seems to have been more interested in assuring herself that Leicester had remained loyal than in punishing him for his part in the fiasco. After subjecting him to a brief period of disgrace, she forgave him and turned to face her Catholic enemies in the North.

In Canto vii, after an eventful trip to the city of the Amazons, Britomart spreads her pavilion close by and prepares for battle. Radigund's first reaction, besides "joyous glee" at the prospect of battle, is the hope "that she the face of her new foe might see" (vii.25), and this detail may refer to Mary's well-known desire throughout this period to meet Elizabeth in personal interview.[27] Like Mary, however, Radigund fails in this desire. Trumpets sound the battle, and Radigund sees only the hard exterior of her opponent's armaments.

Before she engages Britomart, the Amazon propounds the same conditions under which she fought with Artegall. This time, however, her opponent refuses to accept any law but that of chivalry. This point is worth noting because it corresponds with a crucial change in Elizabeth's policy in the years 1569–71. Previously, her ambassadors had been willing to offer, as one term of a comprehensive settlement with Mary, a clause granting the Scottish Queen the right to succeed to the English throne should she outlive Elizabeth and her heirs. However, once Mary's Catholic forces had attempted to overthrow the English government in the Rebellion of 1569 and in the Ridolfi Plot of 1571, Elizabeth changed her policy and never again offered to confirm Mary's right of succession.[28] Like Britomart, Elizabeth was now "fully bent / To fierce avengement" of her opponent's pride (vi.18).

Spenser describes the ensuing battle as cruel and unseemly:

> through great fury both their skill forgot,
> And practicke use in armes: ne spared not
> Their dainty parts, which nature had created
> So faire and tender, without staine or spot,
> For other uses . . .
>
> (vii.29)

The reference to blows against one another's "dainty parts" may have to do with charges of sexual immorality that passed between the two queens during this period. In 1571, Elizabeth allowed the publication of the incriminating letters that had been introduced in Mary's trial, and they were bound together with George Buchanan's *Detectio Mariae Reginae Scotorum*, which alleged that Mary had commited flagrant acts of adultery with James Bothwell. In return, Mary sniped at Elizabeth, on one occasion demanding that a proposed treaty allowing Elizabeth's heirs to precede Mary in the English succession include the requirement that they be "lawful issue."[29]

Equally pointed is Spenser's assertion that "both their skill forgot," for both sides fought badly in the Rebellion of 1569. The Earl of Sussex, who commanded Elizabeth's Northern troops, declined to engage the rebels for more than five weeks and was derided at court for failing to act sooner. When at last reinforcements from the south arrived, the army scattered the rebels and pursued them over the border into Scotland. Then it took terrible vengeance on the English villages that had supported the uprising, hanging more than six hundred suspects without due process of law. This excess is probably reflected in the depredations of Talus, who drives the enemy pell mell "into the towne" and then begins a "piteous slaughter" (vii.35). Similar reprisals took place the following spring, when the English army again invaded Scotland to punish Mary's supporters.[30]

We come, finally, to the point with which we began: the beheading of Radigund; and it should now be clear that it can have nothing to do with the actual execution of Mary Stuart. The dates and circumstances are wrong. As we have seen, the fall of Radigund represents events in the period 1569–71, when Mary had been a rival for the affections of several of Elizabeth's own noblemen and when she had cast reproaches against the honor of the English queen and had struck a painful blow against her in the Rebellion of the Northern Earls. Elizabeth's response had been angry and violent, just as Spenser suggests in describing Britomart's final attack on Radigund (vii.34). It was not until 1587, however, that Mary was finally sent to the block, and Elizabeth's attitude then was quite different. She took extraordinary steps to insure that Mary's second trial was scrupulously legal (at least by the standards of the day), and so reluctant was she to allow the death sentence to be carried out that she seriously alienated Parliament and her own Privy Council.[31] Clearly, these circumstances correspond with Spenser's description of the trial and execution of Duessa in Cantos ix–x, but not with the events surrounding the slaying of Radigund.

It seems likely, therefore, that Radigund's death in Canto vii is merely symbolic. Like the dismemberment of Grantorto in Canto viii, which has nothing to do with the actual demise of Philip II in 1598 but only with the dispersal of his Armada ten years earlier, the slaying is not to be taken literally. Spenser hints at the true meaning when he writes that Britomart "with one stroke both head and helmet cleft" (v.34). As we saw earlier, the poet employs Radigund's golden helmet as a symbol for the crown of Scotland, and the head is, of course, a symbol of supremacy. I would suggest that Spenser has in mind, not Mary's death, but the final and irreparable loss of her right and her power to govern Scotland. In 1571, after Mary was implicated in the Ridolfi plot, Elizabeth sent word to the government in Edinburgh that Mary would never be allowed to resume her throne. Although the English queen had long hoped that Mary might somehow be restored and had therefore declined to recognize the government of Mary's young son, James VI, she now granted that recognition. From 1571 on, the ascendancy of the King's party was virtually assured.[32]

Once we recognize the true meaning of the blow to Radigund's head, then the remainder of the allegory falls neatly into place. Britomart's release of Artegall from prison corresponds with a new mood at court after the Ridolfi Plot. Never again were Elizabeth's chief courtiers involved in Mary's schemes, and Parliament went so far as to pass a bill removing her from the English succession and authorizing her execution without trial should any further insurrection be mounted on her behalf.[33] Britomart's personal reign in Radigone and her reestablishment of male supremacy there reflect the role of English troops in maintaining order in Scotland after 1569. In 1570 and again in 1573, they crossed the border to aid the Protestant party, successfully defending them until a strong new Regent, the Earl of Morton, could take measures to repress Marian dissent and consolidate his power.[34] Finally, the oath of fealty that the magistrates of Radigone swear to Artegall accurately represents the firm alliance between Scotland and England which was established during this period.

One question remains: why did Spenser risk misleading his readers by having Radigund killed, when he might simply have had her deposed? The answer must, of course, be speculative,

but two reasons come to mind. In Book I, when the poet had
been concerned with religion, he had alluded to Mary in the
figure of Duessa. In Book V, where most of the allegory of
Mary's reign explores issues of political justice rather than of
religion, Spenser chose to recast Mary in the figure of Radigund.
In the cantos after the death of the Amazon queen, however,
there is once again a specifically religious point to be made. In
1571, the Pope issued his Bull of Excommunication against Elizabeth and thus transformed her political struggles with Mary
into a religious conflict. Thereafter, all the chief Catholic powers
of the Continent—Philip II of Spain, the Pope, the Guises—
began machinations to depose the heretical English queen. I
would argue that, in order to emphasize the terrible new danger
posed by Mary after the Bull, Spenser chose to represent her once
again in the figure of Duessa.

The shift also reflects a change in Mary's *modus operandi*.
Before 1571, her struggle with Elizabeth was more or less open. It
involved major diplomatic and military confrontations that lend
themselves to the sort of heroic treatment that we see in the
portrayal of Radigund. After 1571, however, Mary was reduced
to scheming of the most ignoble sort, using empty beer barrels to
smuggle letters to shady agents outside her prison and joining
one murderous conspiracy after another. The suggestions of
duplicity in the name "Duessa" become altogether appropriate
again. The glamorous and proud Queen of Scots, figured forth
so grandly in the armor of Radigund, did indeed die in 1571.
Thereafter, all that remained was a bitter, aging woman, living
out her life at Tutbury and Chartley in plots and empty dreams.

VI

The detailed depiction of Mary Stuart as Radigund raises
important questions about the nature and the aims of the historical allegory in Book V. It is often assumed that Spenser handled
topical material allusively and that it is altogether in the service of
the moral and political allegory of the poem. Edwin Greenlaw
once wrote that historical allegory is included only "by way of
illustration or compliment or ornament, never sustained for
long"[35] Albert Gough took a similar—though more radical—
position when he wrote that "a complete and consistent allegory

is not to be looked for. It is Spenser's habit to give a hint of a political meaning, and then to confuse the trail."[36] The allegory of Mary Stuart offers at least one major counter-example to the generalizations of Greenlaw and Gough. It is sustained, coherent, and largely chronological. It can hardly be called "compliment" or "ornament," and if it is confusing, the difficulty lies with our own lack of historical knowledge, not with the allegory itself.

Yet what of Greenlaw's third possibility: that the historical allegory serves as an "illustration" of the principles involved in the moral allegory? Though topical references undoubtedly act in this way throughout the poem, I would argue that they also have a second and more important function in Book V. There, the topical allegory is not intermittent or occasional but pervasive, and it lies at the very heart of the poet's intention. In Cantos iv through xii, Spenser portrays the reign of Queen Elizabeth as a single, momentous struggle against the Catholic forces of the world. In Radigund he presents the rivalry with Mary Stuart in the 1550s and '60s; in the Souldan and Duessa the battles against Philip of Spain and Mary in the 1570s and '80s; in Gerioneo and Grantorto the wars in the Netherlands and Ireland in the 1580s and '90s.[37] Far from being mere illustration, the historical allegory constitutes the main action of Book V. Moreover, the nature of this action is one of Spenser's most conspicuous innovations in the genre of the epic.

In the Letter to Raleigh, Spenser likens The Faerie Queene to the works of "Poets historicall" such as Homer, Virgil, and the Italians. In doing so, he is accepting a fundamental premise of classical epic: that the legendary history of a nation is the matter best suited to educate its people. As Spenser goes on to explain, this is true, in part, because legend provides a store of moral and political exempla. Yet it is also true because history unites the nation in a common view of its origins and its social order, and— through the visions of its founders and heroes—provides a way to establish its claims for the future.

The contemporary references in the Radigund episode and throughout Book V fulfill this larger epic intention. They set forth the greatness of Elizabeth's achievement in preserving justice and Reformed religion in the British Isles and in establishing England as a major force in the Western world. They do so, however, by transforming the present reign of Elizabeth into the stuff of the mythic past. As the poet announces in the procm to

Book III, he intends to fit "antique praises unto present persons." This transformation is Spenser's major innovation in the genre of the romantic epic. Earlier epic poets, such as Virgil and Dante, had alluded to current politics or brought it in by way of illustration, and Ariosto may have had it in mind in brief passages of allegory. Spenser, however, turns it into the main action of an entire book. In portraying Elizabeth and her ministers in the guise of legendary figures, he sets them in a heroic tradition reserved for the descendents of the gods. Their deeds are the beginning of a new destiny for England. Like Aeneas, they must carry on a great battle against an ancient civilization across the sea. Like him, they are destined to found a new and more glorious Troy. Prophetic passages throughout the poem confirm the English in this epic role. Their destiny is emphasized in the Briton Chronicles in Book II, in Merlin's prophecies and Britomart's account of the founding of Troynovant in Book III, and in Britomart's dream at Isis Church in Book V—which comes just before the decisive battle with Radigund.

As Spenser suggests after the death of Duessa, the ultimate significance of the episodes involving Mary Stuart lies in this epic pattern. For three decades, Mary was the single greatest threat to Elizabeth and to the new order that she sought to establish. After the allegorical portrayal of Mary's death, the poet can at last pause to celebrate a true epic victory. He sings of Elizabeth as if she were an ancient hero, honored by the gods, great in England's destiny, exemplary in the classical and Christian virtues. He writes of her (in the figure of Mercilla):

> What heavenly Muse shall thy great honour rayse
> Up to the skies, whence first deriv'd it was,
> And now on earth it selfe enlarged has
> From th'utmost brinke of the *Armericke* shore,
> Unto the margent of the *Molucas*?
> Those Nations farre thy justice doe adore:
> But thine owne people do thy mercy prayse much more.
>   (x.3)

Spenser's adaptation of epic convention to allow this sort of glorification of a living ruler is bold almost to the point of presumption. Yet his words—at least those concerning Elizabeth's role in England's new destiny—were prophetic. By ensuring the survival of the Protestant Reformation, by consolidating a centralized government in England, and by laying the first foundations for the British Empire, Elizabeth did indeed alter the course of Western civilization.

As the Radigund episode reveals, the historical allegory of Book V is not simply a set of illustrations to support the moral allegory. It is also a new form of epic action, comparable in scope and global implications with Virgil's account of the founding of Rome.

Virginia Polytechnic Institute and State University

NOTES

1. See, among others, Albert B. Gough, *The Faerie Queene, Book V* (Oxford, 1918), cited in Edwin Greenlaw, *et al.*, eds., *The Works of Edmund Spenser: A Variorum Edition*, 11 vols. (Baltimore, 1932–57), V, 221 and 246; Edwin Greenlaw, *Studies in Spenser's Historical Allegory* (Baltimore, 1932), pp. 142–47, cited in the *Variorum*, V, 304–306; H. S. V. Jones, *A Spenser Handbook* (New York, 1930), pp. 262–64, cited in the *Variorum*, V, 316–17; Thomas Cain, *Praise in "The Faerie Queene"* (Lincoln, Nebr., 1978), p. 152.
2. I cite the text of *The Faerie Queene* edited by A. C. Hamilton (London, 1977). Archaic spelling inverting i and j, u and v has been modernized.
3. Cain, p. 152.
4. See Donald V. Stump, "Isis Versus Mercilla: The Allegorical Shrines in Spenser's Legend of Justice," *Spenser Studies* 3 (1982), 87–98.
5. Before beginning, one would like to be able to identify Spenser's sources of information. Unfortunately, however, Mary's case was the subject of countless tracts and histories, and we have no way of knowing which of them Spenser may have read. He could, moreover, have learned all that he needed without opening a book, for he served under two officials who knew the case intimately: the Earl of Leicester and Lord Arthur Grey. As I shall discuss below, Leicester was a principal figure in several of the incidents woven into Spenser's allegory, and Grey fought in one of its key battles and was also a commisioner at Mary's trial in 1586. I have, therefore, confined my documentation in sixteenth-century sources to two of the best known histories: George Buchanan's *History of Scotland* and Raphael Holinshed's *Chronicles*. Buchanan is useful because he shares Spenser's bitterly anti-Marian stance and often follows the official English line on Mary's conduct. Holinshed offers detailed accounts of military engagements. For further bibliography, see Kerby Neill, "The Faerie Queene and the Mary Stuart Controversy," *ELH* 2 (1935), 192–214, and James Emerson Phillips, *Images of a Queen: Mary Stuart in Sixteenth-Century Literature* (Berkeley, 1964).
6. George Buchanan, *The History of Scotland*, tr. James Aikman, 4 vols. (Glasgow, 1827), II, 437.
7. Buchanan, *History*, II, 406–420. See also Gordon Donaldson's concise history of the rebellion in *The Edinburgh History of Scotland*, edited by Gordon Donaldson, III: *Scotland: James V to James VII* (Edinburgh, 1965), pp. 85–106.

8. See Buchanan, *History*, II, 420–04. A detailed account of day-by-day military operations and the terms of the subsequent treaty appears in Holinshed's *Chronicles of England, Scotland, and Ireland*, 6 vols. (London, 1808), IV, 188–201.

9. On the strategic importance of Leith, see Holinshed, *Chronicles*, IV, 189.

10. See Buchanan, *History*, II, 441–48, and E. Russell, *Maitland of Lethington, the Minister of Mary Stuart. A Study of His Life and Times* (London, 1912), pp. 146–58.

11. See J. E. Neale, *Queen Elizabeth* (New York, 1934), pp. 106–113, 124, 151–52, 164.

12. Donaldson, *Scotland: James V to James VII*, pp. 66–72, 76–79.

13. See Antonia Fraser, *Mary Queen of Scots* (New York, 1969), pp. 48, 90.

14. See Elizabeth Jenkins, *Elizabeth and Leicester* (New York, 1962), pp. 93–95, 134–35.

15. Buchanan gives detailed accounts of Mary's quarrels with Darnley and charges her with complicity in his assassination. See *History*, II, 471–502, and *Detectio Mariae Reginae Scotorum*, in *The Tyrannous Reign of Mary Queen of Scots*, tr. and ed. W. A. Gatherer (Edingurgh, 1958), pp. 163–80.

16. See Buchanan, *History*, II, 502–27.

17. Jenkyns, *Elizabeth and Leicester*, p. 154. Many critics simply equate Artegall with Leicester, but, as Artegall's connection with the actions of Elizabeth's other ministers shows, he represents no single person but rather the Queen's justice as it was carried out by all her agents. See Greenlaw, *Studies in Spenser's Historical Allegory*, p. 101.

18. Jenkyns, pp. 154–66; Fraser, p. 420.

19. Neale, *Queen Elizabeth*, pp. 179–82.

20. As one of the Scottish commissioners, Buchanan had an insider's knowledge of Norfolk's involvement with Mary. See *History*, II, 540–44.

21. Buchanan, *History*, II, 544–45, 552–54; Neale, p. 180.

22. Buchanan, *History*, II, 569–71; Maurice Lee, Jr., *James Stewart. Earl of Moray: A Political Study of the Reformation in Scotland* (New York, 1953), pp. 273–74.

23. Fraser, *Mary Queen of Scots*, pp. 417–18.

24. Buchanan discusses Norfolk's secret arrangement to send letters to Mary through William Maitland and suggests that the marriage was first negotiated through the wife of Mary's earlier warder, Lord Scrope. See *History*, II, 543–44, 562.

25. See Buchanan, *History*, II, 543–44; Lee, *James Stewart*, pp. 237–41; Russell, *Maitland*, pp. 370–84. Lee and Russell have proposed plausible theories to explain Maitland's bizarre behavior in this incident, showing that it was neither self-serving nor intentionally destructive of Anglo-Scottish relations. To someone like Spenser, however, who knew less about the man and who had more intense feelings than we do about the disastrous results of the Norfolk marriage scheme, Maitland's maneuvering must have seemed plain treachery with but one plausible explanation: that Maitland was trying to curry favor with the English for his own personal advancement.

26. See Neale, *Queen Elizabeth*, pp. 185–86.

27. See Neale, pp. 161–64, 168.

28. Neale, pp. 195–96.

29. Neale, pp. 190, 196.

30. Holinshed's account of the rebellion reveals the bumbling and the excesses of both sides. See *Chronicles*, IV, 234–52. See also Neale, pp. 183–87.

31. See Neale, pp. 272–77.

32. See Neale, pp. 195–96.

33. Neale, pp. 198–201.

34. Donaldson, *Scotland: James V to James VII*, pp. 163–67.

35. Greenlaw, *Studies in Spenser's Historical Allegory*, p. 96.

36. Gough, *Variorum*, V, 211. For arguments against these and other scholars with similar views, such as A. C. Hamilton and Graham Hough, see Frank Kermode, "The Faerie Queene, I and V," in *Shakespeare, Spenser, Donne* (New York, 1971), pp. 33–59.

37. See Jones, *A Spenser Handbook*, pp. 26–71.

DEBRA BELT

Hostile Audiences and the Courteous Reader in *The Faerie Queene*, Book VI

*I*N BOOK V, canto xii of *The Faerie Queene*, Spenser abruptly
introduces the Blatant Beast into his narrative, turning it loose to
attack his characters and to range through the rest of the epic
more or less at will. Readers of the poem have long realized that
this move signals a major shift in tone and narrative strategy.
Assessments of its implications have been skewed, however, by
the collapsing of key distinctions between the Beast and his
associates and by our failure to perceive that Spenser's final book
is rife with echoes from the prefatory addresses to the reader
routinely appended to works published in the 1580s and 1590s.[1]
These prefatory allusions and cross-references supply a conceptual framework from within which to approach a book remarkable for its diversity of incident. The poet's repeated incorporation of motifs from such contemporary documents not only
serves to associate the Beast with the figure of the observer
critical of what he sees and hears but acts unmistakably to add the
concept of the "courteous reader" to the poet's anatomy of
courtesy.

Such additions make the ways preface-writers define courteous and discourteous responses to their labors continuously
available as glosses upon the incidents narrated in Book VI.
Resonating behind the Priscilla-Aladine episode and the encounter with Colin Clout, these allusions help to explain why Calidore as courteous knight should "go to such lengths to protect"
what Richard Neuse has termed "a dubious reputation"[2] and pin
down what he neglects to do when confronted with the vision on
Mt. Acidale. The context provided by these cross-references
suggests that Canto x should be viewed not as an expression of
despair that conditions essential for the practice of poetry are
unattainable,[3] but as an effort to set forth a working model for
the relationship between audience and piper that appears to the
poet most likely to be mutually productive. Such efforts are

consistent with Spenser's overall strategy in Book VI: simultaneously to supply the receptive reader with examples of proper and improper ways to respond to the kinds of incidents that comprise the narrative and to drive home to him the potential consequences that adopting unfriendly or prematurely judgmental postures can carry. These practices mark Book VI as an attempt to deal reasonably with the series of critical audiences with whom Spenser has skirmished throughout the epic, an effort abandoned only in the poem's closing stanzas, where he adopts a more confrontational stance that amounts to an all-out declaration of war.

I

Roma Gill has described some of the ways that what she terms prefatory "conventions of Envy" influence Spenser's "choice of terminology" when he comes to describe the monster who terrorizes his final book, chief among them being Envy's traditional associations with dogs and snakes and her connections with railing, reviling, and backbiting. Yet Envy is in Spenser's narrative a figure separate from the Blatant Beast, portrayed not as the monster's equivalent but as the first in a series of goaders and suborners which includes not simply Detraction, but Decetto, Despetto, and Defetto as well. These figures use the same monster as an instrument for fulfilling different private agendas; to each is ascribed a different motive for turning to what resembles nothing so much as a force conveniently available to any comer who desires to point it and unleash it. Such facts serve simultaneously to highlight the connections between the Beast and his handlers and to insist that the monster remains an entity distinct from them. The final canto of the poem confirms and deepens these distinctions, suggesting that the Beast's motives transcend the idiosyncratic grudges and dislikes in which envy, detraction, and spite are rooted.[4] The picture of the monster "barking and biting all that him doe bate" (VII.xii.40) makes his actions look much more impersonal and dispassionate: like the Renaissance equivalent of the bulldozer or the tank, he simply disables anything that threatens to impede his passage. His aim appears to be the single-minded one of achieving and preserving power.

Such factors suggest that we need to be more careful when we categorize and interpret Spenser's monster. The Beast seems explicitly designed not as the allegorical equivalent of an emotional state, but as an encompassing figure—an envelope whose mouth contains "a thousand tongues of sundry kindes and sundry quality."

> Some were of dogs, that barked day and night,
> And some of cats, that wrawling still did cry,
> And some of Beares, that groynd continually,
> And some of Tygres, that did seeme to gren,
> And snar at all, that euer passed by.
> But most of them were tongues of mortall men,
> Which spake reprochfully, not coring where nor when.
>
> And them amongst were mingled here and there,
> The tongues of Serpents with three forked stings,
> That spat out poyson and gore bloudy gere
> At all, that came within his rauenings,
> And spake licentious words, and hatefull things
> Of good and bad alike, of low and hie . . .
>   (VI.xii.27–28)[5]

Spenser's portrait of the monster—the first good look at him that he has given us—thus draws together many different types of hostile and reproachful voices, insisting upon their connections with one another without blurring the distinctions among them. It is this "sundriness of kind and quality" that needs stressing. Certainly the monster's repertory includes the vices of envy and detraction, as well as those of slander, spite, and deceit. But he seems explicitly designed to contain these vices without being confined by them. Some more comprehensive explanation of his significance to the narrative appears to be required.[6]

More careful attention to the final book's connections with the prefaces should help clarify this significance; for Spenser's use even of the prefatory conventions that Gill correctly identifies is far more systematic than she appears to realize, and his overall debt to these documents is much larger than she imagines. The poet does not merely insert occasional allusions to prefatory conventions into a narrative largely preoccupied with other concerns. Rather, as I shall demonstrate below, he imports wholesale the attributes of a range of hostile and critical figures—and of a complex of ideal readers that would have been instantly recognizable to readers conversant with the dedicatory practices of the era. He uses the context supplied by such attributes to structure and focus the diverse incidents that comprise the final book of the poem.

One finds the

> wicked monster that his tongue doth whet,
> Gainst all, both good and bad, both most and least,
> And poures his poysnous gall forth to infest
> The noblest wight with notable defame
>
> (VI.vi.12)

—the cur whose "venemous despite" is aimed squarely at the work itself—in both literary and non-literary contexts almost exactly as Spenser portrays him. Matthew Grove images himself poised in the act of publication as beset by "manie serpents tongues redie in the waie, . . . and [by] the teeth of . . . manie barking dogs readie to bite." William Clowes characterizes those critical of his work both as dogs who "l[ie] snarling, and scornefully prying into other mens doings, to blemish and deface the same as much as in their power consist[s]" and as figures who

> continually spit foorth poysō out of their noysome and unsauorie mouths, against diuers godly learned, and wel disposed persons, who haue with long and tedious labours published diuers Bookes.

John Stockwood ascribes the troubles encountered by one of his earlier works to "the opprobrious censures of virulent and venemous tongues misdeeming, and thorough misdeeming, misiudging, and most mis-reporting, and mis-speaking of the same"; and Thomas Watson likewise attributes "stormes that may fall vnlooked for" to "the poyson of euill edged tongues." He links his elaborate prefatory remarks to "the feare" he says he had "to be bitten by such as are captious."[7]

Like Spenser's beast, moreover, these prefatory figures "wound" with words,[8] "byte [their victim's] name behind [his] backe,"[9] "carry . . . in their tongues" the wherewithal to "set men's fame on fire,"[10] seek their victims' shame.[11] Like the Beast, they are described as shadowy figures difficult to pin down, said to be always lurking, portrayed as apt to attack suddenly and without warning.[12] Such figures characteristically operate by influencing the opinions of third parties, as does Spenser's monster;[13] like him, they refuse to distinguish between those who deserve criticism and those who do not.[14] They routinely condemn the whole because they find the part faulty; and they magnify errors until they come to seem much larger than they really are,[15] practices which bear striking resemblances to those favored by the Blatant Beast.

Preface-writers share the narrator's conviction that the damage caused by such treatment can be considerable; and they spell out the consequences of this conviction in strikingly similar terms. Like the Hermit (VI.vi.1,9,13), Thomas Watson terms the "bite" that he fears "a hurt remedilesse" which at best may be "salue[d] up with patience." Euerard Digbie's statements are similar; and his vow to limit what he utters in order to stave off what he deems the inevitable effects of critical displeasure closely parallels the one made by Spenser's narrator at the end of Book VI. ("If the enuious toong were but as the winde which changeth often, or as the sting of the little Bee whose greatest swellings are easily asswaged with annointing of sweet honey, then might I aduenture my little boate into the wide Ocean seas: and crie alowd with old Anchises: *Vela dare ventis*," he informs his readers.

> But sith the venimous tong more mortal than the Cockatrice, empoisoneth further than the eye can see, infesting the absent with deadly disgrace: heereafter, *Spes & fortuna valete*, shall be my song, and $\Delta \alpha \theta \epsilon$ $\xi \iota \omega \sigma \alpha \varsigma$ [a locution paraphrased by classics scholar Barry Goldfarb as "avoid public duties and cultivate your own interests"] my full conclusion.)

Such sentiments find echoes in Henrie Howard's mutterings about his "Bandogge" critics ("whelpes of that accursed kinde, which driue men with their bawling, from the conquest of the golden fleese, that is regarded by the worthy") and in Thomas Morley's assertion that the criticism which he anticipates, "couched in the progress of a wayfaring mans passage, might make him retire, though almost at his journeyes end."[16]

Nor are such parallels confined to the Beast or to the narrator of Spenser's poem. When the knight of courtesy confronts the monster, the pair are often placed in postures that mimic those ascribed by preface-writers to hostile figures and to potential defenders against their carping. Samuel Brandon attributes to critics of his *Tragicomedie of Octavia* the same preference for flight over fair fight that Spenser ascribes to the Blatant Beast when confronted by the knight of courtesy (VI.iii.25, VI.xii.25, VI.ix.3 4). Stephen Gosson's vow to

> whippe out those Doggs, which have barked [more?] at mee for writing *The Schoole of Abuse*, then Cerberus did at Hercules for descending to hell; and haue laboured with the venom of their teeth to wound me deeper, then that curst curre, which was the death of Licinius, and the cause of a battaile, wherein Hercules lost his brother Iphiclus,

is even more suggestive, for it places the writer in a Herculean context very like the one ascribed to Calidore during the climactic battle in Canto xii (stanzas 32 and 35). The punishment desired by the translator of *News from Niniue to England brought by the prophet Jonas*—that the *reader*

> helpe to mosell Momus mouth and bridle Zoilus chappes
>   Which like a curre ech willing wight
>   With currish fanges he snappes—

likewise bears an uncanny resemblance to the treatment that Spenser's courteous knight ultimately administers to his monster.[17]

These recurrent parallels suggest that Spenser intended the Beast's connections with such figures from the prefaces not only to be recognized, but to define the monster's function in his narrative. Through his connections with these documents the Beast comes to embody the genus hostile reproacher of which the other unfriendly figures who fill Book VI could be said to constitute the various species. The book itself accordingly emerges as an anatomy of the complexities and difficulties that coping with the behavior of such hostile observers entails.

This suggestion is reinforced, as the quotation from *News from Niniue* makes clear, by persistent similarities between the deeds the courteous knight performs and the actions that contemporary prefaces typically urge upon their ideal readers. Calidore's titular virtue itself constitutes the most obvious of the parallels between prefatory practice and Spenser's narrative, for courtesy not only becomes in the 1580's and 90's the attribute most commonly requested of potential readers, but in preface after preface is cited as the preferred strategy for neutralizing the dangers that faultfinders are said to pose. Appeals "to the courteous reader" may be found in the prefaces to such disparate documents as I. G.'s translation of *Giacomo di Grassi his true Arte of Defence* (1594); John Blagrave's *Astrolabium Vranicum Generale* (1596); Leonard Wright's *A Display of dutie* (1589); Timothy Kendall's *Flowers of Epigrammes* (1577); Thomas Fenne's *Fennes Frvtes* (1590); Thomas Bradshaw's *The Shepherds Starre* (1591); and E. L.'s *Romes Monarchie* (1596). William Clowes, Robert Dormer, John Lane, Henry Lok, Richard Bellewe, and John Dickinson all end their prefaces by entrusting themselves and the fate of their work to the reader's "courteous offices," as do Robert Greene, George Gascoigne, and George Pettie.[18] By 1592, Richard Johnson can define the act of publishing itself as "aduentur[ing] on [his "Gentlemen Readers"] courtesies."[19] Solicitations of the reader's courteous response appear even in religious tracts,[20] suggesting that, fully as much as did the attributes of the Blatant Beast, the concept of "the courteous reader" formed part of a complex of prefatory motifs whose immediate recognizability Spenser could presume without question.

In practice, furthermore, the reader's courtesy and the hostile critic's condemnation are repeatedly, almost ritualistically, associated. Richard Stanihurst in the same breath "craue[s] the good liking of the curteous, and scorne[s] the controlment of the currish"; and the address of the printer of Spenser and Harvey's *Three Proper and wittie familiar letters* (1580) to the "cvrteous buyer (for I write not to the enuious carper)" sets courtesy and hostile criticism directly in opposition to one another. The prologue to Lyly's *Sapho and Phao* (1584) does likewise; and Charles Gibbon similarly links the curious critic to the courteous excuser when he says he means

> not to satisfie such readers which bee rude, but reasonable, not the curious but the curteous, the one will excuse and couer a fault with discretion, the other will but carpe and cauill with cause . . .[21]

Significantly, moreover, the reader's courtesy is often invoked not simply as the natural opposite to but as a potential antidote for the hostile critic's malice. In his preface to *Pandosto* (1588),

Robert Greene proposes that if any should "condemne" his work, he "shroud my selfe vnder the shadowe of [my readers'] courtesies." R. Rabbardes likewise requests the readers of *The Compound of Alchymie* (1591) to "defend me with your curtesies" if "anie carper inueigh against me"; and the printer of Simon Robson's *The Courte of Ciuill Courtesie* (1582) beseeches his readers that they "vouchsafe of [their] great curtesie . . . to defend both [his work] and him that offereth it, from the spightful tongues of malicious carpers."[22] The writer of "the Bookes request" to the readers of *The Contemplation of Mankind* (1571) labels such courtesies "a recompense sufficing well, and countervayling aye, / The blacke reproch that Momus tongue / enforceth daye by daye."

Preface-writers also routinely spell out the actions in which they desire their readers' courteous response to issue. In effect such specifications define what their writers mean by courteous reading; and these definitions resonate behind the actions of Spenser's knight of courtesy in a number of different ways. This is true not only of Calidore's responses to the Beast, but to many of the other figures in Book VI. Repeated prefatory exhortations to the "courteous" to overlook mistakes or to brook rash actions and errors with patience, to "beare with [the speaker] although [he] merit blame," to "correct friendly" or "amend" discreetly rather than condemn vocally and hastily—or at the very least to "passe over" mistakes or indiscretions "with silence"—find their embodiment in Calidore's behavior toward Priscilla and Aladine, for instance, and to some extent in his actions and comments towards Briana and Crudor. A multitude of admonitions to the courteous reader not to read hastily or react precipitately—to "rather continew in suspense, then pronounce rashly," to "staye thy judgement till thou knowe [the writer's] intent and deeme the best till then"—also help to explain what Spenser's chief protagonist neglects to do when confronted with the vision on Mt. Acidale.

II

Prefatory descriptions and definitions of courteous reading offer ample evidence that in cases where the speaker-actor is found to be at fault, the reader is expected discreetly to overlook equivocal actions, to pardon well-intentioned mistakes, and to bring to his task a considerable measure of forbearance. William Vaughan states flatly that "Erre I may in writing, but it is thy part (courteous Reader) to brooke mine errours with patience." The writer of *The Forrest of Fancy* (1579) beseeches his reader to "beare with me though I merit blame"; and Angell Day similarly implores his audience's "courteous forbearance" even "when . . . I cannot cleare me from [my readers'] censures." William Auerell "desires" his "courteous and freendly reader" "to beare with" those "faults" "committed by vnwarinesse and . . . by wearynesse";[23] and a host of exhortations implore such a reader to pardon the "rashness" of the writer's actions.

Preface-writers also insist that when judging equivocal actions or responding to potentially offensive and blameable situations, the courteous reader will take into consideration both the writer-actor's intentions and, where appropriate, his youth and inexperience. The author of *The Forrest of Fancy* asks "each curteous wight to way my good intent . . ."; and Robert Greene characterizes the "mark[ing of] the mynd, and not the matter; the wil, and not the worke" as the "wonted curtesie" for which he "hopes." Anthony Munday defines "courteous readers" specifically as those who "though they finde a scape, will beare with the Authors simplicitie, and consider his good will indifferently, concerning his . . . Adolescency."[24] Ideal readers are likewise routinely asked to view perceived missteps in the context of the doer's overall character and exhorted to bear in mind the frailty of humankind in general. John Brooke counsels the reader of *The Staffe of Christian Faith* (1577) to respond to missteps not by being "red[y] to condemne them, as the enuious doe: but by ascrib[ing] it to mans fragilitie, as Christians ought." "Hoping of [his readers'] courteous acceptance," Richard Bellewe likewise requests the "defence" of "those whose experience teaching them that *Humanum est errare*, knowe how farre easier it is to finde a fault, then to doe that which shalbe without fault."[25]

There is widespread agreement that as a result of such deliberations the courteous reader will at the very least pass over inadvertent or unwary missteps in silence[26]—and that where possible he will mend what is amiss, remembering that he should "rather graunt to save then spill, / to help then work offense." Charles Gibbon reminds his audience that the "curteous" reader "will excuse and couer a fault with discretion"; and Angell Day "prays" his "courteous and learned" readers to "couer [anything

found blameworthy] . . . with the vaile of your courtesie."
Henrie Howard also "wishes" that "eyther [his "faultes and
ouersightes"] were noted with discretion, or concealed with
humanitie." The author of *A Geometrical practical Treatise Named
Pantometria* (1591) "hopes" that "the discrete and modest Reader
will rather of curtesie amend [his "faultes"] than" respond to
them "with . . . cauillation";[27] and James Bell, translator of
Against Jerome Osorius, states flatly that "findying ought amisse,
[the gentle-natured] will with courtesie rather correct . . . then
with carpyng condemne" him.

Calidore's treatment of Aladine and Priscilla in Canto iii—his
consideration of the young couple's intentions; his concealing
behind the veil of courtesy the rash actions which have rendered
them vulnerable to attack; his care discreetly to amend the situation into which Priscilla has backed herself; his decision, in short,
to "rather graunt to saue then spill, to helpe then worke
offense"—embodies and enacts such prefatory admonitions and
assertions. Angell Day's claim that his "courteous readers" will
remember that "in reformation, two notable instances . . . do
craue allowance . . . and these are for a man to finde his defect,
and secondly to haue a will to amend it" suggests a rationale,
moreover, for Spenser's having the couple admit to each other
Priscilla's own role in creating the "ill state in which she stood"
(VI.iii.11). The whole complex of prefatory echoes accordingly
serves to explain why Calidore as courteous knight should "go
to such lengths to protect" what the modern critic Richard
Neuse, reflecting current scholarly opinion about the incident,
dismissively terms "a dubious reputation." For Spenser's handling of the entire episode appears calculated to discourage just
such prematurely reductive judgments. It calls into question the
authority of audiences inclined to make them and insists upon the
serious consequences that mistaken and uncharitable assumptions can carry. It suggests that when one can be assured of the
basic soundness of the doer's character or the essential goodness
of his intentions, courtesy may consist in a discreet overlooking
of potentially equivocal activities.

Certainly the "proof" of Calidore's "kyndely courtesy" consists in Canto iii in getting Priscilla safely reinstalled in the home
and in the good graces of a potentially wrathful parent; and it is in
light of the character of this parent that his actions in the rest of
the sequence should be viewed. For Spenser portrays Priscilla's
father as a man not only predisposed to be hostile to news about

the company his daughter has been keeping (VI.iii.7), but apparently apt to draw from her overnight absence from home the same kinds of conclusions about her moral character as does Neuse, who flattens the nuances of the girl's description of two lovers "ioying together in vnblamed delight" into a bald and disapproving account of "couples copulating in the woods" (374).

The terms in which the courteous knight "present[s] the fearefull lady to her father deare" bear witness to his belief that questions of judgment, reproach, and potential condemnation will be those uppermost in this audience's mind. She is, he says,

> Most perfect pure and guiltlesse innocent
> Of blame, as he did on his knighthood sweare,
> Since first he saw her, and did free from feare
> Of a discourteous knight, who her had reft,
> And by outragious force away did beare:
> Witnesse thereof, he shewed his head there left,
> And wretched life forlorne, for vengement of his theft.
>
> (VI.iii.18)

The heavy and deliberate emphasis upon the girl's "purity" and "innocence" describes the expected area of concern more precisely, locating it in anxiety about what would once have been called Priscilla's honesty or, in a suggestive cliché, her virtue. (This locution neatly telescopes two distinct processes, the questioning of the propriety of her actions and the forming of conclusions about her moral character, into a single word. It thus mimics the move that her father, like Neuse, appears determined to make.) Indeed, the extravagance of the superlatives Calidore piles one atop another hints that the audience to whom he speaks is likely to view anything less than a certification of "perfect purity" and "guiltless innocence" as evidence of absolute corruption. Such an interpretation in turn seems destined to result in a wholesale condemnation that could lead to Priscilla's banishment from the household (VI.iii.11,12,18).[28] Calidore's "counter cast of slight"—concocted "to giue faire colour to the lady's cause in sight" and consisting of a tale that casts Priscilla in the storybook role of innocent virtue threatened by dirty-minded vice—seems similarly designed to play to an intelligence that insists on thinking of young ladies in such black-and-white, stereotypical terms. The use of the legal language of "cause," "oath," and "witness" reinforces the sense that the lady herself is on trial before a reflexively critical, powerful, and quite possibly vengeful judge, one whose first inclination is to assume that she has been doing something worthy of his censure.

Such details serve as pointed reminders that the impulse to condemn Priscilla is at least partly the product of a habit of mind already disposed to interpret her actions in the worst possible light, and that negative conclusions about the girl's moral character can thus hardly be said to be the result of unbiased reasoning, let alone models of good judgment or of clear and charitable thinking. Spenser reinforces these reminders both by allowing the girl to testify in her own behalf (she tells Calidore that she was "ioying together in vnblamed delight" with "him to whom she was foreuer bound"; and one of the sixteenth-century senses of "unblamed" is, after all, "unblameworthy" or "unblameable") and by endowing the couple's actions with a mutual care and compassion that lend considerable weight to their claims about the depth of their affection for one another. The pair's concern "to intimate / Each others griefe with zeale affectionate" and their willingness to grow "forgetfull of [their] owne, to mind [the other's] feares" (VI.iii.12) stand in sharp contrast to the tendency to think first in terms of self and to blame the other party for the situation in which they find themselves that Serena and Calepine, the other couple that figures prominently in Book VI, display. It is a willingness upon which the poet repeatedly insists: see VI.ii.41, VI.ii.43, VI.iii.11—"for first, next after life, he tendered her good."

Yet if Priscilla emerges as a victim undeserving of the condemnation that audiences both within and without the book seem poised to administer, Spenser also insists that the girl herself has helped to make that victimization possible. He has her belatedly acknowledge that she has placed her "good fame" at considerable "hazard"—a conclusion in which Aladine concurs (VI.iii.12)—and he supplements Priscilla's version of the incident with the stranger lady's considerably more suggestive description of the girl sitting "with a knight in ioyous iolliment / Of their franke loues, free from all gealous spyes" and "show[ing to him] all louely courtesyes" (VI.ii.16).

The lady's account is not necessarily incompatible with Priscilla's version of what happened in the clearing. It carries no hint of moral censure: her distaste appears to be not for the activity in which the girl is engaged, but for Priscilla herself, whose attractiveness to her own knight the lady quite plainly resents (VI.ii.17–18). Her stress on "show[ing] . . . louely courtesyes" is, moreover, completely consistent with the concern for the other member of the couple upon which the rest of the episode insists. Yet the presence of such a description in the narrative does demonstrate the ease with which the situation into which Priscilla has placed herself can give rise to potentially scandalous interpretations of her actions. It also drives home the near impossibility of proving oneself undeserving of condemnation if one's audience is predisposed to deliver it. It accordingly calls attention to the depth of Priscilla's *need* for courteous construal of her actions, and it highlights the uncomfortable dependence upon the charity of the observer-audience that such a need creates.

The overall effect of this combination of prefatory echo and allusion with narrative event is thus to create an episode that does not simply talk about the problems involved in courteous construal of actions and incidents, but embodies and enacts them. It calls into question current interpretations of Calidore's behavior, and it stands as an example of what I would argue is Spenser's overall narrative strategy in Book VI, many of whose episodes appear calculated to give the reader examples of ways he should and should not respond to situations like those which comprise the narrative or to impress upon him the consequences that adopting unfriendly, suspicious, or prematurely judgmental postures towards such situations can carry.

Canto x, which appears deliberately constructed to call attention to the connections between the actions it sets forth and the responses that contemporary preface-writers expect from their ideal readers, is a further case in point. Calidore is here cast specifically as a viewer-audience confronted with an interpretive dilemma, a set of images whose significance he wishes to determine and which he therefore feels compelled to identify; but this time his actions and their consequences closely parallel prefatory exhortations about the stance the courteous reader is *not* supposed to adopt. For preface-writer after preface-writer implores his audience not to demand explanations or react to his work prematurely, counseling that audience instead to suspend judgment, to allow the author the benefit of the doubt while the work proceeds to its end, and only then to decide how to respond to it. Increasingly towards the end of the century such actions are linked directly to courteous behavior or made functions specifically of courteous reading.

Contemporary preface-writers are emphatic about the sequence they wish their readers to follow—first read, then judge, they repeatedly admonish.[29] Counsels to experience the work to its finish before judging whether its author's intent be good or ill, to hear it out in its entirety before deciding whether it contains truth or vanity, are routinely proffered even when the prospective reader may, like Calidore, have some reason to question intent and to be wary of provenance. (The 1582 edition of *A Confutation of vnwritten verities* urges its audience to "reade me throughout" before it decides "whether [the work] be / Either good or ill." William Auerell likewise "craues" his reader "to suspend thy verdyt tyll thou hast considered the end"; and T. C. requests his audience's "patience to rest in silence . . . vntill the end" of his *Historie of the Troubles of Hungary* [1600]. Robert Hitchcock makes the reader's willingness to perform such tasks a function of his "good courtesie." G. duVair counsels his readers to "heare . . . to the end without interruption, admonishing that "in doubtfull thinges we must suspend our iudgemēts, till we haue found some reason or ground to stand vpon"; and Richard Mulcaster, whose entire "peroration" is summarized as "a request for curtesie," states flatly that the reader who is "friend to iudgement" "will rather continew in suspense, then pronounce rashlie, till he be throughlie enformed."[30])

During this period before judgment, preface-writers repeatedly caution readers to maintain a strict stance of impartiality—or, preferably, to read "as friends" until the work has run its course. The title page of *A discourse wherin is debated whether it be expedient that the scripture should be in English for al men to reade that wyll* (1554) exhorts its reader, for instance, to "Fyrst reade this booke with an indifferent eye and then [to] approue or condempne, as God shall move your heart." Lewys Euans asks the readers of *The Castle of Christianity* (*c.* 1568–69) to "iudge indifferently" only after they have "reade as friends." Ber[nard?] Garter, in *The Tragicall . . . Historie which happened betwene two English lovers* (1563), is even more explicit: the ideal reader's task, he says, is to "accept my good will, and staye thy iudgement till thou knowe myne intent and deeme the best til then." The timing of the reader's response to what he hears or sees and the sequence he is to follow in formulating that reaction are thus as crucially important to contemporary preface-writers as they are to Spenser's narrative, where Calidore wants the vision to proceed or temporarily to halt for clarification at his convenience rather than in its or Colin's own good time, and where the subsequent events of the canto seem calculated to drive home the potential consequences both to writer and viewer-reader of making such demands upon an author's text.

The cumulative effect of these repeated parallels between prefatory admonition and narrative event is unmistakably to add the concepts of the courteous and hostile reader to the poet's anatomy of courtesy. It is also to make the ways in which preface-writers define courteous and discourteous responses to their labors continuously available as glosses upon the activities depicted in Book VI.[31] For the composite picture that I have been sketching might be as plausibly derived from a reading of Spenser's poem as from a perusal of contemporary prefatory remarks. In both contexts we find, on the one hand, an ideal audience whose courtesy leads him to listen even when the initial appearance seems damning; to hear the speaker through to the end of his statements; to construe kindly and as the writer or speaker-actor intends; to make judgments on an individual, case-by-case basis; to consult a variety of intangible and potentially mitigating factors when deciding whether to praise or blame, defend or condemn; and to be flexible and compassionate enough that absolute freedom from error need not be a prerequisite for favorable judgment or for "pitty" or "mercy" to be shown. On the other, we encounter a set of discourteous and hypercritical observers who attack without a hearing, refuse or respond perversely to pleas for help or mercy, misconstrue ignorantly or deliberately, fail to make distinctions or to consider extenuating circumstances, and generally proceed not according to the dictates of the case at hand but according to a private agenda of their own—and whose discourtesy operates specifically to discourage the would-be doer-writer from heroic action.[32] The constant interplay between narrative event and contemporary prefatory practice ultimately creates a system of cross-references that serves both to illuminate the actions of Spenser's epic and to comment upon the claims and complaints being made by other writers of the era.

For the narrative also ultimately takes issue with several key assumptions upon which contemporary prefatory statement routinely rests. The standard response to the prefaces in general—an accurate one in many cases—has, for example, been that their writers try to shift all blame onto their critics, charging that any objection to the work must be attributable either to the reader's misinterpretation of the text or to the hostile critic's malice. Such claims to absolute innocence are clearly self serving, since they leave out the possibilities that some critical responses may be prompted by legitimate objections to what one reads and that the writer himself may play a role in provoking the blame that his work incurs. Spenser's handling of narrative incident appears specifically designed to concede such possibilities; for he endows the characters of Book VI with a positive genius for getting themselves into compromising or potentially scandalous situations and pointedly insists upon the ways that such victims of hostile attack as Serena, Timias, and Mirabella can not only exacerbate their wounds' effects but be complicit in their own ill treatment.[33] In the Priscilla and Mirabella episodes he stresses the victim's role in inviting the condemnation of those already disposed to render it; and he acknowledges in Canto x that there are limits to the poet's claims to artistic freedom (see pp. 124ff. below). Such tactics appear calculated to arm the work against some of the reasonable objections to which the more extravagant of prefatory commentary is clearly vulnerable.

III

Spenser's narrative strategy thus seems designed to initiate and to preserve a dialogue with the poem's readers. This resembles the two-stage approach outlined by Richard Mulcaster, who claims that his *Elementarie* seeks, "by planting skill in all, to avoid misliking in anie . . . and [to operate so that even potential] mislikers maie be entreated, as to becom frends of foes" (48). Supplying the reader with examples of proper and improper ways to respond to situations like those which compromise the final book of the poem and confronting him with episodes that drive home the potential consequences that adopting unfriendly or suspicious attitudes can carry should theoretically operate to reduce the number of those who unthinkingly assume hostile stances towards the narrative itself, and the concessions cited above ought to "entreat mislikers" by forestalling some obvious objections to the poet's point of view.

The impression of narratorial flexibility and reasonableness that such a strategy fosters also makes it a great deal easier for Spenser to claim immunity from further criticism, for casting himself as a gentleman poet willing to argue for his position by accommodating reasonable objections in effect enables him to portray any remaining displeasure with his narrative as a function of the reader's ill will or inflexibility rather than as a response to offenses or shortcomings with which he as writer may legitimately be taxed. Such practices thus ultimately afford him an excuse to wash his hands of those critics who remain by claiming that he has made every concession he can legitimately make, done everything that it is humanly possible to do. Yet despite its obvious convenience for this purpose, the narrative strategy outlined above does differ markedly from the imperious and contemptuous dismissiveness which have earlier characterized Spenser's handling of those whom he anticipates will respond negatively to his narrative. Demands for the complete capitulation of "witlesse" objectors (Proem, 2) and attempts to exclude as unworthy whole classes of potentially critical readers (Proem, 4) have given way to efforts at inclusion and persuasion, at establishing a common ground on which narrator and a skeptical or even a potentially censorious reader can meet.

The presence of Calidore on Mt. Acidale offers one explanation for such a shift in tactics, as well as for the change in the relative prominence afforded the relationship between the poet and his readers in the closing segments of the epic. For Spenser in Canto x implies that there is simply no evading the specter of one's audience, and therefore no escaping some kind of relationship or interaction between reader and writer. The rest of the book suggests that one can make such relationships constructive or destructive, but it likewise insists that one cannot opt out of them altogether. Ignoring the existence of the Beast no more protects one from his attacks, for instance, than ignoring Calidore's existence would have protected Colin's vision from its observer's actions. Failure to remain aware of the possibility that an observer may wander into whatever activity one is at the moment conducting is in fact often all that is needed to trigger the appearance of such an audience.

The stresses and the strains that these realities place upon poetic composition are reflected in the events of Canto x. Yet the encounter on Mt. Acidale seems designed less to convey the despairing opinion that the conditions necessary for the practice of poetry are unattainable than to provide, partly by negative example and partly by positive demonstration, a working model for the postures the poet feels that both reader and writer must

assume if the inevitable contact between the two is to be prevented from causing irreparable harm. Teaching by negative
example means that the conduct that would have prevented the
loss of the vision must be inferred from its opposite; but doing
things this way does allow Spenser the freedom simultaneously
to sketch the direction in which he believes any workable accommodation between reader and writer must proceed and to drive
home the consequences of a failure to observe the restrictions he
propounds.

The dynamics of this working model are complex. Most
noticeable are the limitations and restrictions under which it
operates, for the relationship that Spenser here envisions is em-
phatically not an equal one.[34] His model for preventive (and
productive) interaction places most of its constraints upon the
reader, demanding that in order to participate in the vision at all
he adopt the role of mute and passive observer "beholding all yet
of [the vision's participants] vnespyde" (VI.x.11). The fate of the
vision Colin is piping and the echoes from contemporary prefaces summarized above imply that this posture must be maintained and the viewer-audience's potential questions and reserva-
tions suppressed until the piping has run its course. Otherwise
the vision vanishes and the reader is left to contend with a
disgruntled poet whose anger must be placated and whose explanation is inevitably a pale substitute for the vision itself. Calidore's eventual response to that explanation—the admission
that he "rashly sought that, which I mote not see" (VI.x.29)—
carries these constraints and restrictions even further, suggesting
that there are elements of the poetic composition the seeing of
which must not be sought, into which a reader simply must not
inquire, on pain not only of losing the experience for himself but
of bereaving the poet-singer of it as well.

Yet if the events of the canto deny the viewer equal status with
the piper, they do not bar him from access to the poet's vision
entirely, even at the preliminary composing stage at which Calidore appears to have encountered it, so long as the viewer does
not make his presence felt. They promise such an observer
generous quantities of explanation and even of fellowship, moreover, after the dance has run its course. These allowances and
promises necessarily place some restrictions upon the freedom of
the poet-piper, who may prefer to proceed unhindered by the
need to explain himself to anyone;[35] and Spenser's handling of
the sequence acknowledges the existence of such restrictions in

other ways as well. For if Canto x stresses the poet's need to "play to please [him] selfe, all be it ill,"[36] taking no thought for any other audience, the description of Colin in Canto ix has already made clear that withdrawal from public scrutiny is not behavior in which the piper is expected to indulge one hundred percent of the time. (See VI.ix.41, where Colin is by consensus selected to pipe the shepherds' dance "as one most fit," a fact which both suggests that his normal activities in shepherd country are of a considerably more social nature and hints that he does not routinely refuse observation or evaluation by some viewer-hearers, at any rate.) Calidore's very presence on Mt. Acidale implies, moreover, that the piper's desire for a controlled environment—a milieu in which he plays to an audience for whose dance he calls the tune and whose actions he therefore can predetermine—is best an ideal and at worst a delusion, a fantasy so remote from actuality that the advent of a single unpredictable real-life reader is all that is needed to remind it of its fictional status and thus to send it vanishing into thin air.[37]

Once his initial pique at losing the vision has dissipated, Colin himself appears to accept this fact with equanimity. It is as much to underscore his acquiescence in the inevitability of audience as for any other reason, I think, that Spenser not only does not have the piper expel his importunate viewer-hearer from his private retreat—an action that would refuse relationship entirely—but shows him willing to dilate the vision's more general significance even when that audience has given him considerable reason to take offense.[38] That Colin not only loses his anger in the course of this dilation but recovers in the process much of the original fervor which inspired the dance[39] suggests, in fact, that such pauses for explanation possess their own attendant pleasures. The piper's willingness to spend "long time" with Calidore "together" pursuing other "discourses" "as fit occasion forth them led" (VI.x.30) reinforces this suggestion, even as the final clause implies that the narrator regards the exchanges born of such pauses not as regrettable though unavoidable necessities, but as actions fitting and proper for all concerned.

The demonstrations of acquiescence in limitations and acceptance of obligations that Calidore's confession and Colin's dilations provide point the way for at least a tentative accommodation between the sometimes antagonistic needs and desires of reader and writer—an accommodation that involves mutual concession and that therefore stresses mutual forbearance. Both the piper's desire for release from public scrutiny (and from its concomitant demands for instant accountability) and that of the reader for adequate information about the significance of and the intentions behind the images that he encounters in the works he reads are, they imply, legitimate impulses. Yet the events of the canto also insist that both observer and piper must recognize that to pursue these impulses without thought for the other parties who may be affected carries, as Mirabella has already discovered, unacceptable consequences not only for these others but for those doing the pursuing as well.

Even in Canto x, however, this mutual accommodation is incompletely realized. Some of the terms of parley must be inferred from Calidore's failure to observe the restrictions the poet propounds; and fully harmless interaction must therefore be imagined in the face of present loss. By the time the poem ends two cantos later, moreover, the poet appears to have abandoned all efforts to reach even such a partial reconciliation with those readers who remain antagonistic to his point of view. For the bitter irony of the final lines of the book (and of the work) amounts to an acknowledgement that the strategy of reason and demonstration, cajoling and cagey defensive posturing upon which his invocation of the reader's courtesy is predicated has itself failed to accomplish the task for which it was designed. It is an acknowledgement that has in fact seemed inevitable almost from the book's beginning, for the act of demonstrating in what that courtesy consists has also served to highlight the double binds, complexities, and contradictions that a reliance upon such offices entails.

It is not simply that the availability of a courteous defender emerges as something the victim of hostile reprehension dare not count upon or that, when such an advocate does arrive, he almost always appears in time not to prevent the attack but merely to pick up the pieces—though for Serena, Priscilla, and Calepine this fact alone would be damning enough. In Book VI the presence of a courteous defender doesn't even always guarantee the administration of comfort after the fact; for as Calepine, Timias, and Enias all discover, instead of delivering the victim from continued abuse, the would-be rescuer is often subjected to the same kind of treatment being administered to the victim he is attempting to defend.

Not only do such courteous ministrations thus not reliably prevent harm; they may actually extend the list of those who are vulnerable to attack. This is in fact doubly true, since Spenser repeatedly demonstrates that the need to cope with the disapproval or criticism of unfriendly audiences may force the courteous defender into equivocal situations which open him to blame from other directions as well. Calidore's efforts to "counter" the preconceptions of an audience who considers anything less than perfect purity evidence of absolute corruption involve a knight who is said to "loathe leasing, . . . / And loue simple truth and steadfast honesty" in the concoction of an outright lie about Priscilla's activities—a fact that critics already disposed to look askance at Spenser's protagonist have not been slow to grasp. The courteous actions that clear Matilde of her husband's blame likewise open Calidore's "less-gifted surrogate" Calepine[40] to the charge that he has abandoned Serena, who later "blames" the knight "for being of his loue to her so light, / As her to leaue in such a piteous plight" (VI.viii.33). Coping with the Blatant Beast, the task with which the knight of courtesy is principally charged, places Calidore in an even more equivocal double bind. If he ignores him entirely, the monster ranges uncontrolled; yet if he pursues him he extends his sphere of influence by pushing him from the court into the towns and villages of Faery Land and eventually all the way to the open fields and into the pastoral world. Whatever he does the knight thus risks reproach and those he is defending risk their very lives.

Spenser's handling of narrative incident thus ultimately suggests that the offices which courteous defenders can provide are at best an imperfect solution to a growing problem, that in practical terms they simply do not afford the victim of hostile reprehension the protection that contemporary preface-writers so sanguinely claim. Such conclusions are unsurprising given the curiously defensive and peculiarly dependent nature of the virtue itself as Spenser portrays it, contingent as it is for its successful operation upon the cooperation of those at whom it is aimed. (Unlike justice, which can be forcibly administered, no one can compel the object of courteous behavior to respond as desired, for instance—and, as Spenser's gloss of the Graces [VI.x.23–24] makes clear, an appropriate response by those on the receiving end of a courteous deed is an essential component of the circuit of exchange that characterizes the virtue in action.) The nature of the adversary that the exemplar of courtesy must handle tends merely to exacerbate this uncomfortable state of dependency, for the fact that the Beast can be tracked only by the trail of spoils he has made repeatedly forces Calidore as courteous knight to respond to situations in which a wound has already been inflicted or displeasure already incurred. Most of his actions thus become exercises not in prevention of harm, but merely in damage control. Courtesy accordingly becomes over the course of the book a *reactive* rather than a fully active virtue, a fact which tends increasingly to confirm its inadequacy as a defense against the displeasure of those determined to attack the performers of the actions they observe.

These inherent problems, double binds, and contradictions help to explain why both courtesy and the strategy of accommodation come to be abandoned in the work's final stanza in favor of a more openly provocative and aggressive narratorial stance, a move that bespeaks not a quitting of the field but yet another change in tactics, a shift to a different strategy for maintaining control over the reception of the narrative. The poet doesn't offer to be silent, after all: he threatens to "seek to please," a phrase that casts him in the role of manipulator and so asserts his mastery of the situation once again—and a locution whose possible meanings could easily include giving readers determined to construe what they encounter as potentially scandalous plenty of material on which to operate. The closing stanza in effect throws down a gauntlet, and the final lines of Spenser's epic become not so much the end of something as the opening salvo in what seems henceforth to be regarded as an outright state of war.

Hillsdale College

Notes

1.   Roma Gill, "The Renaissance Conventions of Envy," *Medievalia et Humanistica*, n.s., 9 (1979), 220–21, is a partial exception; but as I demonstrate below, she has vastly underestimated the extent to which the conventions of the prefaces and dedications of the period inform Spenser's final book.
2.   Richard Neuse, "Book VI as Conclusion to *The Faerie Queene*," in *Essential Articles for the Study of Edmund Spenser*, ed. A. C. Hamilton (Hamden, Conn.: Archon Books, 1972), 378.
3.   This is the conclusion to which critics who talk about Book VI in terms of the collapse of the poet's attempts to find a public role for the practice of poetry generally come. (See, for example, David Miller, who claims that in Canto x the conflicting ideals of poetry "as a form of public action" and poetry as a private act of contemplation irrevocably part company, and who therefore

considers the sequence the place where Spenser's search for a way to reconcile these ideals gives way completely ["Abandoning the Quest," *ELH* 46 (1979): 173–93].) While I view the canto as the concrete expression of a desire to "play to please my selfe . . . / Nought weigh[ing] who my song doth prayse or blame," I would point out that such a desire has been evident at least since *The Shepheardes Calender*, from which the preceding quote is taken, and that it is therefore nothing especially new or radically different. What *is* new is the presence in Book VI of outside observers who do not immediately comprehend the significance of the vision or its usefulness for the poet; and it is in the clashes between the needs and desires of the reader–observer to have the vision explained and the desire of the piper to pipe only to an ideal audience to which he does not have to justify himself or hold himself accountable that the significance of the incident appears to lie. The structure of the vision itself suggests that both these desires are legitimate needs and that the only resolution between them must come from forbearance and a giving up of claims to complete independence on the part of both poet and reader. See pp. 124ff. below.

4.   See V.xii.31ff., for instance, especially stanza 35. See IV.viii.26 for similar claims about Sclaunder.

5.   All citations are to *Spenser: Poetical Works*, ed. J. C. Smith and E. de Selincourt (Oxford: Oxford University Press, 1912).

6.   For other such explanations, see Jane Aptekar, *Icons of Justice: Iconography and Thematic Imagery in Book V of* The Faerie Queene (New York: Columbia University Press, 1969); Harry Berger, Jr., "A Secret Discipline: The Faerie Queene, Book VI," in *Form and Convention in the Poetry of Edmund Spenser: Selected Papers from the English Institute*, ed. William Nelson (New York: Columbia University Press, 1961), 35–75; A. Leigh DeNeef, "'Who Does Now Follow the Foule Blatant Beast': Spenser's Self-Effacing Fictions," *Renaissance Papers 1978*, 11–21, and *Spenser and the Motives of Metaphor* (Durham, N.C.: Duke University Press, 1982); Leslie Hotson, "The Blatant Beast," in *Studies in Honor of T. W. Baldwin*, ed. D. C. Allen (Urbana: University of Illinois Press, 1958), 34–37; Merritt Hughes, "Spenser's 'Blatant Beast'," *MLR* 13 (1918), 267–75; Richard Neuse, "Book VI as Conclusion to *The Faerie Queene*," 366–87; James Nohrnberg, *The Analogy of "The Faerie Queene"* (Princeton: Princeton University Press, 1976).

7.   Except where noted, all citations are to the preface to the reader of the work indicated. Groves, *The Most Famous and Tragicall Historie of Pelops and Hippodamia* (1587). Clowes, *A Prooued Practise for all young Chirurgians, concerning burnings with Gunpowder* (1588). Stockwood, trans., *A Fruitfull Commentarie vpon the twelue small Prophets* (1594). Watson, *The Hekatompathia, or Passionate Centurie of Love* (1582), ed. S. K. Heninger, Jr. (Gainesville, Florida: Scholars' Facsimiles and Reprints, 1964). John Partridge describes the proverbial critic Zoilus as a "Cur dog" with a "tongue that hath annoyde / Great workes which haue employde / continually to frame / A happy common weale (*The Treasurie of Commodious Conceits* [1573]).

8.   See Thomas Delapeend, trans., *The Historie of John Lorde Mandozze* (1565). Clowes' dogs similarly "wound [euen] the dead with speeches of defame."

9.   Delapeend. "Monsters right they be," he adds, "who do not spare to speake all that they may."

10.   John Eliot, *Ortho-epia Gallica, Eliots Fruits for the French* (1593).

11.   Henry Petowe, *Philochasander and Elanira* (1599).

12.   Hugh Plat, *The Jewell House of Art and Nature* (1594); Thomas Churchyard, *A Scourge for Rebels* (1584).

13.   John Eliot, *Ortho-epia Gallica*; "Nicholas Bowyer in commendation of" George Whetstone's *Rocke of Regard* (1576); William Chauncie, *The Rooting out of the Romishe Supremacie* (1580).

14.   Lodowicke Lloyd, *The Pilgrimage of Princes* (1573); William Clowes, *A Prooued Practise. See also W. F., The Strange, Wonderfull and bloudy Battell betweene Frogs and Mise* (1603).

15.   Simon Robson, *The Choise of Change* (1585); Richard Percyvall, *Biblioteca Hispanica* (1591).

16.   Watson, *Hekatompathia*. Digbie, *Euerard Digbie, His dissuasiue from taking away the lyuings and goods of the Church*. Howard, *A Defensatiue against the Poyson of Supposed Propheies* (1583). Morley, dedication to *Sextvs Madrigales*. *The Triumphes of Oriana* (1601).

17.   S[amuel] B[randon?], "Prosopopeia al libro" (1598), Aiii-r:

> When barking enuie saw thy birth,
>
> It straight contemnd the same;
>
> And arm'd his tongue, to giue a charge,
>
> Thy weakenesse to diffame.
>
> But seeing honors golden hooke,
>
> So linckt to vertues lyne:
>
> He fled away as halfe afraid,
>
> Yet ceast not to repine.

The concept is a commonplace. Gosson, *The Ephemerides of Phialo* (1579), ed. Arthur Freeman (New York: Garland Publishing, 1973), A1r. "The Translator [Thomas Tymme] to the Reader" of *News from Niniue* (1570). Momus and Zoilus are popular contemporary terms for hostile critics.

18.   Clowes, *A . . . Book of Obseruations, for all those that are burned with the flame of Gunpowder* (1596). Dormer, *The Famous Hystory of Herodotvs* (1584). Baynes, *The prayse of Solitarinesse* (1577). Lane, *Tom Tel-troths Message, and his Pens complaint* (1591). Lok, *Sundry Christian Passions Contained in Two Hundred Sonnets* (1593). Bellewe, *Les Ans du Roy Richard le Second* (1585). Dickinson, *Arisbas* (1594). Greene, *Planetomachia* (1585). Gascoigne, preface to Sir Humphrey Gilbert's *A Discourse of a Discoverie for a new Passage to Catalia* (1576). Pettie, trans., *The Civile Conuersation of M. Steeuen Guazzo* (New York: AMS Press), 1967.

See also Richard Barnfield, *Cynthia* (1595); Anthony Munday, *The History of Palmendos* (1589); Anthony Munday "to all curteous and freendly Readers" in commendation of T. F.'s *Newes from the North* (1579); James Yates, *The Castell of Courtesie* (1582); George Whetstone, *The Rocke of Regard* (1576); W. Auerell, *The life and death of Charles and Iulia* (1581); Angell Day, *The English Secretorie* (1595). "T. E." likewise "commits" R. P.'s translation of *The Second Part of the Mirrour of Knighthood* (1583) "to [its readers'] courteous consideration." Richard Mulcaster appeals in the peroration to his *First Part of the Elementarie* (1582) to his "good cūtrimen and curteous readers"; and the closing pages of that tract collectively constitute what the marginal gloss calls "a request for curtesie." The writer of *Tarltons Newes out of Purgatorie* (1590) likewise "hopes" of [his Gentlemen Readers'] courteous censure"; and George Turberuile appeals to his readers' "wonted curtesie in perusing Bookes" (*The Eglogs of the Poet B. Mantuan* [1572]).

19. Johnson, comp., *The Nine Worthies of London* (1592).

20. R. P., *The Second part of the Booke of Christian Exercise* (1591), addresses his preface to the "courteous reader"; and Charles Gibbon's *Remedie of Reason* (1589) appeals "To the Christian and courteous Reader." The preface to Lambertus Danaeus' *A Fruitfvll Commentarie upon the twelue Small Prophets*, trans. John Stockwood (1594), appeals "to the courteous and Christian reader"; and William Whatelie, *A Caveat for the Covetous* (1609), likewise entitles his preface "To the Courteous Reader."

21. Stanihurst, *The First Fovre Bookes of Vergils Aeneis* (1583). Gibbon, *A Work Worth the Reading* (1591).

22. For similar observations, see Thomas Morley, *A plaine and Easie Introduction to Practical Mvsicke* (1597). James Yates also considers it the province of his "courteous construers"

> my indeuour to protect,
> From truthlesse tongues, which tattle tales but fained
> And glorie great when others are disdained

(*The Hold of Humilitie, Adioyned to the Castell of Courtesie* [1582]).

23. Vaughn, *The Golden Grove* (1598). Day, *The English Secretorie* (1599), ed. Robert O. Evans (Gainesville, Florida: Scholars' Facsimiles and Reprints, 19679). Auerell, *The life and death of Charles and Iulia.* John Sharrock, *The Valiant Actes and Victorious Battailes of the English nation* (1585), "beseeches" his readers if they "finde a scape" to "passe it ouer with patience"; and Emmanuel Forde implores "the Curteous Reader" "if you find any imperfections, [to] passe them ouer with a careless respect" (*The Second Part of. . . Parismus, the renowmed Prince of Bohemia* [1599]). The author of *A defence of the Honeur of . . . Marie Quene of Scotland* exhorts his readers to "rather curteouslye of frendly faueur pardon many great faultes, than curiously with rigorouse censure to condemne one little"; and Leonard Wright tells the reader of *The Hunting of the Anti-christ* (1589) that "the wise and learned [have] courteously. . . pardon[ed] my imperfections, accept[ed] my good will, and consture[d] all things to the best." "Tollerating" the less than perfect and excusing inadvertent or unthinking mistakes are likewise said to be the province of Angell Day's "learned and courteous readers" (*The English Secretorie* [1599]). Lodge's preface to *Rosalynde* (1596) "welcomes" "courteous gentlemen, that favor most, backbite none, and pardon what is ouerslipt." The writer of *The Boock of Physick* (trans. 1599) requests that his "most curteous Reader" "rowle vp all [his] faultes together, and cast them into oblivione, and look not anye more back vppon them to returne a newe remembrance thereof."

24. Greene, *Mamillia* (1583). Munday, *The Mirrour of Mutabilitie* (1579).

25. Bellewe, *Les Ans du Roy Richard Le Second.*

26. Greene hopes that "the courteous Readers" of *Pandosto* (1588) "will requite my trauell, at the least with silence." The preface to *Greenes Farewell to Folly* (1591) implores readers "curteouslie to passe ouer my vnskilfull presumption with silence." John Farmer, *Cantvs* (1599), likewise specifically leaves his "labors to [his readers'] favorable iudgement, to keepe secret what may be amisse." William Byrd (*Psalmes, Sonnets, and Songs of Sadness and Piety*, 1588) "desires" that "faults by mee committed" "eyther with courtesie . . . bee

concealed" or that "in friendly sort" he "bee thereof admonished . . ." For similar comments see Ludowicke Lloyd, *The Pilgrimage of Princes: Tarltons News out of Purgatorie* (1590); Lyly, *Euphues and His England* (1597).

27.   For "rather graunt to saue then spill," see Thomas Hill, *The profittable Arte of Gardening* (1568). Gibbon, *A Work Worth the Reading* (1591). Howard, *A Defensatiue against the Poyson of Supposed Prophesies* (1583). Thomas Digges, *A Geometrical treatise called Pantometria* (1571). Day, *The English Secretorie* (1599).

28.   This threat of disinheritance holds over Priscilla's head a potential loss whose implications extend far beyond the simple deprivation of property today associated with that concept. By disowning her, her father would separate her from her home and family, the entities which have given her her name and that have hitherto provided the context in which she locates and so defines herself— given her by the measure by which she knows who she is. Such considerations give added resonances to Priscilla's worry "to what case her name should now be brought" (VI.iii.6), for the potential consequence of her father's mistaken assumptions is condemnation to a state not merely of monetary or even of legal, but of existential limbo. To have him take the action he threatens and she fears would be almost to have him try to negate her very being, to wipe her out of existence as far as he is concerned, to say, as Shakespeare's Lear will say, "I have no such daughter."

29.   This sequence is firmly established. "Reede over, then iudge, / Condemne not before," "The Bookes Request" admonishes the reader of Janus Dubravius's *A New Booke of Good Husbandrie* (1599), trans. George Churchey. Anthony Munday exhorts "all curteous and freendly Readers" of *A breefe Aunswer made vnto two seditious Pamphlets* (1582) "when [they] haue red, [to] iudge then." For similar admonitions see the preface to William Fulke, *A Comfortable Sermon of Faith in temptations and afflictions* (1574) and the title page of Michael Woode's *A Dialogue . . . concernyng the chyefest ceremonyes* (1554). The burden of such writers' advice seems not to be "don't judge," but "don't do so prematurely or with preconceptions."

30.   Auerell, *The life and death of Charles and Iulia*. Hitchcock, *A Pollitique Platt for the honour of the Prince . . .* (1580). G. du Vair, *The Morall Philosophie of the Stoicks*, trans. T. I. (1597), 192. Mulcaster, *Elementarie*, 47, 201.

31.   This relationship with the prefaces applies not simply to the episodes in which Calidore appears, but to other episodes of book as well. The Mirabella sequence first mentions that lady in the context of subjection to public shame, for instance; and in Canto vii the hostile attitudes Scorn and Disdain are introduced into the narrative as characters. (Writers of contemporary prefaces regularly attribute such stances to those who may criticize their work.) In the course of the episode both Timias and Enias also fall victim to the pair's mistreatment; and Spenser devotes considerable time to detailing the effects that this treatment produces. Such a conceptual framework could also apply to the Briana and Turpine episodes: both are cast as observer–audiences, and their actions closely mimic the traits of the discourteous reader described below.

32.   The prefaces frequently attribute the writer's discouragement directly to the reader's discourtesy. The reader of Joshua Silvester's translation of *The Triumph of Faith* (1592) is promised "some greater seruices to come, if vntimelie by thy discurtesie I bee not discouraged . . ." James Yates, *The Castell of Courtesie* (1582), "craues" "the courteous and friendlie reader" to

> let . . . with courtesie,
> This simple worke be skande,
> . . . .
> Least that thou doe discourage me,
> if skoffingly thou deeme.

33.   Serena is shown "loosely wandring . . . about the fields, as liking led /
Her wauering lust after her wandring sight" (VI.iii.23), a description that at
best hints at a pre-existing wavering of purpose, a loosening of self-possession,
upon which the Beast obligingly pounces. Timias' predisposition to impetuous
challenges likewise makes it possible for Despetto, Decetto, and Defetto to use
the Beast as "baite" to "draw [the boy] . . . into the daunger of defame"
(VI.v.14–15). The relationship between the monster and his victims as Spenser
portrays it thus comes to resemble that between germs in the air and the hosts in
which they ultimately lodge; for while these outside forces are the proximate
causes of disease, they do not do their damage unless their chosen host provides
a suitable medium in which to incubate and ripen to maturity.

Spenser also makes it clear that the victim's collaboration in his fate may
extend into the aftermath of the attack, during which he can considerably
exacerbate the damage that has been done to him. Neglecting the wounds can
allow them to fester and turn deadly (VI.vi.3); and desire to avoid further pain
may make the victim perversely responsible for the continuation of his own
affliction. Fear of "villany to be to her inferd" prompts Serena's flight from
Scorn and Disdain, for instance, an action that deprives her of the chance to be
rescued by Arthur and plunges her into the wilderness where she encounters the
cannibals, figures whose status as observers who intend their victims ill is
insisted upon at considerable length. Timias's "secrete shame" leads him to
"shut vp all his plaint in priuy paine" (VI.v.24), a reaction that deprives him of
the sympathetic hearing touted throughout *The Faerie Queene* as a sure way to
ease suffering. His encounter with Scorn and Distain renders him "unwilling to
be known or seene at all," even by an Arthur anxious to help him. Like
Mirabella, whose acquiescence in her punishment leads her to refuse release
from the clutches of Scorn and Disdain, the squire thus clings perversely to his
own affliction.

34.   This point needs stressing, for Book VI shows not, as A. Leigh DeNeef
claims, a Spenser in the process of gracefully giving up possession of his
narrative (*Spenser and the Motives of Metaphor*, 140), but a poet desperately
running through a series of maneuvers that may conceivably allow him to
remain in control of it. In Canto x the poet clearly remains master of the
situation: Spenser couches Colin as the bestower of knowledge, Calidore as the
receiver of the information that Colin chooses to impart; and the canto's
allegory of benefits received and requited also implies that the knight is obli-
gated to respond to Colin's actions in certain specified ways. Colin's gloss of the
graces in fact sets up the score 2:1 in favor of the writer. (See stanza 24:

> And eeke them selues so in their daunce they bore
> That two of them still froward seem'd to bee,
> But one still towards shew'd her selfe afore;
> *That good should from vs goe, then come in greater store.*)

It is a proportion that E. K. has much earlier affirmed. ("Therefore," he says in
The Shepheardes Calender [*Aprill*], the Graces

make three, to wete, that men first ought to be gracious and
bountiful to each other freely, then to receiue benefits at
other mens hands curteously, *and thirdly to requite them
thankfully.* . . . And Boccace saith that they be painted
naked, . . . the one hauing her backe toward vs, and her face
fromwarde, as proceeding from vs: the other two toward
vs, *noting double thanke to be due to vs for the benefit, we haue
done.*)

35.   They mean, for example, that even in the preliminary composing stage at
which Calidore appears to have surprised the vision—a stage before it is ready
to be "put forth to the view of the world," as preface-writer after preface-writer
describes the act of publication—the responsible poet's vision cannot be totally
self-regarding or hermetic. If it were, it would be intelligible only to the piper
and of no benefit to any larger community; and he could therefore be charged
with indulging in the idleness so abhorrent to contemporary critics of poems
and plays.

Colin's vision clearly fulfills this criterion. Indeed, its structure is emblematic
of the way the ideal poetic construct operates. It consists of an outer ring of
naked maidens, anonymous yet said to rivet the attention even of the casual
observer; a middle ring containing the Graces, allegorical figures whose significance is accessible to a learned community and capable of being imparted to a
teachable audience like Calidore; and an inner core of personal inspiration
whose meaning appears not entirely communicable and into whose sources the
reader simply must not inquire. (The designation of the figure at the center of
the concentric circles as she "who made [Colin] pype so merrily, as neuer none"
makes clear her connections with the personal needs, the idiosyncratic impulses
and desires, in which the vision is rooted—with its motive forces or its "secret
thoughtes," as Henrie Howard puts it [*A Defensatiue against the Poyson of
Supposed Prophesies*]. And it is for bereaving Colin of this personal element at the
core of the vision that Calidore's confession apologizes:

Now sure it yrketh me, . . .
Thus to bereaue thy loues deare sight from thee.
Now gentle shepheard pardon thou my shame,
Who rashly sought that that I mote not see. [VI.x.29])

Colin's gloss for the Graces also suggests that the significance of the allegorical and iconographic elements of the vision to piper and to reader-viewer may
differ—even that some of their functions are reserved for the piper. (The syntax
of his dilation differentiates, for example, between the Graces as "sweet Good-
desses, all three, which *me* in mirth do cherry"—a statement that Spenser
underlines by allowing it to end a stanza—and these ladies as those who "*on men*
all gracious gifts bestow / Which decke the body or adorne the mynde"
[VI.x.22, 23].) These figures clearly have significance and some applications
even for the casual observer, however, and it is this general significance upon
which Colin's dilation concentrates.

36.   Quotes are from *The Shepheardes Calender* ("June," 72ff).

37.   It is certainly in all senses a fiction: it contradicts even the "facts" set forth
in his own earlier compositions, to which the narrator seems pointedly to direct
the reader's attention in stanza 16. Colin's idealized portrait of the lass "to

whom [he] pyp[es] alone"—a receptive Rosalind "present there with [him] in place"—contrasts sharply, for instance, with his complaints in the "Januarye," "June," and "December" eclogues about that lady's recalcitrance, her withholding of her presence, and the disdain and scorn with which she responds to his piping ("Januarye," 63–66). His inability to inspire in this audience the response that he desires is the reason the shepherd ultimately gives for breaking his pipe ["Januarye," 67–72].) The vision on Mt. Acidale seems designed specifically to arrange these harsh realities more to his liking, to conform them to his own desires.

The dance that Colin has conjured also rearranges such realities as hierarchy and societal position to suit its purposes, making worthiness the sole criterion for eminence and the poet-piper sole arbiter of worth. Its idealized portrait of the properly graceful interaction between poet as bestower of benefits and reader as grateful receiver and requiter seems calculated to provide an alternative to Spenser's own prior complaints about the recalcitrance of the audiences he says have been critical of his own handiwork and to the actions of the Beast that he details in Canto xii.

38.   By having Colin enact the stances preface-writers repeatedly request their audiences to adopt, Spenser also of course dramatizes his piper's willingness to abide by the same restrictions he is asking the courteous reader to respect. (Compare Colin's bearing with well-intentioned if misguided actions, even when they cause him grave offense, to the prefatory exhortations on pp. 115ff., for instance. See also Anthony Munday, who asks the "courteous reader" to "beare with my rudeness if I chaunce to offend you"—*Zelauto, The Fountaine of Fame* [1580]. Bartholomew Chappell requests that such a reader "pardon my presumption"—*The Garden of Prudence* [1595]; and in his preface to *Pandosto* Greene likewise calls courtesy the proper response to "rashness.") The statement in Nicholas Breton's preface to *The Wil of Wit, Wits Will, or Wils Wit, chuse you whether* (1597)—that

> perfect courtesie dooth beare with imperfect knowledge, . . . and there-
> fore the best will giue good woords, whatsoeuer they think, to incourage
> a forward will to doo better, when indeede it were a fantasticall heade that
> could doo worse—

could stand as an emblem for the manner in which Colin treats Calidore. Such facts lend a twist to Daniel Javitch's contention in *Poetry and Courtliness in Renaissance England* (Princeton: Princeton University Press, 1978) that the poet in this canto replaces the courtier as exemplar of courtesy. I would simply argue that Spenser uses Colin's example to encourage the courteous reader to respond in kind, as Calidore eventually does.

39.   See stanzas 27–28. The vision itself is never completely recovered, of course. What is regained is instead a version for public consumption that recaptures some of the fervor of the original. As the apology to Elizabeth (stanza 28) makes clear, this reconstituted version, unlike its predecessor, remains uncomfortably aware of the need to anticipate the responses of and then to placate an exceedingly powerful audience with a known capacity to take offense.

40   The phrase is Donald Cheney's. See *Spenser's Images of Nature: Wild Man and Shepherd in "The Faerie Queene"* (New Haven: Yale University Press, 1966), 195.

MARGARET P. HANNAY

"My Sheep are Thoughts": Self-Reflexive Pastoral in *The Faerie Queene*, Book VI and the *New Arcadia*

C ONSCIOUS THAT direct speech risked the queen's disfavor, Sir Philip Sidney and Edmund Spenser attempted to teach Queen Elizabeth to read their pastoral fictions aright, hoping that she would reward the flattery and follow the admonition underlying it, as recent scholarship has demonstrated.[1] Although we are intensely aware of their political use of the pastoral genre ("under hidden forms uttering matters as otherwise they durst not deal with"),[2] a subtle strategy for insuring the desired Right Reading has escaped notice: in the *New Arcadia* and in *The Faerie Queene*, Book VI, Sidney and Spenser mirror the queen's act of reading wi∴in the narrative. Conscious of potential misprision where the highest is represented by the lowest, both poets dramatize within the work the process of teaching a princess to read a pastoral fiction.

The pastoral adventures of Sir Calidore in *The Faerie Queene*, Book VI, who temporarily abandons his knightly quest and dons shepherd's apparel to win the fair Pastorella, echo the adventures shepherd's apparel to win the fair Pastorella, echo the adventures of Prince Musidorus, who also interrupts his knightly adventures and takes on the identity of the shepherd Dorus to win the Princess Pamela in the *New Arcadia*. In both tales, much of the action is controlled by a knight teaching a princess to read his fictional roles. The aim of the shepherd knights is thus the same as the aim of Sidney's Right Poet—that is, to include the reader in the activity of making by embodying the Idea through imitative action. To read aright, the princess (and, by implication, the queen), must reverse the mimetic process and "transfer the text into an Idea . . . by understanding why and how the text is metaphoric," in A. Leigh DeNeef's terms.[3] As the shepherd/knight wishes to demonstrate his real status to the princess to win her heart, so the poet/courtier wishes to demonstrate his real worth to the queen to win a position at court. Despite the vast difference in their social status, for both poets the problem of Right Reading is given urgency by their own experience of envy and resultant slander, embedded in the narrative by Sidney through the Cecropia/Amphialus plot, allegorized by Spenser in the Blatant Beast.

The self-conscious fictions of the Elizabethan court, encouraged by Elizabeth herself in the cult of the Faerie Queen, were usually dramatized in three roles, the Petrarchan, the pastoral, and the chivalric. Similarities between Book VI of *The Faerie Queene* and the *New Arcadia* are not limited to those of plot, but extend to the complex interplay of these roles. In each work the Petrarchan role is less successful than the pastoral in winning the shepherdess/princess; nevertheless, the shepherd/knight is forced to drop the pastoral disguise and return to the court in his true identity, defined in terms of chivalry and signified by the change of clothing. In the *New Arcadia*, there are three knights who present self-conscious fictions to princesses: Pyrocles, Musidorus, and Amphialus. In Book VI of *The Faerie Queene*, Spenser ignores the tale of the Amazonian Pyrocles entirely, echoes the tale of Musidorus, and incorporates an ironic element from the tale of "the courteous Amphialus" which may help to explain the dubious success of Calidore, the knight of courtesy.[4]

In the Musidorus and Calidore plots, the similarities are striking enough to be significant despite their common sources and their adaptation of standard plot elements from the pastoral romance tradition, such as disguised princes and princesses, the interrupted quest, identifying birthmarks, singing shepherds, encounters with wild animals, attacks by outlaws, kidnapping, extended separation of the lovers, and so on.[5] Both Musidorus and Calidore apparel themselves as shepherds to be near the women they love; each wooing is much impeded by a real shepherd (Dametas and Coridon); each shepherd/knight rescues the princess from a wild beast while the real shepherd displays his "cowherd feare" (x.35); each woman comes to love her shepherd knight just before she is captured by rebels and reported dead.[6] After the real shepherds have failed to save the princesses, each knight doffs his shepherd guise to take up arms and rescue his princess.

Spenser treats this romance with less irony than does Sidney.[7] A characteristic difference in these tales appears in the motif of the royal identity revealed by a birthmark, a device at least as old as Odysseus' scar, and one commonly employed in pastoral to establish the royal lineage of the shepherds.[8] Spenser plays it straight: Pastorella's "rosie marke" on her "yuory chest," seen by her old nurse, reveals her to be the lost child and heir of Bellamour and Claribell (xii.15). She is thereby restored to her true position at court, so that Calidore may return to his quest without worry for her. Humphrey Tonkin suggests that her suitability for the court may be seen in the mark itself, the flower, which connects with the Flower of Courtesy.[9] In contrast, Sidney puts an ironic twist on the birthmark tale: Dorus tells Pamela the story of how Prince Musidorus was discovered by a birthmark of a lion's paw on his neck "as I might . . . show this of my neck to the rare Mopsa" (138). Such self-revelation, of course, proves nothing at all, despite his veiled suggestion that Pamela send to Thessalia to check on his credentials, an action she predictably rejects as contemptible.

Another characteristic difference is that even incidents which appear the same lack the same motivation because in Spenser's version there is no equivalent of Cecropia, who seeks the kingdom for her son. Amphialus had been the only heir of Basilius until the king—an old man—wed the young Gynecia, who bore him Pamela and Philoclea. He might well have taken for his device "Speravi" under erasure, Sidney's own device after the birth of Leicester's son. As Richard McCoy has demonstrated, Amphialus reflects something of Sidney's own position.[10] In The Faerie Queene, as in the classical pastoral romance, there is no political motivation: it "chaunst" that the wild beasts simply appeared as they do in Montemayor and other pastorals; in the Arcadia, they are deliberately starved and then loosed by Cecropia. Similarly, in The Faerie Queene "it fortuned one day" that the brigants suddenly attacked the shepherd community on a whim, invaded and destroyed their houses, murdered the shepherds, and took Melibee and "all his people" captive, including Pastorella and Coridon (x.39–40). In the Arcadia, the peasant revolt is instigated by Clinias as another of Cecropia's attempts to gain the kingdom for her son Amphialus, adding an element of political intrigue to the plot.

Still, despite these differences in motivation, Sidney and Spenser use this shared plot to demonstrate the necessity for a correct reading of the pastoral genre. Calidore and Musidorus each present the beloved woman—a princess in shepherdess guise—with a pastoral fiction that she must learn to read. Calidore, presenting himself as a knight to a woman who believes that she is a shepherdess, first attempts the Petrarchan role but discovers that he can win her love only by taking on the transparently fictional role of shepherd. Although Pastorella herself believes the story of her humble origin, her royal position is revealed to the reader in our first glimpse of her, seated higher than the rest, encircled with a "girland . . . of lovely lasses" and piping shepherds (ix.8), as Queen Elizabeth had been described in *Aprill* and as the fourth grace is displayed on Mt. Acidale.[11] Although Calidore apparently accepts her role as shepherdess, or perhaps as "soueraine goddesse" to shepherds, it is only after he has decided that "her rare demeanure" made her "worthy . . . to be a Princes Paragone esteemed," that he falls in love. His initial reaction is described in suitably Petrarchan terms:

> He was vnawares surprisd in subtile bands
> Of the blynd boy, ne thence could be redeemed
> By any skill out of his cruell hands,
> Caught like the bird, which gazing still on others stands.
>
> (ix.11)

Overcome by love, he attempts to woo Pastorella in the presence of the shepherds, hoping that she would be a more astute reader than they: "And euermore his speach he did apply / To th'heards, but meant them to the damzels fantazy" (ix.12).

His success is dubious, for she is not the courtly reader he had hoped. It is Colin Clout's pastoral songs which draw her, not the Petrarchan poems of Sir Calidore:

> But she that neuer had acquainted beene
> With such queint vsage, fit for Queenes and Kings,
> Ne euer had such knightly seruice seene . . .
> Did little whit regard his courteous guize,
> But cared more for *Colins* carolings
> Then all that he could doe, or euer deuize:
> His layes, his loues, his lookes she did them all despiz.
>
> (ix.35)

Only when Calidore, has doffed "his bright armes, himself addresst / In shepherds weed," and taken in hand "in stead of steelehead speare, a shepheards hooke," adopting a pastoral fiction, does Pastorella begin to favor him (ix.36). Yet after the pastoral world is destroyed, he is instrumental in revealing to Pastorella the fiction of her own pastoral identity and in restoring her to her rightful position at court, a position which—given her reaction to Sir Calidore in knightly garb—must have been initially painful to her, although Spenser presents it without irony. Pastorella is, after all, the pastoral, raised in the country but originating in court; she is much less a real person than Pamela or Philoclea.

Musidorus is faced with a more complex situation than Calidore. His princess knows her role as shepherdess is a fiction but believes that his role as shepherd is truth. Pamela's disdain for her own condition is apparent even in Pyrocles' first description of her: "The fair Pamela, whose noble heart I find doth greatly disdain that the trust of her virtue is reposed in such a lout's hands as Dametas, had yet, to show an obedience, taken on shepherdish apparel . . . but believe me she did apparel her apparel, and with the preciousness of her body make it most sumptuous" (83). The allegorical nature of her condition is made known in her jewel, "a very rich diamond set but in a black horn" with the inscription "Yet still myself" (84). To win her love the Prince Musidorus becomes Dorus, the same sort of shepherd that she is, with his "sheep hook so finely wrought that it gave a bravery to poverty; and his raiments, though . . . mean, yet received . . . handsomeness by the grace of the wearer" (105). The allegorical nature of his identity is even more evident in his song:

Come shepherd's weeds, become your master's mind:
Yield outward show, what inward change he tries.

(105)

Because he must reveal his true identity as an allegorical shepherd to Pamela in the presence of the obtuse reader Mopsa (herself a comic inversion of Virgil's Mopsus from the fifth Eclogue), Musidorus adopts a series of strategies to control Pamela's reading, even as we have seen that Calidore's words were ostensibly addressed to the shepherds, "but [he] meant them to the damzels fantazy" (ix.12).

As the shepherd Dorus, Musidorus's first strategy is to assume his own clothing and demonstrate his knightly skill on horseback as a shepherd pretending to be a knight, thereby presenting truth through a dual fiction. The modern reader may be amused by

Pamela's admiration of Dorus's athletic prowess: she seems in awe that he rides "as if centaur-like he had been one piece with the horse" (153). This scene is not as frivolous as it may appear, however, for Musidorus demonstrates horsemanship to establish his true position in society—shepherds cannot ride. Because of the cost of equipment and training, knightly exercises were *de facto* restricted to the wealthy, as Maurice Keene reminds us.[12] The comic Dametas demonstrates that a knight in shepherd's attire may demonstrate his love, but a shepherd in knight's attire is merely ridiculous: he is tossed "from the saddle, to the mane of the horse, and thence to the ground, giving his gay apparel almost as foul an outside as it had an inside," disproving his earlier claim that "he wanted but horse and apparel to be as brave a courtier as the best" (154), and implying that Dorus could be a prince without the apparel. Pamela, an astute reader, understands that Dorus rides at the ring and dances the matachin in armor in order "to make me see that he had been brought up in such exercise" (154).

A second strategy is to tell his own story as if it were that of another: "In this entangled case, [Prince Musidorus] clothed himself in a shepherd's weed, that under the baseness of that form he might at least have free access to feed his eyes" on her. "In which doing . . . he hath manifested: that this estate is not always to be rejected, since under that veil there may be hidden things to be esteemed" (136). Musidorus here presents fiction so self-conscious that it becomes, as Montrose has suggested, virtually "metapastoral" (49), thereby proving that—at least in this case—a true example hath as much force to teach as a feigned example. Musidorus later explained the strategy to Pyrocles: "Thus having delivered my tale in this perplexed manner, to the end the princess might judge that he meant himself who spake so feelingly," (137) he was free to explain that Musidorus had taken the role of shepherd. Later Musidorus slips into the first person, causing him to blush and Pamela to smile at the inadvertent abandonment of his fiction (173).[13]

His third strategy, equally metapastoral, is singing "to show what kind of shepherd I was":

> My sheep are thoughts, which I both guide and serve:
> Their pasture is fair hills of fruitless love:
> On barren sweets they feed, and feeding starve:
> I wail their lot, but will not other prove.

My sheep-hook is wanhope, which all upholds:
My weeds, desire, cut out in endless folds.
    What wool my sheep shall bear, whiles thus they live,
    In you it is, you must the judgment give.

(138)

His song is a fully selfconscious presentation of the pastoral convention, explaining clearly the allegory of his present lowly position in this transparent appeal for a correct reading. The character here usurps the traditional role of the sophisticated narrator appealing to the reader over the heads of naive characters.[14]

Musidorus' final strategy is to give Pamela a letter which declares his love in Petrarchan hyperbole, using that combination of the pastoral and the Petrarchan which had become a standard part of the pastoral romance. Although he believes that all his strategies are failures—"Howsoever I show I am no base body, all I do is but to beat rock and get foam" (141)—they are in fact successful. Unlike Pastorella, Pamela values "such knightly seruice" and tells Philoclea, "Who think you is *my* Dorus fallen out to be? [Italics added] Even the Prince Musidorus, famous over all Asia for his heroical enterprises." How can she "abstain from loving him who . . . is content so to abase himself as to become Dametas' servant for my sake?" (152) Disdaining her own enforced disguise as a shepherdess, she can rightly read the pastoral fiction of her shepherd/prince: "Tell me, sweet Philoclea, did you ever see such a shepherd? Tell me, did you ever hear of such a prince?" (155).

Accepting his identity as Prince Musidorus, Pamela concludes that "since my parents deal so cruelly with me, it is time for me to trust something to my own judgment" (155), even as Pastorella chooses to love Calidore. Yet Pamela has another fictional identity—that of the unattainable mistress—to maintain for some time yet, lest she be too lightly won. She was apparently correct to do so, for as soon as she declared that "if she had been the princess whom that disguised prince had virtuously loved, she would have requited his faith with faithful affection," Musidorus attempts to kiss her. "For this favour filling him with hope, hope encouraging his desire, and desire considering nothing but opportunity," he seized that opportunity as soon as Mopsa disappeared: "Love, that never stayed to ask reason's leave . . . made the too much loving Dorus take her in his arms, offering to kiss her, and as it were to establish a trophy of his victory" (309). The kiss is clearly a euphemism, since this scene replaces the attempted rape of the *Old Arcadia*, the most disturbing scene in the romance. While Pamela slept, "she was in a shrewd likelihood to have had great part of her trust in Musidorus deceived and found herself robbed of that she had laid in store as her dearest jewel—so did her own beauties enforce a force against herself" (*OA*, 306). As Caroline Lucas has recently demonstrated, the woman reader is apt to feel betrayed in this sophisticated passage, for "the passive mode effectively appears to remove responsibility and blame from Musidorus, and the metaphorical terms in which it is couched at first gloss over his offence" until Sidney makes explicit reference to his "tyrannical fire of lust."[15] Because the revised *Arcadia* displaces the lust of Musidorus onto Amphialus, Pamela in the next chapter is captured and taken to Amphialus; this technique of externalizing a state of mind is closer to that of *The Faerie Queene* than we usually find in Sidney, bringing to mind such personifications of lust as the forester who pursues Florimell. The lust of Amphialus is curiously further displaced on to a woman, however, for the injustices against the women originate with his wicked mother Cecropia: she captures, imprisons and tortures Pamela, Zelmane, and Philoclea. Even lust is explained in the *Arcadia* as an instrument of Cecropia's political strategy: she tells Amphialus that a woman's "no" means "yes" and urges him to use force to gain the princess—and thereby the kingdom.[16] Amphialus's sins against the princesses are largely those of omission: he courteously rejects the idea of rape, but he refuses to grant them their liberty, and he does not insure that they are well treated.

Like Pastorella, the princesses Pamela and Philoclea are abducted from their pastoral world. Through their experience, Sidney and Spenser both make statements about the nature of the pastoral: the pastoral fiction itself is destroyed by physical attack. When brigants capture Pastorella, Calidore must abandon his pastoral identity and assume his role as knightly warrior to rescue her. Significantly, he maintains his shepherd's guise as he follows Coridon to the brigants' caves:

> So forth they goe together (God before)
> Both clad in shepheards weeds agreeably,
> And both with shepheards hookes: But *Calidore*

Had vnderneath, him armed priuily.

(xi.36)

The pastoral disguise gains him entrance but during the night he
must switch roles, demonstrating, as DeNeef suggests "the failure of the pastoral ultimately to sustain itself."[17]

Sir *Calidore* him arm'd, as he thought best . . .
But *Coridon* durst not with him consort,
Nor durst abide behind, for dread of worse effort.

(xi.42)

The real shepherd displays his "cowherd fear" while the shep-
herd/knight "Like as a lion mongst an heard of dere . . . did hew
and slay, / Till he had strowd with bodies all the way" (xi.49)[18]
The pastoral role may win Pastorella's love, but only the chivalric role can free her. The shepherd Coridon is incapable even of
defending himself; it takes the knight to restore his flocks. Similarly, when Pamela is captured and imprisoned, the cowardly
shepherd Dametas cannot help; the fictional shepherd Dorus
must assume his knightly role to save her. The lowliness of the
shepherd role is emphasized by Musidorus' self-condemnation
when he cannot defeat Amphialus: he is unworthy "to be friend
to the most valorous prince that ever was entitled valorous
[Pyrocles] . . . worthy for nothing but to keep sheep." He
admonishes himself, "get thee a sheep-hook again, since thou
canst use a sword no better!" (409). All praise his valor, but once
again Musidorus believes that he has failed. Although the *New
Arcadia* ends before the siege of Amphialus' castle is over, we
may assume from the *Old Arcadia* that Musidorus will be successful in rescuing Pamela and in reuniting her kingdom.

The inability of the pastoral to sustain itself and the consequent
need for chivalric intervention would appear to substantiate
Renato Poggioli's observation that the literature of chivalry
arises from the need to provide justice in the pastoral world.[19]
Sidney, however, adds a further twist to the pastoral and chivalric fictions: "the knight of the sheep," who seems to be an avatar
of the author, comes to rescue Musidorus—the shep-
herd/knight/poet in effect rescues his own pastoral knight who
is attempting to rescue the innocent. After Musidorus and Amphialus seriously wound each other, Musidorus is attacked by
the brothers of Anaxius, who significantly are "not recking law

of arms nor use of chivalry" (411). His death would have been
certain were he not rescued by "the Knight of the Sheep" and his
unnamed companion, "the Knight of the Pole."[20] "The Knight
of the Sheep" is "all in green, both armour and furniture," so that
"it seemed a pleasant garden wherein grew orange trees which,
with their golden fruits cunningly beaten in and embroidered,
greatly enriched the eye-pleasing colour of green. In his shield
was a sheep feeding in a pleasant field, with this word, 'Without
fear or envy'" (411–12). Again, Sidney presents us with a double
fiction. The shepherd/knight Musidorus is saved only by another knight in pastoral guise. The self-conscious nature of the
pastoral is emphasized in the earlier description of Philisides:

> An Iberian, whose manner of entering was with bagpipes
> instead of trumpets, a shepherd's boy before him for a page,
> and by him a dozen apparelled like shepherds (for the fash-
> ion, though rich in stuff) who carried his lances which,
> though strong to give a lancely blow indeed, yet so were
> they coloured, with hooks near the morne, that they pret-
> tily represented sheephooks. His owne furniture was
> dressed over with wool, so enriched with jewels artificially
> placed that one would have thought it a marriage between
> the lowest and the highest (255).

This, too, is virtually metapastoral, with the bagpipes replacing
the epic trumpets, the rich apparel of the mock shepherds, the
jewels half-hidden in the wool, the lance cleverly disguised but
maintaining its true knightly function, even as Philisides and
Musidorus and Calidore do themselves. It is truly a "marriage
between the lowest and the highest," but the opposite of Dametas' pathetic attempts at that same marriage. To emphasize the
difference between the heroic shepherd/knight and the comic
knight/shepherd, Philisides' disguise is cleverly inverted in the
device which Dametas displays on his shield in his mock combat:
"a plough (with the oxen loosed from it), a sword (with a great
number of arms and legs cut off), and lastly, a great army of pen
and ink-horns, and books" (381). Dametas' device echoes the
three-fold identity of Musidorus (shepherd, knight, poet), but he
has it all wrong.

In both the *New Arcadia* and *The Faerie Queene*, the protagonist
wins the princess's heart through a pastoral fiction but wins her
person only through assuming his true identity and undertaking

feats of chivalry. This process is inverted by "the courteous Amphialus." Through the agency of his wicked mother Cecropia, Amphialus has the person of Philoclea secured; his problem is to win her heart. Like Calidore, he first chooses to adopt a Petrarchan pose, but he misreads the role: assuming the allegorically Petrarchan garb of a man imprisoned by love, he imprisons his love. He dresses carefully, choosing garb of black velvet and satin with a collar partially set in diamonds and pearls and partially set in rubies and opals, combining "shining ice" and "a fiery glistering—which he thought pictured the two passions of fear and desire wherein he was enchained" (321). However, the real contraries are in his behavior, as Philoclea sharply reminds him:

> You call for pity—and use cruelty; you say you love me—and yet do the effects of enmity; you affirm your death is in my hands—but you have brought me to so near a degree to death as, when you will, you may lay death upon me, so that while you say I am mistress of your life, I am not mistress of mine own: you entitle yourself my slave—but I am sure I am yours (322).

The rather dense Amphialus still attempts to maintain the Petrarchan fictions in the face of her good sense by attributing his actions to "that tyrant love . . . It is love, not I, who disobey you" (323). He obviously does not understand the nature of literary devices, including personification. He also literalizes the convention of the disdainful mistress, using it in the age-old strategy of blaming the victim ("It is yourself that imprison yourself; it is your beauty which makes these castle-walls embrace you"), a view he maintains even in his last battles, despite its patent absurdity (323). His self-justification echoes the narrator's justification of Musidorus' attempted rape that we have noted in the *Old Arcadia*: "her beauties enforce a force against herself" (*OA*, 306). In fact, Amphialus may be the more chivalrous of the two in this instance, for Musidorus is foiled by the attack of enemies, while Amphialus reassures Philoclea that "the uttermost forces he would ever employ to conquer her affection should be desire and desert" (324). Philoclea does not trust him, however, so she threatens suicide to save her honor, thereby casting "the cold ashes of care . . . upon the coals of desire," an ironic reference to his device of ice and fire (324). Even his sending a boy to sing her a conventional Petrarchan love song of his own composition does not impress her. His Petrarchan role utterly fails to win Philoclea. Because he has chosen the wrong role in the Petrarchan imagery of imprisonment—taking the part of the jailor instead of the prisoner of love—he has insured that her role as disdainful mistress becomes not literary fiction but truth. The Petrarchan role is as ineffective for Amphialus as it was for Calidore.

The second fiction Amphialus adopts is the chivalry which should be truth: like Calidore and like the captain of the brigants, he fights to keep his princess from the invaders.[21] Amphialus, however, misreads the chivalric role when he attempts to win Philoclea's love by fighting off her *rescuers* in truly heroic feats of single combat: "no sword paid so large a tribute of souls to the eternal kingdom as that of Amphialus; who . . . remembering they came to take away Philoclea . . . did labour to make valour, strength, choler and hatred to answer the proportion of his love—which was infinite" (370). Philoclea, forced to watch the slaughter of her friends from a window, gives a rather different interpretation of his actions, as she tells her wicked aunt Cecropia: "Alas . . . simple service to me, methinks it is, to have those who come to succour me destroyed! If it be my duty to call it love, be it so; but the effects it brings forth, I confess I account hateful" (370). Not surprisingly, Amphialus fails in both these attempts to control her reading of his fictions, both Petrarchan and chivalric. He never attempts the one role which had won Pastorella for Calidore and Pamela for Musidorus, a transparent pastoral fiction, since that role requires a humility noticeably lacking in his character. Richard McCoy believes that love indeed reduces Amphialus to a "plaintive supplicant."[22] That would certainly be Amphialus' own view, but hardly Philoclea's or Sidney's, for one of the most engaging aspects of Book III is Philoclea's witty and outspoken rereading of the Petrarchan phraseology that Amphialus uses in an attempt to justify her imprisonment.

The failures of Amphialus may cast light on one of the central controversies about Book VI of *The Faerie Queene*, the success of Calidore's quest and the adequacy of the virtue of Courtesy.[23] Sir Calidore may ultimately fail in his quest because of the inadequacies of Courtesy itself, inadequacies more fully presented in "the courteous Amphialus" (123), as he is invariably termed. The paradox of Calidore's dubious success may thus be partially

explained through his dual role; he is, we may say, both Musidorus, the pastoral knight, and Amphialus, the "courteous
knight," inadequate to the spiritual demands of chivalry.

There is a fascinating parallel between these two knights of
courtesy, Sir Calidore and Amphialus. Although Amphialus is
the one who best fulfills the role of antagonist in the *New Arcadia*,
he is consistently described as noble, valiant and courteous, and
"had won immortal fame both of courage and of courtesy" (317),
like Calidore. When he is introduced, we are told that he is
"never uncourteous" (27), yet each of his courteous acts is tinged
with irony, a pattern echoed in *The Faerie Queene*. Both courteous knights blunder in and destroy true love, both return a
woman home to her parents—thereby preventing her
marriage—and both spy in a manner reminiscent of Acteon.[24]
By spying on that which they "mote not see" (x.29), each knight
is ultimately responsible for the destruction of the pastoral
world. Amphialus' passion for Philoclea, derived from seeing
her bathing, is the lust which impels the capture of Philoclea and
destruction of the pastoral idyll in Book III. Similarly, Calidore
appears courteous in his contrition for disturbing the Graces, yet
he apparently knows that he will break the dance if he is seen
(x.11); although he originally interprets the Graces' departure as
"ill fortune" (x.20), he later admits that he had "rashly sought
that, which I mote not see" (x.29). The disappointment makes
Colin Clout break his bagpipe (x.18), thereby destroying the
poetic vision that upholds the pastoral fiction, for the brigants
attack almost immediately thereafter.[25]

Like Calidore, Amphialus performs well all the public and
private roles of chivalry. He sets up an excellent defense against a
siege, he excels in single combat on horse or on foot, he writes
love poems, and even knows how to dress allegorically—yet
something is subtly wrong with him. He may well be motivated
by love, as Hamilton suggests,[26] but he seems to lose sight of the
ends of his actions, and they almost invariably have tragic results. There is considerable pathos in this man who means well,
but destroys nearly everything he touches. For example, when
he courts Queen Helen for his friend Philoxenus, she falls in love
with him, not with his friend. He courteously refuses to fight
with Philoxenus over Helen, but accidentally slays his friend in
front of Philoxenus's father, who dies of grief. Throwing away
his armor in remorse—as he later throws away his sword after
slaying Parthenia—hardly solves the problem. While he is en-

gaged in single combat he is oblivious to his departing troops and could have lost his army if he had not been reminded of his duty of commanding (474–75), thus achieving defeat by victory. The ineffectiveness of his courtesy may be best illustrated by his sparing of the young basely-born Phebilus, who hopelessly loves Philoclea: "But what good did that to poor Phebilus, if escaping a valiant hand, he was slain by a base soldier who, seeing him so disarmed, thrust him through?" (471)—thereby demonstrating the vulnerability of courtesy to brutal rudeness. His holding of Philoclea put not only her in danger, but also Pamela and Pyrocles, and led to the death of immeasurable numbers of Arcadians and of his own people. The most tragic deaths are those of Argalus and Parthenia, that couple which exemplifies the best of married love; both are slain by Amphialus (as is particularly appropriate, in so far as he, like Calidore, frequently separates lovers). His remorse is shown in his "detesting his fortune that made him unfortunate in victory" (398), but of course remorse brings none of his victims to life.

Similarly, Calidore seems to wither all he touches. He may have saved Priscilla's reputation by the tale he tells her parents (iii.18), but his action prevents her marriage to her beloved Aladine with whom she was "forever bound"; presumably she will now be forced into the marriage with the "great pere" that she had originally fled (iii.7). It may well have been "his fortune and not his fault" (iii.21) that he interrupts Calepine and Serena as they make love in the forest, but he demonstrates the most appalling insensitivity by swapping adventure stories with Calepine while Serena is carried off and wounded by the Blatant Beast (iii.22–24). The subsequent misadventures with Sir Turpine and with the cannibals are also the direct result of Calidore's blunder.

His very presence seems to herald destruction of the pastoral mode. Melibee's praise of the shepherd's life emphasizes freedom from that envy and malice symbolized by the Blatant Beast, yet it is Calidore who, after all, has herded the beast into their midst:

> Him first from court he to the citties coursed,
> And from the citties to the towns him prest,
> And from the townes into the countrie forsed . . .
> From thence into the open fields he fled,
> Whereas the Heardes were keeping of their neat,

And shepherds singing to their flockes, that fed,
Layes of sweete loue and youthes delightfull heat:
Him thether eke for all his fearefull threat
He followed fast, and chaced him so nie,
That to the folds, where sheepe at night doe seat,
And to the litle cots, where shepherds lie
In winters wrathfull time, he forced him to flie.

(ix.3–4)

On his arrival in Arcadia he insults Melibee with his offer of
money to buy a pastoral interlude. Melibee's praise of the shepherd's life emphasizes freedom from that envy and malice symbolized by the Blatant Beast: "Therefore I doe not any one enuy,
/ Nor am enuyde of any one therefore" (ix.21). Yet Calidore has
herded the beast into their midst and himself provokes envy
when he mocks Coridon with his superficial courtesy, thereby
undermining him with Pastorella. Not surprisingly, "gealousie"
was ready to devour Coridon, who is denied even the pleasure of
maligning his rival. Calidore is so clever in giving his own prizes
to Coridon that he "Could not maligne him, but commend him
needs" (ix.45). Machiavelli himself could not have devised a
better scheme for humiliating a rival.

Calidore's presence coincides with the destruction of the pastoral by brigants, and seems in some unspecified way to provoke
it. All the shepherds are slain, save the rather cowardly Coridon.
When Calidore returns, he is distraught when he sees "the shepheards cottage spoyled quight" (xi.25). "The playnes all waste
and emptie did appeare: / Where wont the shephcards oft their
pypes resound, / And feed an hundred flocks, there now not one
he found." Calidore might eventually restore Coridon's flocks,
he might save Pastorella and restore her to the court, but the
pastoral community is gone. It will not be rebuilt by Pastorella,
who is left with her newly-found royal parents, nor by Calidore,
who leaves both Pastorella and the community to follow "his
first quest" in his double-edged search to avoid dishonor and to
gain "fame, / As through the world thereby should glorifie his
name" (xii.12). There is no indication that he ever returns to
Pastorella or to the pastoral mode. Action wins over contemplation, the chivalric over the pastoral, ambition over contentment.

True, his abandonment of his quest leads to the vision on Mt.
Acidale and to its temporary fulfillment; the Blatant Beast is
bound and muzzled. Yet as Richard Helgerson observes, "the

dominant sense of Book VI is one of disillusionment, of the disparity between the poet's ideals and the reality he envisions . . . the failure of courtesy . . . dramatizes Spenser's implicit avowal that the potential ideal which his epic was designed to embody has been defeated by a world hopelessly antagonistic to its realization" (331). From Book IV on, "chivalry is reduced to empty forms" (333). By the end of Book V, "the chivalric ideal as a way of dealing with the problems of ethics and politics now seems like a hopeless dream" (334); the court has abandoned moral aspiration for fashion. In a world without clear moral governance the Blatant Beast takes over as "the perfect expression of a mass society: impersonal, anonymous, indiscriminate, and unendingly clamorous" (338). Calidore himself is not improved by experience; instead, "he gradually loses all semblance of the ideal virtue set out in the Proem" (245). As Richard Neuse concludes, Calidore lacks "the spiritual faculty that would allow him to sense the mystery of courtesy."[27] This makes Book VI far darker than the *Arcadia*, for there "the courteous knight" who gets it all wrong is the antagonist; we still have the protagonists Musidorus and Pyrocles to demonstrate true courtesy.

The similarites between *The Faerie Queene* VI and the *New Arcadia* are not just those of plot, but the complex interplay of the pastoral, chivalric, and Petrarchan roles. As the Graces disappear when an intruder appears, so does the pastoral fiction. Courtesy is inadequate to maintain that fiction of the idyllic world; once the fiction is disturbed the knight must reassume his arms and go back to battle. The usual pattern of the court to pastoral interlude and return to court is maintained in both works. Calidore, however, merely returns to the chivalric role as he takes up his quest, leaving Pastorella, and fulfilling the quest only in his own lifetime. Andrew Ettin has noted that the pastoral usually precedes marriage and family responsibilities; so do the Petrarchan and the chivalric.[28] If Sidney did not intend to change the ending of the *Old Arcadia*, Pyrocles and Musidorus will go beyond the chivalric to the kingly, taking up marriage, family responsibilities, and the task of ruling the state. Their success presumably does not end with death, for the narrator concludes his tale with reference to the son of Pyrocles and Philoclea (Pyrophilius) and Musidorus and Pamela's daughter (Melidora) "who . . . may awake some other spirit to exercise his pen in that wherewith mine is already dulled" (*OA*, 417).

A correct reading of their pastoral romance is the more necessary because both Sidney and Spenser present a double fictionalization, an assumed pastoral identity for the author and an assumed pastoral identity for the protagonist. One may well experience what Greenblatt, referring to the Bower of Bliss, calls "the reader's sense of encountering in Spenser's poem the process of self-fashioning itself."[29] Sidney portrays himself as the shepherd/knight/poet Philisides, an appropriate guise for a knight who began writing a pastoral romance during his exile from court. Spenser, a person of lower social rank, had more freedom to portray himself as the shepherd/poet Colin Clout, as Richard Helgerson has demonstrated.[30]

Book VI of *The Faerie Queene* conflates their real and fictional worlds insofar as Calidore represents the pastoral knight Philisides, Sidney himself. In his dedication of *The Shepheardes Calender*, Spenser had appealed to Sidney as a defense against envy, but by 1596 Sidney could no longer protect the poet from the Blatant Beast. As Sidney's epitaphs repeatedly assert, envy had slain Philisides. If there is any truth to the tradition that Sir Calidore figures Sir Philip Sidney, then Calidore's quest for the Blatant Beast, the "monstrous pet" of Envy and Detraction (V.xii.37), is particularly appropriate, for envy and the accompanying slander were the bane of Sidney's family.[31] Sir Philip himself wrote two defenses against slander, one defending his father's governance in Ireland, and one defending his uncle against the libellous tract Known as *Leicester's Commonwealth*.[32] More importantly, Sidney and his family believed that the advancement he sought was blocked by envy at court. When Sidney had presented himself as Philisides, he incorporated into that image the conflict between the pastoral ideal and the reality of court: his device represents the pastoral ideal of a peaceful world, but his arms fit him for the actual world, ruled by fear and envy. Sidney's family believed that he was indeed slain by envy, for he died in a campaign that they believed was doomed by lack of the Queen's support, a situation they attributed to envy at court.

This is a constant theme in the epitaphs. Just as he pictured himself as Philisides in a pastoral world "Without fear or envy", so Mary Sidney pictured his "Angell Spirit" in heaven "where never Envie bites."[33] "The Dolefull Lay of Clorinda" similarly portrays him enjoying heavenly bliss "from iealous rancor free."[34] Yet Spenser, too, came to see that words, not deeds, determine public character, as he declared in "The Ruines of Time": "Deeds doe die, how euer noblie donne." It is only "wise wordes taught in numbers for to runne" which "Live for ay . . . Nor age, nor envie shall them ever wast."[35] The theme of envy significantly recurs in each of the pastoral elegies printed in *Astrophel*. "The mourning Muse of Thestylis" by Lodowick Bryskett praises Sidney's verse that will extend his fame "that enuies rage, nor time might end the same" (sig. H2). "A Pastorall Aeglogue" speaks of Philisides as the greatest among Albion's shepherds: "Who vneath / Enuie could touch for vertuous life and skill; / Curteous valiant, and liberall" (sig. H3). "An Elegie . . . for his *Astrophill*" is even blunter: Sidney was "by enuie slaine" (sig. K1[v]). Accepting that accusation, "An Epitaph upon the right Honourable sir Phillip Sidney knight" portrays even envy mourning: "Enuie her sting, and spite hath left her gall, / Malice her selfe, a mourning garment weares" (sig. K3). "Another of the same" repeats the motif: "enuie strangely rues his end, in whom no fault she found" (sig. K3[v]).

As Envy was believed to have defeated Sir Philip Sidney, even so the Blatant Beast finally triumphs after Calidore's death, coming out of the fiction to attack the author:

> Ne may this homely verse, of many meanest,
> Hope to escape his venemous despite,
> More then my former writs, all were they clearest
> From blamefull blot, and free from all that wite,
> With which some wicked tongues did it backebite,
> And bring into a mighty Peres displeasure,
> That neuer so deserued to endite.
> Therfore do you my rimes keep better measure,
> And seeke to please, that now is counted wisemens
>   threasure.
>
> (xii.41)

In dedicating *The Shepheardes Calender* to Sidney as "the president / Of noblesse and of chevalree," Spenser had appealed to Sidney as a defence, advising his book that "if that Envie barke at thee, / As sure it will, for succoure flee / Under the shadow of his wing."[36] No longer can Sidney serve as a bulwark between the poet and envy, for envy has slain Philisides himself. Lacking that protection, the poet must appeal to his audience—and to his queen—for a correct reading, even as the fictional princes appeal to their princesses.

In the ultimately cheerful world of the *Arcadia*, the Petrarchan and the pastoral must give way to the chivalric. Yet from the ending of the *Old Arcadia* we may surmise that the chivalric too is inadequate to restore harmony. Musidorus and Pamela fail in their attempt to bring back aid, for they are captured by rebels very like Spenser's brigants. When it comes, salvation is miraculous—the resurrection of Basilius. The progression of Petrarchan/pastoral/chivalric/spiritual follows that of Sidney's own works, from the Petrarchan in *Astrophil and Stella*, to the chivalric in the *Arcadia*, to the spiritual in his *Psalmes*. Significantly, Philisides comes to rescue Musidorus, the shepherd/knight/poet rescuing his own pastoral knight. The parallel process in *The Faerie Queene* is more complex because of the nested narrators: Spenser, the epic narrator, and Colin Clout. In *The Faerie Queene* the Petrarchan gives way to the pastoral and the pastoral to the chivalric on two levels, that of Calidore's experience and that of the narrator's. Ominously for the poet, the vision on Mt. Acidale is destroyed by the pastoral knight Calidore and so Colin breaks his pipe: the pastoral persona is destroyed by his own creation.[37] This destruction immediately precedes the destruction of the pastoral world which is, in some sense, upheld by Colin's poetry. Then the chivalric or epic narrator is also destroyed at the end of Book VI when the Blatant Beast leaps out of the poem to attack the author himself.

Within the fiction of the *New Arcadia* and *The Faerie Queene*, the princes win their shepherdess/princesses by employing Petrarchan, pastoral, and chivalric roles, but ultimately all fictions fail, slain by envy. For the authors as well, all fictions fail as protection against the Blatant Beast. Sidney himself, his friends believed, was "by enuie slain"; in "Astrophel" Spenser allegorizes his battle wound as the attack of "a cruell beast of most accursed brood" who "with fell tooth accustomed to blood, / Launched his thigh" (f. 2v). Spenser's poetic persona faces a similar death when the Blatant Beast leaps out of the poem to attack the author. Their fictions and their lives gain meaning only when these Right Poets receive a Right Reading. If they cannot hope for such readers on earth, perhaps they will become such readers in heaven: *The Faerie Queene* concludes with a final prayer for "that Sabaoths sight" (VII.viii.2) which would enable the author to read truths beyond this mutable world.

Siena College

Notes

1. Sidney apparently began his *Arcadia* at Wilton when he was in disgrace for his letter on the proposed Alençon marriage; he never did achieve the position his friends and allies anticipated. Spenser ends Book VI with mention of "a mighty peres displeasure," usually understood to refer to Burghley, who was angered by "Mother Hubberds Tale." Documentary evidence of Spenser's disgrace has been discovered by Richard Peterson, presented at "Spenser at Kalamazoo," International Medieval Congress, Western Michigan University, 12 May 1990.

On the political functions of the pastoral, see Sidney's "A Defence of Poetry" in *Miscellaneous Prose of Sir Philip Sidney*, ed. Katherine Duncan-Jones and Jan Van Dorsten (Oxford: Clarendon Press, 1973), 95–96; Louis Adrian Montrose, "'Eliza, Queen of shepheardes' and the Pastoral of Power," *ELR* 10 (1980), 153–82 and "Of Gentlemen and Shepherds: the Politics of Elizabethan Pastoral Form," *ELH* (1983), 415–59; Annabel Patterson, "Under . . . Pretty Tales": Intention in Sidney's *Arcadia*," *Studies in the Literary Imagination* 15 (1982), 19 and *Censorship and Interpretation: Conditions of Writing and Reading in Early Modern England* (Madison: University of Wisconsin Press, 1984) and *Pastoral and Ideology: Virgil to Valery* (Berkeley: University of California Press, 1987); David Norbrook, *Poetry and Politics in the English Renaissance* (London: Routlege and Kegan Paul, 1984); Alan Sinfield "Power and Ideology: An Outline Theory and Sidney's Arcadia," *ELH* 52 (1985), 259–77; John Bernard, *Ceremonies of Innocence: Pastoralism in the Poetry of Edmund Spenser* (Cambridge: Cambridge University Press, 1989).

2. *The Countess of Pembroke's Arcadia (The New Arcadia)*, ed. Victor Skretkowicz (Oxford: Clarendon Press, 1987), 24. Future references will be given in the text.

3. A. Leigh DeNeef, *Spenser and the Motives of Metaphor* (Durham, N.C.: Duke University Press, 1982), 8.

4. Spenser had already used the Amazonian theme in the Radigund episode in Book V.

5. For the standard pastoral plot elements and the way in which Spenser and Sidney use them, see Gilbert Highet, *The Classical Tradition: Greek and Roman Influences on Western Literature* (London: Oxford University Press, 1949), 164; *The Works of Edmund Spenser: A Variorum Edition*, ed. Edwin Greenlaw et al. (Baltimore: Johns Hopkins University Press, 1938) VI, 372–74, 376–81; Humphrey Tonkin, *Spenser's Courteous Pastoral: Book Six of The Faerie Queene* (Oxford: Clarendon Press, 1972), 285, 296; H. C. Chang, *Allegory and Courtesy in Spenser* (Edinburgh: Edinburgh University Press, 1955), 114–51. Harry Berger lists the series of motifs used in Book VI which are derived from these plots in "A Secret Discipline: *The Faerie Queene* Book VI," in *Form and Convention in the Poetry of Edmund Spenser: Selected Papers from the English Institute*, ed. W. Nelson (New York: Columbia University Press, 1961), 39. Dorothy F. Atkinson traces Spenser's debt to the Mirrour of Knighthood in "The Pastorella Episode in *The Faerie Queene*," *PMLA* 59 (1944), 361–72.

6. *Edmund Spenser: The Faerie Queene*, ed. Thomas P. Roche, Jr. (New Haven: Yale University Press, 1978), 996. Future references will be to this edition.

7.   For example, by choosing to echo the adventures of Musidorus, who-disguises himself as a shepherd, rather than his younger cousin Pyrocles, who disguises himself as an Amazon, Spenser omits the sharpest irony of the *New Arcadia*, for Sidney's comedy often begins with farce that later develops tragic undertones. The scene where Zelmane (Pyrocles in his Amazon garb) watches Philoclea bathe is a hilarious version of the Acteon story; laughing at Pyrocles' discomfiture, we do not yet realize that this farce will have tragic consequences because Amphialus is watching Philoclea too (195–98). Amphialus' glimpse of Philoclea is sufficient to produce the vehement passions that impel the plot of Book III. While the brigants certainly destroy the pastoral world of *The Faerie Queene* as thoroughly as Amphialus does the Arcadia idyll, there is nothing initially amusing about their attack.

8.   Chang notes the use of the birthmark in Heliodorus, Tasso, and Boiardo; for example, 117 n.3.

9.   Tonkin, 149.

10.   Richard C. McCoy, *Sir Philip Sidney: Rebellion in Arcadia* (New Brunswick, N.J.: Rutgers University Press, 1979.)

11.   The ever-literal E. K. annotates "Aprill" to explain to the obtuse reader that Rosalind is not a real shepherdess but a "Gentle woman of no meane house." He must fear that we are as dense as Mopsa.

12.   Maurice Keen, *Chivalry* (New Haven: Yale University Press, 1984), 1–2, 12–13. Sidney's pride in his own skill in horsemanship is revealed in his advice to his brother Robert, in his own course of study in Italy, and in the opening of his *Defence of Poetry*, where he mentions studying horsemanship under John Pietro Pugliano, 73. See also Musidorus's praise of Pyrocles, who was so skilled that no "man living . . . could perform any action, either on horse or foot, more strongly, or deliver that strength more nimbly" (164).

13.   On the function of the narrators in the *New Arcadia*, see S. K. Heninger, Jr., *Sidney and Spenser: The Poet as Maker* (University Park: Pennsylvania State University Press, 1989), 489–97.

14.   On the deceptively naive narrative voice of pastoral, see Hallett Smith, *Elizabethan Poetry* (Cambridge, Mass.: Harvard University Press, 1952), 18; William Empson, *Seven Types of Ambiguity* (London: Chatto and Windus, 1949), 114–15; Paul Alpers, "Empson on Pastoral," *New Literary History* (1978), 102–23 and "What is Pastoral?" *CI* 8 (1982), 437–60.

15.   Caroline Lucas, *Writing for Women: The Example of Woman as Reader in Elizabethan Romance* (Milton Keynes: Open University Press, 1989), 128.

16.   See McCoy, 173.

17.   A. Leigh DeNeef, "Ploughing Virgilian Furrows: the Genres of *Faerie Queene VI*," *John Donne Journal* 1 (1982), 156.

18.   The lion image, although traditional, may be another echo of Musidorus, who is identified by the mark of a lion's paw.

19.   On justice and the pastoral, see DeNeef, 152–66; and Renato Poggioli, *The Oaten Flute: Essays on Pastoral Poetry and the Pastoral Ideal* (Cambridge: Harvard University Press, 1975), Chapter 10.

20.   "The Knight of the Sheep" is not named as Philisides here, but the identification may be implied; cf. Maurice Evans, ed. *The Countess of Pembroke's Arcadia* (Harmondsworth: Penguin, 1977), 857, 862.

21.   On the parallel between Amphialus and the captain, see Chang, 128.

22.   McCoy, 188. As Andrew Ettin argues, pastoral fiction is usually presented from a male viewpoint. Sidney, however, occasionally shows the woman's point of view: *Literature and the Pastoral* (New Haven: Yale University
Press, 1984), 146. This consciousness of a female audience probably comes from
the influence of his sister Mary Sidney, Countess of Pembroke, to whom the
Old Arcadia is dedicated. It was written "only for you, only to you," Sidney
says in his dedication, "most of it in your presence" (*OA*, 3). This must imply
that they talked about the story as he was writing it.

23.   Anthea Hume says that Calidore is the knight most in possession of his
virtue, despite his failures: *Edmund Spenser: Protestant Poet* (Cambridge: Cambridge University Press, 1984), 139. David Shore argues that Calidore is con-
strained by expediency; he "acts with the greatest courtesy man can display,"
although courtesy often shades into policy—*Spenser and the Poetics of Pastoral: A
Study of the World of Colin Clout* (Montreal: McGill-Queen's University Press,
1985), 161. See also MacCaffrey, 397; Berger, 39; Richard Neuse, "Book VI as
Conclusion to *The Faerie Queene*." *ELH* 35 (1968), 329–53.

24.   Note that the pictures in Kalendar's summer house include "Diana, when
Acteon saw her bathing, in whose cheeks the painter had set such a colour as
was mixed between shame and disdain," 15. The Acteon image is here explicit
in *Arcadia*; in *The Faerie Queene* it is implicit in the confrontation between
Calidore and the Graces, and in the story of Faunus, Book VII. On Acteon, see
Tonkin, 308–309, and Maureen Quilligan, *Milton's Spenser: The Politics of
Reading* (Ithaca: Cornell University Press. 1983), 193.

25.   For a more sympathetic reading of Calidore on Mt. Acidale, see Bernard,
155–59.

26.   A. C. Hamilton, *Sir Philip Sidney: A Study in His Life and Works* (Cambridge: Cambridge University Press, 1977), 139.

27.   Neuse, 325.

28.   Ettin, 149.

29.   Stephen Greenblatt, *Renaissance Self-Fashioning: From More to Shakespeare*
(Chicago: University of Chicago Press, 1980), 175.

30.   Or at least this is the impression Sidney attempts to convey, calling his
works his "toies" in the dedication to the *Arcadia*, declaring that he fell into the
name of a poet in his *Defence*, and, if the deathbed statement is authentic, asking
to have his work destroyed. Richard Helgerson demonstrates how this fits the
literary mold of the times, "The Elizabethan Laureate: Self-Presentation and
the Literary System," *ELH* 46 (1979), 193–220, and *Self-Crowned Laureates:
Spenser, Jonson, Milton, and the Literary System* (Los Angeles: University of Los
Angeles Press, 1983). See also Isabel G. MacCaffrey, *Spenser's Allegory: The
Anatomy of Imagination* (Princeton: Princeton University Press, 1976), 359.

31.   MacCaffrey, 357. On blame and slander as "Tropes of Personal Rivalry,"
see Frank Whigham, *Ambition and Privilege: The Social Tropes of Elizabethan
Courtesy Theory* (Berkeley: University of California Press, 1984), Chapter 5.

32.   "Discourse on Irish Affairs" and "Defence of the Earl of Leicester," in
Miscellaneous Prose, 8–12, 129–41.

33.   "To the Angell Spirit," in *The Triumph of Death and Other Unpublished and
Uncollected Poems by Mary Sidney, Countess of Pembroke (1561-1621)*, ed. Gary F.
Waller (Salzburg: University of Salzburg Press, 1977), 94.

34.   "The Dolefull Lay of Clorinda," in *Astrophel. A Pastorall Elegie vpon the death of the most Noble and valorous Knight, Sir Philip Sidney* (London: William Ponsonby, 1595), sig. G2ᵛ. On the countess's authorship, see Margaret Hannay, *Philip's Phoenix: Mary Sidney, Countess of Pembroke* (New York: Oxford University Press, 1990), Chapter 3.

35.   Edmund Spenser, "The Ruines of Time," in *The Yale Edition of the Shorter Poems of Edmund Spenser*, ed. William Oram *et al.* (New Haven: Yale University Press, 1989), 249.

36.   Edmund Spenser, *The Shepheardes Calender*, in Oram, 2.

37.   On the failure of the pastoral and of the chivalric in *The Faerie Queene*, see DeNeef, "Virgilian Furrows," 152–57 and "'Who now does follow the foule Blatant Beast': Spenser's Self-Effacing Fictions," *Renaissance Papers 1978*, ed. A. Leigh DeNeef and M. Thomas Hester (Durham, N.C.: Southwestern Renaissance Conferences, 1979), 11–21. On Calidore as an avatar of Spenser, see Bernard, Chapter 5.

STANLEY STEWART

Spenser and the Judgment of Paris

*E*VER SINCE the eighteenth century, critics have recognized a
link between Spenser and the Judgment of Paris tradition. Edmund Malone sees Peele's *Araynement of Paris* (1584) as a parody
of *The Shepheardes Calender*, and recently, such critics as Thomas
P. Roche, Jr. and Louis A. Montrose have extended the connection, the latter, for instance, construing the Judgment of Paris as
encoding a critique of the Elizabethan system of patronage, and
Spenser's Colin as "a perverter of pastoral."[1] In the following
pages I propose to examine the literary and iconographic context
of the Judgment of Paris tradition as Spenser received and revised
it, especially as it concerns felt tensions between the imagined
worlds of epic and pastoral. Although Paris belonged to both
worlds, the manner in which the two were intertwined in
Spenser's revised narrative of the Paris myth has not been fully
elucidated.[2] Without doubt the Paris narrative was popular with
Renaissance poets.[3] We have Peele's *Araynement*, Sidney's *Arcadia*, English translations of Guido delle Colonne's *Destruction of
Troy*, Chapman's translation of the *Iliad*, and many less ambitious treatments of the story in such works as Boccaccio's *De
Claris Mulieribus*, Tottel's *Miscellany*, Whitney's *Choice of Emblems* and T[homas] H[eywood]'s epyllion, *Oenone and Paris*.
Thomas Watson's *Hecatompathia* has a sonnet on the subject, and
his translation of Coluthus' *Helenae Raptus* into Latin in 1586
prompted John Trussell's English version in 1595. But the most
popular work on the subject was George Turbervile's translation
of Ovid's *Heroides* (1567).

In Spenser's treatment of the Paris myth marriage is perhaps
the most important theme. Traditionally, the tale involves inter-
woven strands of narratives recounting rivalries and discords at
weddings and in marriages. The tendency in criticism from
Fulgentius on has been to construe the Judgment of Paris as a
choice between the sensual appetite, on the one hand, and intellectual, moral, and spiritual impulses, on the other. There is
evidence to support this line of argument—from paintings of

161

Lucas Cranach and commentaries of Fulgentius and Ficino (among many), which associate the Judgment of Paris with the Choice of Hercules.[4] Hence, the apparent collapse of Paris's tripartite decision in Fulgentius (contemplative, active, voluptuary)[5] into the duality of Sallust, who holds that "the golden apple denotes the world, which, on account of its composition from contrary natures, is not improperly said to be thrown by Discord . . . And a soul living according to sense, (for this is Paris) not perceiving other powers in the universe, asserts that the contended apple subsists alone through the beauty of Venus."[6]

I will argue that, notwithstanding its moral overtones, in Spenser, the Judgment of Paris represents a poetic choice. Spenser's protagonists *do* face ethical dilemmas, but their alternatives go hand-in-hand with mutually exclusive poetic forms— or, rather, with forms that seem to preclude mutual assimilation. Book II of *The Faerie Queene* is about morality as self-discipline. But morality in this private mode can be exercised to the uttermost without reference to procreation, that is, asexually. Book III, which concerns love as an active, outgoing virtue, involves sexual union and regeneration. In Spenser's poetic system, this virtue entails aesthetic configurations: how couples look together is as much a matter of art as it is of nature.

It is not my aim to trivialize the ethical dimension of Spenser's handling of the tradition. Rather, my thesis is that Spenser received a metaphoric system and narrative line from the literary and iconographic context of a largely Ovidian tradition, and proceeded to reshape it to quite different ends. Through the centuries, in art and in literature, especially in poetic transformations of Ovid's *Heroides*, Paris remained a complex figure, a composite of often conflicting, even contradictory, roles: prince/shepherd, warrior/coward, husband/adulterer. Above all, Paris was a lover, and Spenser makes him a father, too. In *The Faerie Queene*, Spenser refashions Paris as a restless knight, but, as we shall see, Paridell preserves many of the features of his primarily Ovidian precursor. For pastoral and epic, Spenser draws on appropriate, though different, aspects of the tradition; but taken together, *The Shepheardes Calender* and *The Faerie Queene* exhibit intricate variations on the possibilities of Paris as a character. Most important, Spenser represents Paris in his less familiar role as a poet whose destiny, shaped in part by the gods, was to choose between the worlds of pastoral and epic.

I

On its surface, the Paris myth has everything: love, longing, jealousy, intrigue, betrayal, courage, cowardice, conniving, war. Moving from fabulous events foreshadowing his birth to accounts of his death and efforts of Oenone to revive him, the richly embroidered narrative imbedded in Spenser's revised narrative reflects an understanding of the way in which individuals shape history as much by their limitations as by their virtues. Perhaps the most striking traditional apposition is that between epic scenes of battle and those of bucolic retreat. Consider Plate 1. Such treatments of "the archetype of the shepherd"[7] (typical of the dozen or so paintings of the subject by Cranach) are anachronistic. Cranach knows that, since the Judgment is only now taking place, Paris ought not to be in armor. The Trojan War lies a long way off, in space as well as in time. For, although sources vary, many hold that the Judgment of Paris took place on Mount Ida (a fact of literary topography important in both the "August" eclogue and Book VI of The Faerie Queene).[8] And yet here he is (in an apposite treatment Mercury awakens him [Plate 2]), prepared for battle, not for watching sheep. In the Metropolitan Judgment (Plate 3), Cupid bends his bow, and, in the distance, we see the battlements of Troy.[9]

Spenser's refashioned tale casts Paris as an ineffective warrior and stresses domestic aspects of received tradition. Even the entry of Paridell—Spenser's Paris—into the narrative seems to happen by accident, not as a consequence of Paridell's chivalric aims or skills. He comes along ("faire pricking on the plaine")[10] just as the narrator, having told of Florimell's fate at the hands of Proteus, returns to Satyrane and the Squire of Dames. Of course the seemingly random flow of disparate narratives (Chrysogene, Venus, Diana, Belphoebe, Amoret, Florimell, the Squire of Dames) elaborates a common motif of the "incessaunt paine" with which the male exerts his "power or skill" to "do service unto gentle Dames" (III.vii.54). This male inclination to pursue feminine beauty wherever and whenever such pursuit is physically possible exhibits one aspect of the process represented in the "Gardin of Adonis," and so is part of the divine order under which all species reproduce themselves. Spenser's story of Paris starts here, with Paridell—his breast bearing the emblem of a burning heart (reminiscent of Hecuba's dream and Cassandra's

PLATE 1. Lucas Cranach, *The Judgment of Paris* (*c*. 1537). Courtesy of the St. Louis Art Museum.

PLATE 2. Lucas Cranach, *The Judgment of Paris* (*c*. 1516–18). Courtesy of the Seattle Art Museum.

PLATE 3. Lucas Cranach, *The Judgment of Paris (n.d.)*, *The Metropolitan Museum of Art, Rogers Fund. (28.221)*

prophecy)—pursuing Florimell, whose death he refuses to accept. Determined to "savegard" her (III.viii.46), he wanders the earth, an exile from his native country, on an epic quest "for faire Ladies love, and glories gaine" (III.ix.37). It appears that to him sexual conquest and epic glory are one and the same thing.

In *The Faerie Queene*, Spenser plays with differences between these categorical opposites. Not only was the Rape of Helen—Petrarchan banners and battlefields aside—not the stuff of epic poetry, but in the typical view represented in Thomas Heywood's *Troia Britanica* (1609), Paris was (in contrast to Hector) "effeminate,"[11] attractive—made for love, not war. A seventeenth-century engraving (Plate 4) of "Paris to Helen" in *Ovids Heroicall Epistles* (1637) illustrates how readers of the 1630 *Faerie Queene* might have taken Spenser's representations. "*The Argument of the fifteenth Epistle*" explains Paris's proposal that Helen "disgrace her husband" by going "with him to *Troy*, where he would keepe her by force."[12] In the context of the lovers' correspondence, the illustration conveys more than a little irony. In the background, the cavalry, flanked on both sides by infantry, stand at the ready. Tips of the soldiers' lances form three parallel lines, which extend from the farthest rank toward Paris, who is occupied, not by war, but by demands of literary composition. He wears no helmet, possesses no weapon, has no horse, and wears sandals.

The illustration is divided into two parts, one depicting armed legions ready to fight, the other representing Paris, possessed by love and focused on its attendant function: writing to and about his mistress. In effect, the illustrator conveys a proleptic sense of Helen's laconic remark on the gulf between reality and her lover's written word. Paris had, indeed, claimed to be fierce: "Nor *Menelaus* shall / of greater courage bee / Than Trojan *Paris*, nor in armes / more stiffe and stoute than hee."[13] Recalling his valiant exploits as a child, Ovid's Paris proclaims himself in martial prowess second only to Hector in the world.

Helen's response is masterfully ambiguous, full of taunts and innuendoes. Again, the illustrator of the 1637 Wye Saltonstall translation captures the sense of her unerring rejoinder to Paris's claim to valor. In Plate 5, Helen is seated in a posture strikingly like that of her lover. We see the same platform, the same outcropping, even the same rock and wall-hanging. Like Paris, she is engaged in writing, but the presence of Eros, holding an inkwell and supplementary quills, marks a difference in candor.

PLATE 4. "Paris to Helen," *Ovids Heroicall Epistles* (1637), sig. H4ᵛ.
Courtesy of the Henry E. Huntington Library and Art Gallery, San
Marino, California.

PLATE 5. "Helen to Paris," *Ovid's Heroicall Epistles* (1637), sig. I4ᵛ. Courtesy of the Henry E. Huntington Library and Art Gallery, San Marino, California.

In the distance, a ship—presumably, the fateful one on which she will soon embark—sails away. The contrast between the two engravings underlines the surface candor of Helen's confessional epistle. Admitting her own motivations, Helen sees Paris as the thrall of Venus, not of Mars: "The truth is thus, that from your words / your feature differs quite . . . Love *Paris*, and let men of force / go fight in fielde for thee" (sig. O3).

Spenser makes rich use of the tension in Paris's character between the bravado and armor of Mars and the motives and manners of Venus. Britomart's early and easy victory over Paridell not only exposes his low station as a warrior, but also provides an appropriate prelude to description of his quest "for faire Ladies love, and glories gaine" (III.ix.37). In both love and war Paridell is the worthy inheritor of the Paris tradition:

> From him my linage I derive aright,
>   Who long before the ten yeares siege of *Troy*,
>   Whiles yet on *Ida* he a shepheard hight,
>   On faire *Oenone* got a lovely boy,
>   Whom for remembraunce of her passed joy,
>   She of his Father *Parius* did name;
>   Who, after *Greekes* did *Priams* realme destroy,
>   Gathred the *Trojan* reliques sav'd from flame,
> And with them sayling thence, to th'Isle of *Paros* came.
>   (III.ix.36)

Britomart's interruption of Paridell's narrative should not mislead us into overlooking the paradoxical attitudes reflected in his account. For after his fulsome praise of Helen as the "flowre of beautie excellent" (III.ix.25), Paridell reveals that he is descended from Oenone, the wife whom Paris abandoned and betrayed for Helen. As the notes to the Spenser Variorum indicate (III, 281), Paridell's genealogy is partly adapted from Joannes Tzetzes.[14] Since Tzetzes' *Works* appeared in Greek and Latin twice during the sixteenth century, it is possible that Spenser knew it. But there is very little similarity between the name attributed by Tzetzes (Corythus) and the one that Spenser chose for the son of Paris and Oenone (Parius). It seems to me more likely that Spenser took the accounts of the doomed marriage between Paris and Oenone from the *Heroides* and Smyrnaeus, and dreamed up their progeny on his own. Be that as it may, Spenser's choice emphasizes the affinity between father and son, paralleling that between ancestor (Paris) and descendant (Paridell). Likewise, Spenser stresses this link by delineating Britomart's compassion for the Trojans, which reveals an emotional tie to Paridell, with whom she shares her "countries cause, and commune foe" (III.ix.40). Further, these emerging tales of odyssey tell of two lines of descent from Priam's house, one (including Britomart's offspring) leading from Aeneas and Creusa, the other from Paris and Oenone.[15] Since the tale of Paris is also that of the Rape of Helen, we cannot disentangle Paridell's narratives from Spenser's theme of marriage and legitimacy. Britomart wants to hear the familiar tale of Troy's most famous exile, Aeneas, whose wife, Creusa, was the sister of Paris. But in more than their common theme of military ruin and retreat, Paridell's two tales are parallel. (We are reminded that Virgil's Juno thinks of Aeneas as the "second Paris.")[16] Not only are they about a single Trojan family, but they share a common narrative core. In this context, Britomart's interest and compassion are not at all out of place, for the parallel narrative lines recount the exiles and separations suffered by legitimate and illegitimate offspring of the first family of Troy.

The characters are further linked in that, like Paridell, Britomart is an exile from her "native soyle" (III.ii.7) on an apposite quest, having left "greater *Britaine*" to find "*Arthegall*" (III.ii.8), whose "manly face" (III.ii.24) she has seen in Merlin's glass. As Merlin's allopathic treatment of Britomart's Love-wound suggests, Book III is about the power of Love, but also about its divine source: "Most sacred fire, that burnest mightily / In living brests, ykindled first above, / . . ." (III.iii.1). We understand that in the "*Castle Joyeous*" sexual impulse is more or less undiscriminating as to object and means of satisfaction; nobody asks Britomart for that "loves choise" (IV.ix.37) set out by Prince Arthur as the goal of chivalry. Because of that "sacred fire," which presents a world of difficulty, Britomart has left her homeland to seek a man she has not even met. And yet, Platonic Love and Faeryland aside, Artegall is, as the documentary record shows, "sprong of seed terrestriall" (III.iii.26).[17] Spenser refashions Merlin's prophecy as English readers might have read it in Malory's *Morte d'Arthur* by infusing it with a substance reminiscent of Book VI of the *Aeneid*, in which Aeneas is provided a glimpse of the earliest branching of Priam's line in the *gens Julus*. Thus, in Spenser, difficulty and delay are part of a divine scheme. Spenser's Merlin succours Britomart with assurance—akin to the promise Michael will make to Eve in *Paradise Lost*—that recognition of the triumph of her fertility requires historical perspective.

It is in this panoramic historical context that Artegall's exploits find poetic emphasis in Spenser. All lines—mythic and historical—lead back to Venus: goddess, guardian of Troy, and (as the mother of Aeneas) benefactress of the British race. But more than a shared interest in history links Britomart and Paridell, for both are lovers, and yet eventually "lustfull *Paridell*" ends up—manipulated by Duessa and Ate—the adversary of Sir Scudamore and Britomart. If at times Britomart suffers in a frenzy of desire for Artegall, in Spenser's narrative these natural impulses are intertwined with ethical and aesthetic qualities, such as those apparent in the contrast between her responses and those of Hellenore. In the context of the thematic importance of fidelity in the Paris myth, we need to recall the obvious: Hellenore is married, Britomart is not. And yet we know that a deeper decorum than may be apparent in this fact binds Britomart to Artegall. Spenserian decorum permits—indeed, drives couples toward—sexual union. But the key to Spenser's notion of sexual joy and harmony is not simple-minded monogamy. Whereas pairs should make sense within the natural order, Hellenore and Malbecco are "Unfitly yokt together" (III.ix.6). Nor does the difference in their ages tell the whole story of their joyless union, for the narrator emphasizes Malbecco's avarice above all else. The natural order is plenitude incarnate. Unless forms constantly move into the "*Gardin of Adonis*," other forms cannot constantly be moving out. Hence, the sense we have of Malbecco as a grudging, hoarding personality: "But all his mind is set on mucky pelfe" (III.ix.4). In his household, monogamy is no more aesthetically pleasing or unforced than is promiscuity in the "*Castle Joyeous*." Spenser revises the Paris story in such a way as to intensify, not the moral theme, but the moral ambiguity of the situation. Indeed, unlike the Menelaus of Homer and Ovid, Malbecco is a curious mix of features common to other Spenser villains, notably Despair. The ugliness in his household emanates from his inappropriate pairing with Hellenore.

Again, Spenser provides a disjunctive pair to elucidate different aspects of the same human dilemma. How is it possible for a woman to be beautiful and yet free to choose her mate? It does not help to point out that Britomart has feminine appeal. She certainly does, but if Florimell went around in armor half the population of Faery Land would be spared the trouble of chasing her. The difference is one of presentation; it is Florimell's striking, feminine vulnerability—which is not the true opposite of Hellenore's enforced (and faulty) inaccessibility—that sets the male species in motion. Because of her martial appearance, men often end up fighting Britomart; with Florimell, they are more inclined to fight each other.

So Hellenore, like Britomart, is amply endowed with many of the physical attributes of Florimell. As Spenser's Helen, she is, after all, associated with Venus. Spenser interweaves his Helen narrative with those of eight females. Four are sisters, the other four are alike in certain ways, but quite dissimilar in others: Venus/Diana, Amoret/Belphoebe, Florimell/the snowy Florimell, Britomart/Hellenore. The more the vaunted particularities of history unfold, the more familiar becomes the outline of their uniform truth. Myths of romance separate male from female, which nature yearns appropriately to rejoin. I say "appropriately" because Spenser provides Hellenore, as he does Paridell, with a defensible reason for her betrayal. In Spenser, nature and true art agree that there are enough attractive men and women to go around. Mismatches derive from physical or spiritual distortions and denials of nature. Thus, regardless of the eligibility of various young men about court, Spenser pairs Amoret from the moment of her exit from the "*Gardin* of *Adonis*" as a woman: "But she to none of them her love did cast, / Save to the noble knight Sir *Scudamore* . . . for evermore" (III.vi.53). While Florimell is pursued by all men and the only god with whom she comes in contact, she simultaneously longs for and seeks her appropriate male counterpart. Thus, Spenser envisions a high decorum of legitimacy as an aspect of the natural order, which runs counter to the Paris tale. For if he was "the archetype of the shepherd," Paris was also a notorious adulterer. Not only was Helen a married woman, but in Ovid's *Heroides*, Paris (unlike Paridell) was at the time of the Rape of Helen, himself a married man.

Spenser's revised treatment of Hellenore defies easy comparison with sources, though allusions to many authors, major and minor (including medieval and Renaissance mythographers) have been identified. In fact, although these many sources present a complicated story, this much seems clear: Spenser's treatment (III.ix.30–31; III.ix.52–53) is largely a revised narrative of Helen's "Epistle to Paris" in Ovid's *Heroides*. For instance, like

her beautiful predecessor in the *Heroides*, Hellenore plays the
wine game in a wanton flirtation with Paridell (III.ix.32), which
mutual lapse may support Kathleen Williams's description of
Paridell as a "learned lover."[18] In this connection, the iconography of the Paris tradition often juxtaposes contrasting tableaux
of Paris in the house of Menelaus. Like Plate 5, Plate 6 illustrates
Helen's epistolary recollection of the "wine game." This woodcut depicts the eternal triangle as well as the difference in rank
between guest and host. None too subtly, Helen's letter points
out that Menelaus is not only a husband with certain rights, but
also a king whose hospitality did not earn the seductive behavior
of "a shamelesse guest" (sig. N5): "Againe you sigh as fast, /
another time you take / The Cup, and where I dranck even there
/ your falsed thirst doth slake" (sig. N4v). It is worth noting that,
in much the same manner as the contrasting scenes represented in
Plate 6, the three contiguous panels illustrating Helen's letter in
the 1542 edition (Plate 7) emphasize her husband's rank and
generosity in contrast to the undeserved discourtesy of the wine
game.

PLATE 6. "Helena Paridi," *Heroides* [Tusculani, 1538], sig. H3. Courtesy of the Henry E. Huntington Library and Art Gallery, San Marino,
California.

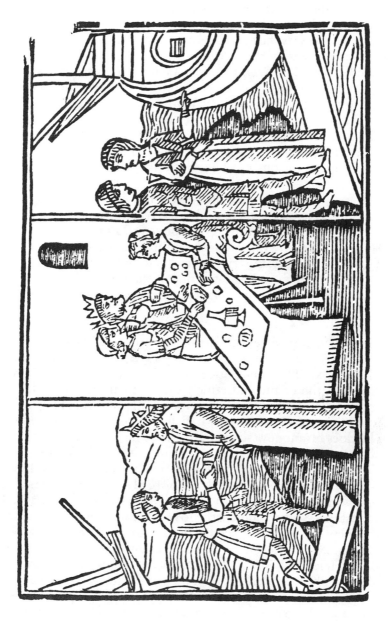

PLATE 7. "Paris Helenae," *Heroides* (Venice, 1542), sig. K3. Courtesy of the Henry E. Huntington Library and Art Gallery, San Marino, California.

The result of Spenser's revision is, then, a "second Helen,"[19] "Empoisned . . . with privy lust," who is a perfect match for Paridell: "Ne was she ignoraunt of that lewd lore, / But in his eye his meaning wisely red, / And with the like him answerd evermore" (III.ix.28). While Ovid's Helen records a narrative of discourtesy on the part of an ungrateful guest in the household of a gracious king,[20] Spenser's Helen is not a reproachful narrator, but held in reproach *by* the narrator for overtly planning, not only how to "Cocquold" Malbecco, but ("As *Hellene*, when she saw aloft appear / The *Trojane* flames" [III.x.12]) how to rob him as well. From the outset, she is both proficient and "prophane":

> Now *Bacchus* fruit out of the silver plate
> He on the table dasht, as overthrowne,
> Or of the fruitfull liquor overflowne,
> And by the dauncing bubbles did divine,
> Or therein write to let his love be showne;
> Which well she red out of the learned line,
> A sacrament prophane in mistery of wine.
>
> (III.ix.30)

Critics have noticed eucharistic overtones of this passage.[21] We now know that Ben Jonson glosses Spenser's "streame of Balme" (I.xi.48) as "The Euch[arist],"[22] but surely the emphasis here is on the comic and ethical rather than sacramental. Malbecco may be possessive, but it does not follow that Hellenore is therefore free from reproach. If he is flawed in regarding his wife as he does his money, so is Hellenore in her avarice unlike Helen and more like Jessica, who makes off with Shylock's money.

Thus, whereas Ovid's Helen claims her innocence in having resisted the rape by Theseus, Hellenore plays Love's games as she has before ("Ne was she ignoraunt"; "Which well she red"). To suggest that Spenser indicts the lovers for violating the Christian sacrament of marriage seems to me to overlook the grossly unaesthetic figuration of Malbecco embracing Hellenore.[23] Ovid's Helen makes no sexual complaint about her husband; and unlike Malbecco, Menelaus is a king. For that matter, the entire panoply of associations of the Paris story is, in Spenser's revision, radically reduced.[24] Hospitality extended by a head of state is transformed to incivility to travellers on the part of an aging, miserly head of household, who possesses, not a crown and the daughter of Zeus, but a castle and a "lovely lasse" whom he "keeps" along with his other possessions in desperate isolation. The contrast is between the epic Rape of Helen and the comic Rape of Hellenore. Unlike Menelaus, rather than pursuing the errant couple in a heroic rescue attempt, Malbecco follows lamely, only to suffer the self-inflicted wound ("and eke himselfe torment" [III.x.3]) of voyeurism: the miser watches others spend his "mucky pelfe."

II

We have seen that Paridell, Parius, and Paris are—all—exiles from their "native soile." But where is the "native soile" from which their ancient line was exiled? The answer lies in the Ovidian tradition and in Spenser's recasting of it. In the *Heroides*, Oenone writes to her erstwhile lover and mate "from *Ida*" (sig. D2^v), a *locus amoenus* which she recalls to his memory: the flocks, the groves, their "homely bed" on "simple stacks of strawe" (sig. D3). She wants him to see that this rural paradise of licit love is better than the world he has chosen to enjoy with Helen. Illustrators of the *Heroides* often depicted this aspect of the conflict in her narrative by apposition between a *locus amoenus*, on the one hand, and, on the other, scenes of court or battlefield.

For example, in three contiguous panels of the 1542 *Heroides* (Plate 8), we see, on the left, Oenone and Paris. Beyond, a forest may be seen, and to the right, a mountain. In the middle panel, trees fill the horizon, and in the foreground, Paris herds cattle. The panel to the right depicts the Judgment of Paris. Of the goddesses (whose nudity renders Oenone's modesty the more apparent), Venus, the most visible, faces Paris, pointing as if to demand the prize. In contrast, even though "Epistle XV" is written by Paris, the accompanying illustration (Plate 7) seems to emphasize his least admirable traits. He reminds Helen that his love for her carries high auspices ("no / small God doth ayde my case" [sig. L4]), which fact effectively exculpates him from blame. Thus Paris presents himself as the victim of his family background, of Hecuba's dream, and of Mercury (who made him "Judge of formes" [sig. L6]). Further, Paris advances a self-serving version of the Judgment itself, which proceeded as a contest between "powre or vertue," until Venus offered him "*Ledas* dearling" (sig. L6^v). Even his deforestation of the slopes

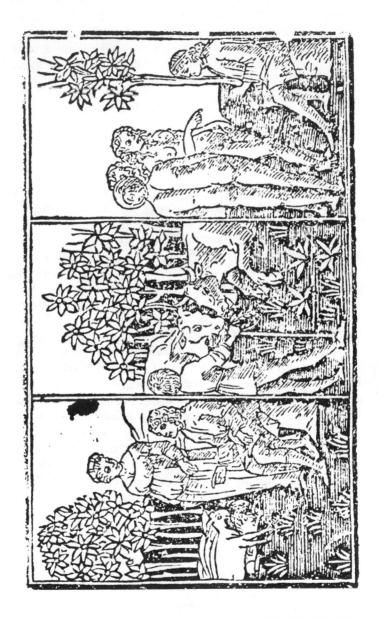

PLATE 8. "Oenone Paridi," *Heroides* (Venice, 1542), sig. D2. Courtesy of the Henry E. Huntington Library and Art Gallery, San Marino, California.

of Ida for lumber to build a ship (the bow of which frames the three tableaux depicting "Paris to Helen") fits his persuasive definition of the causes behind the Rape of Helen. To the left, Menelaus greets Paris as he descends the gangplank. On the right, accompanied by Paris, Helen (pointing as if with hesitation) ascends the same plank. Linking the two maritime scenes is a long table, where Paris is entertained by Menelaus and Helen. The viewer knows that these scenes represent an egregious violation of the laws of God and man. Indeed, Paris himself admits that Menelaus is a gracious host: "Thy husbande tooke mee guest, / with whome I harbourde thoe: / And not without the Gods advise / he practisde that I knowe' (sig. L8).

Turning again to *The Faerie Queene*, we see that Paridell's quest resembles Calidore' s "Great travell" (VI. ix.2) before "he pursew'd the chace" (VI.ix.5) into Pastorella's valley, which rustic retreat, in turn, is reminiscent of the Idaean region enjoyed by the youthful Paris and Oenone. Indeed, Spenser explicitly associates this *locus amoenus* with the landscape depicted in the *Heroides*. For when it appears that Pastorella prefers "*Colins* carolings" to Calidore' s "courteous guize" (VI.ix.35) , the knight ("doffing his bright armes") refashions himself as "*Phrygian Paris* by *Plexippus* brooke, / When he the love of fayre *Oenone* sought, / What time the golden apple was unto him brought" (VI.ix.36). Changing clothes in an effort to ingratiate himself with Pastorella, Calidore dis["guizes"] himself as Paris *before* his Judgment of the Goddesses and his separation from Oenone. As juxtaposition of the two tryptiches (Plates 7 and 8) suggests, we have two Parises, one a simple, active, loving shepherd and husband, the other an idle, duplicitous courtier and guest. Further, these two characters in contrasting landscapes with different preoccupations are separated by a scene of the Judgment.

The narratives of Ovid and Spenser employ parallel figures: Calidore/Paris, Pastorella/Oenone. Pastorella belongs to a world—like Oenone's—untrammelled by change. Before Calidore came along, young men had tried unceasingly and unsuccessfully to obtain her love. Yet she retains her innocence, and, until the Judgment, so does Paris. In a reversal of the Paris story, Calidore enters this *locus amoenus* as an experienced interloper. It is in frustration that he tries to fabricate a personality appropriate to the place and to his suit of Pastorella. In the context of the contrasts developed in the work, Calidore sees in her the outward signs of innocence, which overwhelm him ("Caught like the bird" [VI.ix.11]). It turns out that, like Paris, Pastorella too was raised by shepherds, after having been abandoned by her family. It is in the context of the clash between court and country that Calidore's blazon to the happy life can be seen as implacably repudiating his own vocation and commitment: "How much (sayd he) more happie is the state, / In which ye father here doe dwell at ease, / Leading a life so free and fortunate, / From all the tempests of these worldly seas . . ." (VI.ix.19). In this lovely *beatus ille* passage, Calidore recognizes a plurality of "states" of which that signified by his armor is less "free and fortunate." But his theme has poetic implications, for knights and epic go hand in hand. Epic is about "warres, and wreckes, and wicked enmitie" (line 6), not "felicitie" (line 9). Thus, long before he doffs his Troynovant wardrobe, Calidore rejects the claims of epic and self. It follows that Pastorella's world is at odds, also, with that of Gloriana.

In this context, Calidore's sudden infatuation with the trappings of pastoral reflects more than uneasiness with the values of knighthood, though the values of Gloriana's court are hard to separate from the martial arts. It is a case of Calidore's yearning for alternatives excluded by his calling and quest. When two worlds—one of innocence, the other of experience—collide, experience wins. But, as we shall see, it wins only a Pyrrhic victory. Calidore's courtliness includes a number of associated skills. He has learned, as good courtiers should, "all kind courtesies" (VI.ix.34) to capture a young lady's affection. Thus, when the standard fare fails (and Pastorella still prefers the local hero, Colin Clout), he knows enough to put on the trappings of rusticity and innocence. And the narrator knows that to look like Colin, Calidore must look like Colin's original: Paris before the Judgment.

To say that the Renaissance saw in the young Paris all that was good and beautiful in man untouched and unsophisticated by cities is to underestimate the power of the myth. From Homer on, sources agree on his surpassing good looks, but in the High Renaissance his beauty prior to the fatal arbitration on Mount Ida lent itself to philosophical idealization. The great fresco ceiling of the Farnese Gallery is a case in point. Here, Annibale Carracci depicts Paris in his unspoiled perfection (Plate 9): the ideal rustic, seated in an arcadian landscape, with no evidence of the Judgment to be seen. Part of a larger allegorical expression, Carracci's

PLATE 9. Annibale Carracci, *Mercury and Paris* (1597–98). Gallery, Rome. Courtesy of Archivi Alinari.

fresco works by carefully balanced appositions. Thus, prelap-sarian Paris is neatly juxtaposed against Pan and Diana (Plate 10), achieving, as John Rupert Martin observes, a contrast between upward and downward movements between earth and heaven.[25]

According to tradition, this ideal Paris was transformed, but by events not wholly in his control.[26] Jupiter named him arbiter of beauty because, as a shepherd, he was unspoiled, but his vocation came about when, motivated by Priam's fear of the prophecies of ruin that Paris would bring to Troy, Hecuba placed him in the care of shepherds in the region of Mount Ida.[27] Further, there would have been no Judgment of the Goddesses on Ida had Jupiter been willing to risk offending two of the goddesses by resolving the dispute himself; nor would there have been any dispute in the first place had Peleus and Thetis not offended Ate by excluding her from the wedding feast. As we see in Joachim Wtewael's fascinating treatment of the subject (Plate 11), that Bacchic celebration, Ate's retribution, and the Judgment of Paris are inextricably intertwined. In this context, rustic inno-cence, tenuous at best, is swept away by circumstances. And what is true of innocence is true also of the Fall. As Paris protests in letters to both Helen and Oenone (in the Renaissance, Aulus Sabinus's "Paris to Oenone" was usually printed with Ovid's *Heroides*), from the beginning, events were out of his control.

But the shepherd's fate—Ate's "Fatum Troie" in Peele's *Ar-aynement of Paris* (1584)—results from a specific Fall. Thus, in *The Faerie Queene* as in Peele's *Araynement*, Ate's "fatall frute"—the apple that "partiall *Paris* dempt it *Venus* dew" (II.vii.55)—fetched from the golden tree of Proserpine, represents an intricately-woven cluster of associations: pagan Hades, Chris-tian Hell, Garden of Hesperides, Mount Ida. By extension, Guyon's "deadly fit" (II.vii.66) resembles impairments suffered by Paris after his experience with the golden apple. Tantalus, Pilate, and Paris are all linked (II.vii.63) with the fruit of Proser-pine's Tree and the golden apple from the Garden of Hesperides—all "damned soules" and figures of the Fall—of Troy and of man.

Because of his fall from innocence into experience, then, Paris is a countertype as well as a type of the shepherd. This dialectic explains why, in the "Julye" eclogue, Spenser juxtaposes Paris and "the first shepheard," Abel (in the literal, historical sense of the term [line 127]) and Christ (in the figurative, allegorical sense of high priest).[28] In contrast to the true shepherd, Paris was a self-

PLATE 10. Annibale Carracci, *Pan and Diana* (1597–98). Farnese Gallery, Rome. Courtesy of Archivi Alinari.

PLATE 11. Joachim Wtewael, *The Judgment of Paris*. Courtesy of the
National Gallery, London.

willed exile from the pastor's life. We cannot miss the proleptic quality of the elegaic motif here, which is echoed almost verbatim in the "December" eclogue, as the speaker reminisces about the cost of Paris's love for Helen: "But nothing such thilk shephearde was, / whom *Ida* hyll dyd beare, / That left hys flocke, to fetch a lasse, / whose love he bought to deare . . ." (lines 145–48).

A glance at the iconography of Ate's golden apple may help here.[29] Noting that the ball in Peele's *Araynement* is *"trundled . . . into place,"*[30] R. Mark Benbow suggests that the ball may be "too large to be carried" (III, 115). Although it has an ordinary "Rynde" with an ordinary variant of the usual inscription ("PULCHERIMAE"), the "golden Ball" in Richard Barnfield's *Cynthia* is likewise "trindled from above"[31] by Juno, and in Peele's play, just as, earlier, Ate (*"cum aureo pomo"* [III, 65]) carries it offstage, Juno later *"taketh the ball up"* before the three goddesses read the inscription: *"Detur Pulcherrimae"* (p. 78). Although "trundle" is probably more or less synonymous with "roll along a surface" in these contexts, the idea seems to be that, after the storm, Peele's Ate appears onstage and rolls rather than throws the ball among the goddesses—presumably, toward Juno.

The importance of this moment is in accord with the emphatic doubling of the apple's delivery in many Renaissance representations. In the lovely painting of *The Judgment of Paris* by the Master of the Argonaut panels, for instance (Plate 12), a single tree separates two asymmetrically designed spaces. To the left, Venus holds the ball, pointing to herself, as Juno appears to remonstrate. Zeus points toward the other scene, where Paris sits (surrounded by trees, a dog [a symbol of Mercury], and the animals in his charge), handing the globe to Venus. The balls bear markings, as if inscribed with text (as on the left) or (right) a zodiacal configuration. In perhaps the most famous *Judgment of Paris* of all (Plate 13), Rubens depicts Discord in the clouds— apple held aloft—while beneath her Mercury presents the golden apple to Paris. Again, Joachim Wtewael's magnificent *Judgment of Paris* (Plate 11) represents two dramatic delivery scenes.[32] On the left, we see Paris, dressed as a shepherd, receiving the apple, while the goddesses look on. But on the right and slightly in the background, Wtewael depicts the earlier episode at the wedding feast of Peleus and Thetis. Thus, as the guests celebrate the nuptials of Peleus and Thetis, the excluded deity descends with

PLATE 12. The Master of the Argonaut Panels, *The Judgment of Paris* (*c.* 1480). Courtesy of the Fogg Art Museum, Harvard University.

PLATE 13. Peter Rubens, *The Judgment of Paris* (1632–35). Courtesy of the National Gallery, London.

the apple in her hand—to "trindle" it into the one place most likely to wreak vengeance. among the three goddesses with the strongest claims on Jupiter.

In this iconographic context the globe, so vindictively introduced, is itself a richly metaphoric figure. To an audience accustomed to representations and explanations of the *"sphaera,"* Ate's golden ball signifies the world,[33] which is how the figure is used in the Cranach *Judgment* in the Wallraf-Richartz Museum (Plate 14), and how it is used in the monogrammist HE's variation on the theme, *Queen Elizabeth and the three Goddesses* (1569).[34] In Spenser's mythology, this golden apple (Augustine's pun on *malo* [apple/misery] *aureo* is relevant here), brought from Proserpine's tree, melds with that taken by Atalanta from the Garden of Hesperides. To eat of this fruit of the Judgment is to change the world forever. Thus, Paris exchanges his shepherd's weeds for a warrior's armor. Spenser's version reverses the procedure. Sources do vary on how Paris returned to the civilized world. But they agree on the promise made by Venus—that Paris would enjoy the love of Helen; the story soon places Paris in the household of Menelaus, far from the unspoiled region of Mount Ida, far from the natural ease of his licit love under the order of marriage, but close to the world of time and consequences, close to the alternatives of love and war that we associate with epic.

Comparison between two of the nearly dozen canvasses painted by Lucas Cranach on the Judgment of Paris may help clarify this point. At first glance, the St. Louis Art Museum *Judgment* (Plate 1) has much in common with ten other Cranach paintings of the subject, including the Wallraf-Richartz Museum *Judgment* (Plate 14). Both pictures suggest, as does the Seattle Art Museum version (Plate 2), acquaintance with Guido's account of the Judgment of Paris as transpiring in a dream.[35] Thus, in all three paintings, Mercury holds the globe for which the goddesses contend. The inscription in the Cologne painting (Plate 14) seems to suggest—not one of the variations usually inscribed ("*Detur Pulcherimae*"; "That appul was with gold begrave, / And sayd the fayrest it shuld have")—but "MORT" (Plate 15). For Spenser, the nexus of tree, apple, and Fall from a primitive, idyllic state of innocence, might well have suggested just such a cluster of associations as we find in Barnfield's description of Paris: "Wrapt in the Mantle of eternall Night . . . And under him, awayting for his fall, / Sat Shame, here Death, and there sat fell Despight."[36]

PLATE 14. Lucas Cranach, *The Judgment of Paris* (*c.* 1512–14). Courtesy of the Wallraf-Richartz Museum, Cologne.

PLATE 15. Detail of Plate 14.

III

It appears, then, that Calidore's victory as the "Phrygian swayne" is one of literary culture. Embodying as he does the "greatest grace" in Gloriana's court, he knows the multifarious techniques of pleasing others: "he could wisely use, and well apply" (VI.i.3) the elements of "gracious speach" and "manners mylde" (VI.i.2) that courtly education imparted. He is the fictive representation of values, including literary knowledge, defended in such works as della Casa's *Art of Civill Conversation*. Because of his reading Calidore knows how to look and act like Paris in his pre-Judgment state. Only in that condition was Paris a shepherd and poet, creator and subject of pastoral: a naive and natural singer of songs. Accordingly, in imitating Paris, Calidore transforms himself into a Colin Clout *manqué*.

Thus, literary sophistication is also a disguise. Calidore's efforts to compete with Colin are among the many instances of the male impulse to pursue or otherwise seek to possess Florimell or her surrogate of the narrative moment. Although he does not actually chase Pastorella, like Paridell and the Foster, Calidore is impelled—with all males—toward feminine beauty. In Spenser, this male characteristic is, at one level, undifferentiated. Thus, Calidore's desire for Pastorella gives him one thing—perhaps the only thing—in common with the local swains ("eke many a one / Burnt in her love" [VI.ix.10]). At other levels, differences, which are more than cosmetic, remain. For instance, the elegant means by which Calidore-as-Paris ingratiates himself with Pastorella reflect the social abyss between the common folk and a knight-errant of Gloriana's court.

In the context of the endless process "eternall fate / Ordained hath" (III.vi.32) in "the first seminarie" (III.vi.30) of "dame Nature," the foregoing remark should not be taken pejoratively. Indeed, such a construction would reflect too great an emphasis on moral virtue as defined by nineteenth- and twentieth-century formulae, which tend to erode the boundary between useful and pernicious deception. And yet it is just such an ethical distinction that Spenser fictionalizes and defends in the Priscilla episode. Comparison between the two narratives suggests that, in the latter case, Calidore's behavior is neither high-minded nor base, but human, male, and, like the energies generated within the "*Gardin of Adonis*," ordained: "That substance is eterne, and bideth so, / Ne when the life decayes, and forme does fade, / Doth it consume, and into nothing go, / But chaunged is, and often altred to and fro" (III.vi.37). Calidore tries every way he knows to succeed where local suitors have failed, even playing the part of a shepherd and writing songs, and yet he fails to evoke the desired response. A prudish reading of this narrative must not avert attention from the fact that Calidore's dilemma is at once poetic *and* male. If he supplants Colin in Pastorella's affections, he gets Pastorella—all of her—body as well as soul. But he will have neither a poetic model to emulate nor a worthy competitor with whom to share Pastorella's affection.

This is clearly a poetic problem. In order for Calidore's suit to succeed, he must use his courtly repertoire in a new way. Merely dressing or singing a part will not do; he must *be* a poet, which means that he must not appear to be himself, a hero on an epic quest. As Spenser presents Calidore presenting himself in "His layes" as well as in "his loves [and] his lookes" (VI.ix.35), he fictionalizes a poetic no less than an ethical dilemma. Were Pastorella merely attractive—or as unsophisticated as Kathleen Williams thinks—Calidore would confront a different problem with different possibly helpful alternatives. Trial and error might well match "goodly manners" and "civill conversation" (VI.i.1) to the particular moment in such a way that the courtier prevails where rustics faltered. But Pastorella happens to be a literary critic. In this one area her taste for "heightened simplicities" (Williams, p. 199) has been determined by "heightened" sophistication of her experience with "*Colins* carolings." Calidore understands this. Thus, when he disguises himself as "*Phrygian Paris*" before the Judgment he aims to match, not Coridon and the shepherds (whose collective "art of simplicity" has gotten them nowhere with Pastorella), but Colin. Indeed, by giving the "garlond," "crowne," and place in the ring to Coridon, Calidore reminds everyone of Colin's superiority to Coridon, thus, courteously justifying his own condescension toward the more humble competitor. True courtier that he is, Calidore would compete only against a master singer.

Spenser critics are indebted to Northrop Frye and Kathleen Williams for their shared vision of the coherence of *The Faerie Queene*.[37] And yet, insofar as their view of wholeness idealizes Calidore, Colin, the Mount Acidale episode, and the conception of pastoral—insofar as it sees in the dance of the nymphs and Graces an image of circular perfection and completion in the larger narrative—it distorts Spenser's complex resolution and sometimes even more complex non-resolution of disparate motifs. The textual and contextual evidence suggests disruption no less than harmony. If we look to the Ovidian context to which Spenser owes the most here, the relevant images and associations suggest, not love and art, but resentment and loss. For when postlapsarian Paris abandoned Oenone to gain renown as an unconstant lover, he left behind him not only his wife, but his poetry.

In the Renaissance, music and poetry were as much a part of the Paris tradition as were his adultery and good looks. For instance, in the *Heroides*, Paris is a "gentle *Phrygian* swain" used to playing "a sweet, though rurall strain" on his country "Pipes." Similarly, in Coluthus's *Helenae raptus*, before the Judgment Paris spent much of his time wrapt in song, praising Pan and Hermes.[38] Again, in T[homas] H[eywood]'s *Oenone and Paris* (1594), the speaker declares that Paris in his early days on Mount Ida used "to chaunt a ryme."[39] Indeed, in this Renaissance epyllion, which is largely drawn on Ovid's *Heroides*, Oenone remembers Paris accompanying her "With bagpypes shrill and oken quills contented" (p. 23) as she danced and sang. Not only was he Oenone's legitimate spouse, but he was a musician, playing his "rurall musicke" on "boxen pypes and countrey Tamburines" (p. 25), a playmate of "Faunus and olde Sylvanus." The sense that she would recall to his mind is one of serenity and song: "And every shepheardes swayne will tune his ode: / And more then these, to welcome thy abode" (p. 26).

As in Heywood's version of Ovid's "Oenone to Paris," so in Spenser's revision of the nymph's complaint, themes of love and poetry meld, and as they meld, images and figures from various contexts and from different segments of the same narrative are brought together, eliciting thematic developments and tonal shifts which may elude a modern reader. For instance, on its surface, the singing-match in the "August" eclogue might seem a frivolous, improbable setting for Colin's lament, which is replete with figures of melancholy and loss: "wastefull woodes," "tricklinge teares," "carefull cryes," "wild woddes" (lines 151–66). Not only are the nights full of ghastly sounds, but Colin's lyrics are so relentlessly sad that they make Willye's witty rejoinder to Perigot's claim (that he can find no "salve for [his] sore [line 104]) ridiculous by comparison.

The Spenser Variorum credits W. L. Renwick with first pointing out Willye's playful echo from Ovid's "Oenone to Paris": "Woes me, that love no pow'rfull hearb can cure!"[40] And yet in that Ovidian context Spenser's echo and the transition from singing-match to love complaint are neither frivolous nor inappropriate. By invoking that context Spenser accomplishes more than an antique echo from the literary past, more even than mere recollection of Oenone's recriminations against Paris for the pain a constant lover must endure. His more complex and intense effects result from the fact that Spenser reverses the Ovidian situation completely. In the "August" eclogue it is the shepherd and lapsed poet—Colin as Paris—who does the complaining. And, complex though it may be, Colin's lament lacks the ethos of Oenone's letter, which upbraids Paris with the many reasons why his love belongs, by right, not to Helen, but to her. In contrast, Colin pledges to waste away until death. Spenser does echo the line from *Heroides*, but he does so to intensify his theme of poetic folly by suggesting this question: Why, after so long an ordeal, does Colin cling so hopelessly to the lone theme and poetic type of his unrequited love for Rosalind? As Spenser's readers would know, the answer to that question lies in a significant omission. Nowhere in the "August" eclogue—in fact, nowhere in *The Shepheardes Calender*—do we find reference to any claim apposite to Oenone's: that is, of Colin's *right* to Rosalind's love.[41] Even so—propriety of claim notwithstanding—Colin politely and poetically threatens to kill himself.

If this echo from Ovid's *Heroides* meant anything to Spenser's readers, it probably conveyed such bittersweet irony. The more irrational Colin's impulse seems to be—the less proportion there exists between his feeling for Rosalind and hers for him—the greater the contrast between his manufactured grief and Oenone's sense of the "undeserved wrongs" (sig. D2ᵛ) done to her. At least from Oenone's point of view, the Paris who has left her cannot serve as a model for a decent lover—or poet—to emulate. Not only did he forget that she was his "approved wyfe" (sig. D5), helpful and loyal during his early years of exile, but that she was in every way, including rank, his—and Helen's—superior. They were, after all, mere mortals, while she (like Venus herself) was born "the offspring of a flood" (sig. D2ᵛ). So when Paris abandoned her, he separated himself, not only from his word, but from the natural order: "When pastor

Paris shall revolte / and *Oenons* love forgoe: / Then *Xanthus* waters shall recoile, / and to their Fountaynes floe" (sig. D3^v).

As a "Pegasian Nymph," Oenone was by name and reputation associated with Mount Ida and the Helicon, and so with poetic inspiration.[42] Thus, by recalling his pledge of faithfulness, Oenone also characterizes the place of her lover's poetic word in the scheme of things. By leaving her, Paris alters the operations of the world, which, in the context of Mount Ida and the waters of Helicon, suggests that he has turned away from poetry and music. As Oenone interprets events, Paris turns, not to love, but to violence. It is important for Paris to remember that it was she and not Helen who was beloved of Apollo, "The builder of Troy,"[43] not its destroyer. Apollo, "so famed for his lyre," was, as mythographers reminded Renaissance readers, "the head or guide of the Muses,"[44] whom Paris abandoned for the devices and fate of war.

It is this ligature between unrequited love and failed minstrelsy that fuses the singing-match and Colin's "August" lament. It is evident from the outset that Perigot has suffered in ways linked—from the "Januarye" eclogue on—to Colin's career. As the calendar structure suggests, Perigot is, as Colin soon will be, in the December of life. Though less obvious than that between Cuddie and Colin, the association between the two singers is still the central point of fusion between the two parts of the eclogue. Recurrence of the conflict between youth and age, the apparent theme of the prelude to the singing-match, masks a deeper tension in both parts of the eclogue between the demands of love and those of art. Although in judging the contest Cuddie finds that Perigot's performance "Little lacketh . . . of the best" (1. 127), Willye taunts Perigot as an arthritic "has-been." It is a melancholy fact of this Spenserian "life" that Willye thinks of poetry and youth as inextricably connected. He may be tactless and brash, but intuitively he "knows"—and Spenser seems to let his knowing go unchallenged—that poetic composition, part of "dame Nature's" endlessly turning wheel of life, is coterminous with a youthful capacity to make love.

Spenser's daring thematic innovation is evident if we compare the "August" eclogue with the singing-matches in Theocritus and Virgil, where the contests emanate from disagreements not at all like those between Perigot and Willye. In Theocritus (Idyll 5), after mutual accusations of thievery, a goatherd (Comatus) and a shepherd (Lacon) agree to wager a kid and a lamb to resolve

their quarrel; Morson gives the lamb to Comatus, requesting
that a platetul be sent to him in due course. In Virgil (Eclogue 3),
after arguing about the ownership of a goat, Menalcas and Damoetas turn to wrangle over their singing skills. Damoetas wants
to risk a cow on his talents; pleading poverty, Menalcas puts up
"two beechen cups" ("*pocula ponam / fagina*" [lines 36–37]). Palemon calls the match a draw. In other words, the singing-
matches to which the "Argument" draws attention ("*made in
imitation of that in Theocritus* [and] *Virgile*") end with the settled
judgments of Morson and Palemon. In contrast to these supposed models, Spenser's singing-match is not so much ended as
held in abeyance by Cuddie's decision. By decreeing an "enter-
chaunge of gyfts," Cuddie opts for a tie. But where Theocritus'
Idyll 5 and Virgil's Eclogue 3 stop, the "August" eclogue begins
anew, as Cuddie changes the rules of the game by declaring a
non-participant to be the winner of the contest:

> But tell me shepherds, should it not yshend
> Your roundels fresh, to heare a doolefull verse
> Of Rosalend (who knowes not Rosalend?)
> That Colin made, ylke can I you rehearse.
>   (lines 139–42)

It is one thing to point out that Willye's "undersongs" put him at
a disadvantage, though with the best of wills this cannot be
regarded as high praise. But in this announcement (thinly disguised as a request) Cuddie goes beyond the restraints of that
tactful judgment to suggest that the singing-match had only
piqued a cultivated appetite for more satisfying poetic fare. It is
clear that Cuddie's critical opinion touches on Colin's poetic
ambition as well as on his poetic skills. Colin Clout's lyrics
satisfy more discriminating tastes because his "doolefull verse,"
with its richer elegaic tone, typically put more facile "roundels"
to shame ("yshend": *OED*). Thus, Cuddie affirms the Renaissance hierarchy of poetic forms and Colin's relative skill in
mastering the superior of the two forms considered in this extended format of the singing-match.

Of course, Cuddie's remark is double-edged, for by now
every country piper knows that, although Colin has excelled the
locals by mastering the lover's lament, he has not improved upon
it. Nor has he developed his talent by undertaking more demanding forms. Bluntly, Colin would not have to work very

hard to beat Perigot, who, with his family preoccupations, only
marginally betters sing-song Willye. Indeed, Colin's success in
one form is the signal instance of his ruin as a poet. As promised
(or threatened) in the "June" eclogue, "carefull *Colin*" (line 113)
is interested in one and only one motif, one and only one vocation, one and only one poetic kind:

> Nought weigh I, who my song doth prayse or blame,
> Ne strive to winne renowne, or passe the rest . . .
> I wote my rimes bene rough, and rudely drest:
> The fytter they, my carefull case to frame:
> Enough is me to paint out my unrest,
> And poore my piteous plaints out in the same.
>
> (lines 73–80)

Like the Paris of Ovid, Smyrnaeus, and Coluthus, Colin proposes to give his all—youth and age, body and soul, service and
craft—to Love. So, he is the figure linking themes of sexuality
and poetic composition, underlying preoccupations of the "August" eclogue. Although the speaker in "August"'s "Argument" airily refers to Theocritus and Virgil, the eclogue actually
begins with Willye's insulting challenge to a singing-match and
Perigot's subsequent confession of his current poetic incapacity.
To the extent that Perigot does not deny Willye's opinion of old
age (choosing, if equivocally, to blame his reticence on Love,
whose mischief he knows both as parent and sometime lover),
the more experienced poet reflects darkly on Colin's future as a
poet.

Responses to Cuddie's judgment further underline this generational conflict. Conceding that Willye had to make do with the
more restrictive "undersongs," Perigot is satisfied with Cuddie's
ruling. On the other hand, Willye remains in a combative mood,
likening the match to the Judgment of Paris: "Never dempt more
right of beautye I weene, / The shepheard of *Ida*, that judged
beauties Queene" (lines 137–38). The relevance of this allusion to
the woodcut for "August" (Plate 16) and for the "August"
eclogue itself has not, I think, been fully explained. The most
ambitious treatment of the relation between the woodcuts and
the text of Spenser's pastoral, generally, is Ruth Samson Luborsky's "The Illustrations to *The Shepheardes Calender*."[45] In
this learned essay Luborsky comments on "the narrative mode"
of the "August" woodcut: "Two events are shown: the singing

PLATE 16. "August," *The Shepheardes Calender* (1579), sig. H3v. Courtesy of the Henry E. Huntington and Art Gallery, San Marino, California.

match with its actors and prizes, and a subject mentioned in the contest" (pp. 35–36). Actually, as Luborsky herself implies, the illustration is divided into three parts, each represented on a different plane. Participants in the singing–match appear on a rectangular plateau, the singers with their arms outstretched. Cuddie accompanies them on an oboe-like instrument. In the foreground are the spotted sheep and mazer. A stand of trees providing the backdrop to the scene lends a sense of leisure appropriate to pastoral. As we have seen, this is a setting familiar in illustrations of the Judgment of Paris. At a distance, on land sloping upwards, we see men working the harvest. Theirs is a world presumably at some remove from the singing-match. The workers seem as oblivious to the singers as the singers are to occupations of harvest-time. The worlds of pastoral and georgic may be mutually dependent in basic ways, but here activities of work and composition seem only remotely connected. Indeed, except for the reference to the mazer (fit for "any harvest Queene" [line 37]), the text of the "August" eclogue makes no reference whatsoever to harvesters or harvest. In fact, the poem moves ever further from such practical problems as readers might associate with farmers to those of the gifted poet in love.

Seeming if anything even more out of place, on a third, intermediate rise, stands a woman. Her left arm extends toward the scene of competition. In her left hand she holds a round object, which appears to bear a marking (Plate 17). I am aware that Luborsky sees this woman is a "conventional" representation of Virgo, similar that found in Le grant kalendrier (Plate 18). But comparison between Plates 17 and 18 shows that the substance of the zodiacal representation in Le grant kalendrier is concentrated in the background—the upper left corner, to be exact—of the August cut. In Le grant kalendrier, as in The Kalender of Shepherdes, Virgo bears a stalk.[46] In the latter example, Virgo is seated among clumps of foliage, which signify the fructification on which harvest depends. It may be, as Luborsky suggests, that the designer of the cut in Spenser's work was told: "copy 'Bellibone' from Le grant kalendrier" (p. 36); but, if so, the designer made one important modification: Virgo is carrying a stalk, though "bouncing Bellibone" is not. In The Shepheardes Calender, the harvesters behind Bellibone work the field, but Bellibone seems no more mindful of them than are the participants in the singing-match. Further, we notice that "Bellibone" has, as

PLATE 17. Detail of Plate 16.

August

PLATE 18. "Aoust." *Le grant kalendrier et compost des bergiers avecq leur astrologie* [Paris, n.d.], fol. 9ᵛ. Courtesy of the Henry E. Huntington Library and Art Gallery, San Marino, California.

Virgo in both representations does not, a rounded object in her hand. The detail on Plate 17 reveals a difference in or on the surface of the sphere, marking a declivity at one pole of the rounded object, a declivity such as those typical of the golden apple or ball in tableaux of the Judgment of Paris, the very tableau suggested by Willye as analogous to the present competition.

Indeed, it seems that in the "August" eclogue the theme of time's passage and the proprieties of the season have melded with themes from classical singing matches *and* representations of the Judgment of Paris to invest Colin's lament with a deepening tone of inevitable defeat. Observers familiar with Renaissance illustrations of the Judgment of Paris will recognize the irony of Spenser's reversal of the situation, with "bouncing Bellibone" as the rustic inheritor of the prize. Even if, in his jaundiced outlook, Willye misses the implied imperative of the moment ("The night nigheth fast" [line 95]), time is on the wing, not just for Perigot, but for Willye and Colin as well. The gatherers are in the field; and both figuratively mark poetic work left unfinished. For as time passes and life winds down, the younger generation is poised to repeat the mistakes of its predecessors. Perigot provides a foretaste of the Colin of "December," on whose toolately wiser rhetoric of the ruinous cost ("so deare" [line 152]) of his love for Rosalind the *Calender* will close: "And thus of all my harvest hope I have / Nought reaped but a weedye crop of care . . . Soone as the chaffe should in the fan be fynd, / All was blowne away of the wavering wynd" (lines 121–26). Seasons may change, but the life-pattern of Colin's poetic career unfolds with a solemn sameness. He simply cannot get beyond the lament for unrequited love:

> Adieu delightes, that lulled me asleepe,
> Adieu my deare, whose love I bought so deare:
> Adieu my little Lambes and loved sheepe,
> Adieu ye Woodes that oft my witnesse were:
> > Adieu good *Hobbinol*, that was so true,
> > Tell *Rosalind*, her *Colin* bids her adieu.
> > > (lines 151–56)

While others perceive a conflict here between poetic generations (the new poets and their ancient models with their constraints of form and subject), Harry Berger, Jr. observes that the *puer senex* motif in *The Shepheardes Calender* reflects two poetic value systems, one of youth, the other of age.[47] Thus, paradoxically, Thenot seems to grow younger as Colin grows older: son becomes father, eternal return, and so on. And yet, I would argue, although'time passes, Colin's song stays the same. Indeed, the contrast between Perigot and Colin—and Berger's own sense of "the 'paradise principle'"—points away from dialectical movements, one toward the grave and the other toward the cradle. Of this generational conflict, and of the place of poetry and love in the Spenserian scheme of things, it must be said that Perigot, talented or not, does in fact generate, while Colin does not. And in a poem in which the governing figure of seasonal progress suggests an endless continuum of birth, life, and death, this difference bears structural weight.

Berger's closing remarks link Colin's plight with Spenser's description of the "*Gardin of Adonis,*" an association which, again, suggests a rectilinear progress. In the context of the Paris fable, such a movement presents Colin as a fallen shepherd and poet, who separates himself from the source of poetic *and* human generation. Perigot is, as Colin is not, a father. But in *The Faerie Queene*, the same subtext is rendered in a different way. Before the Fall, Paris fathers a son; poetic composition and biological generation are intertwined in Spenser's cosmic poetics. Paris fell from the timeless regions of Ida into history, from pastoral creator into epic subject, and his voice as a singer disappeared. Colin falls not only from youth into age; everybody does that. He lives his life without fathering a child (because of his immature attachment to an unobtainable woman), and, for precisely the same reason, he fails to generate the various kinds of poetry that are, in nobility, as far above the lover's complaint as the complaint is above the singing-match.

Through his interlocutor in the "August" eclogue, an aging, absent Colin wins the singing-match, but he also takes over completely to reiterate his funereal theme of "June," and thereby to foreshadow the elegiac tone of "December." But this is not a voice so different from the already aged Perigot's. Nor is it that of a fledgling poet preparing himself to "make a greater flyght." Rather, it is a proleptic glimpse of the elegies of "November" and "December"—the chosen form and voice of the pastoral poet as well as Spenser's funeral elegy to pastoral as a poetic form. As Richard Helgerson rightly observes, E. K. remains unaware of many of the poetic questions Spenser represents in

The Shepheardes Calender.[48] Unlike Colin, Spenser neither limits himself to the lover's lament nor to the multifarious possibilities even of the eclogue.

In the context that we have been discussing, Spenser's uneasiness with the limitations of the pastoral form is as evident as Cuddie's doubt about the serious purpose of the singing-match. Like the Colin of "December" and the lover of Colin's "August" lament, Perigot's old story ends in "newe" if predictable "mischaunce" (line 12). This universal tale of love and woe overwhelms generations ("Love hath misled both my younglings, and mee" [lines 17–18]) and ruins poetic careers.[49] I have argued that, besides Virgil and Theocritus, Spenser has a figurative model in mind to fit—and evoke—that gathering sense of impending doom: "Ah, Paris! . . . Then didst thou yeeld Oenone pricke and prayes, / Which now is buryed in eternall dayes."[50] Accordingly, Spenser's Colin-as-Paris is like the Paris of Book VI, who, in turn, is reminiscent of the exile from Mount Ida in *Heroides*: deprived of love, cast out from the *locus amoenus* of his youth, no longer at one with the gods of nature and the joys of poetry. The Judgment of Paris precedes his exile from the poetic environs of Ida (pastoral poetry) to the world of war epic poetry). Perhaps this sounds like a return to ethical motifs from which this argument set out to separate itself. But Paridell is not the son of Adam; nor is Colin (like the "goodly swayne" become Acrasia's plaything) enervated by lust. I think, rather, that Spenser's allegory here is only incidentally moral, and primarily aesthetic. When Paris fell, the gods gave him, not a spade, but a sword. He fell not into work (the georgic), but to war (the epic). In mortal combat Paris found the inevitable truth of Hecuba's dream and of Cassandra's prophecy. Likewise, in epic Spenser found the most compelling figuration of the consequences of sexual competition. In writing, the poet goes beyond Colin's self-pity concerning love denied to explore in cosmic scope the full power of Love, whose "substance is eterne," but whose narrative is written in the lives of the "endlesse progenie" of Venus (III. vi.30), responding to "the mightie word" of "th'Almightie lord" (III. vi.34): such sons and daughters of Venus as Paridell and Britomart. Paris was not perfect. Rather, his Judgment makes him, in his imperfection, the spiritual father of Artegall and Colin as well as of Paridell. Britomart's feelings of kinship toward Paridell show warmth, understanding, and good sense—attitudes not inappropriate to the ultimate union, with its projected progeny, of Britomart and Artegall, nor to the figurative son of the unfallen Paris—the uncompromised heir to that unspoiled poetic domain on Mount Ida: Edmund Spenser.

University of California, Riverside

NOTES

In all quotations I have regularized i/j and u/v, expanded contractions and ignored meaningless capitals and small capitals. Unless otherwise noted, all books published before 1700 bear a London imprint. For their help with revision of this essay, I am grateful to Elizabeth Story Donno, Robert F. Gleckner, Richard Helgerson, Annabel Patterson, James A. Riddell, and Thomas P. Roche, Jr.; they are not responsible for whatever faults remain. Martin C. Ridge (Head of Research, Huntington Library) and The British Academy assisted this project with a generous grant, which allowed me to spend the summer of 1988 in London, working on Spenser.

1. Cf., for instance, Edmund Malone, *The Plays and Poems of Wiliam Shakespeare*, 21 vols. (London, 1821), II, 248–49; Thomas P. Roche, Jr., *The Kindly Flame: A Study of the Third and Fourth Books of Spenser's Faerie Queene* (Princeton: Princeton University Press, 1964), esp. 63–64; and Louis Adrian Montrose, "Gifts and Reasons: The Context of Peele's *Araynement of Paris*," *ELH*, 47 (1980), 433–61.

2. For discussion of the ancient and medieval backgrounds of the tradition, see Margaret J. Ehrhart, *The Judgment of the Trojan Prince Paris in Medieval Literature* (Philadelphia: University of Pennsylvania Press, 1987), ch. 1, esp. 231n. Ehrhart's fine book appeared after I had completed this essay. Although readers will note some overlap of interests, differences in emphasis should be evident as well.

3. Numerous works shaped aspects of the Paris tradition in Spenser's time; besides Homer's *Iliad*, Virgil's *Aeneid*, and Ovid's *Heroides*, more important sources include Quintus Smyrnaeus, *The Fall of Troy* (4th cent.); Lucian, *Judgment of the Goddesses* (4th cent.); Coluthus, *Helenae Raptus* (5th cent.); Benoît de Sainte-Maure's *Roman de Troie*, especially Guido della Colonne's version, *The Destruction of Troy* (13th cent.), familiar in England through Lydgate and Malory. Major commentaries are Apollodorus, *The Library* (2nd cent.); Fulgentius, *Mythologies* (5th cent.); Bernardus Silvestris, *Commentary on the First Six Books of Virgil's Aeneid* (12th cent.); and Cristoforo Landino's allegorization of the *Aeneid* in *Camaldolese Disputations* (14th cent.).

4. See *Marsilio Ficino: The Philebus Commentary*, trans. and ed. Michael J. B. Allen (Berkeley, University of California Press, 1975), p. 482; Max J. Friedlander and Jakob Rosenberg, *The Paintings of Lucas Cranach*, rev. ed. (Ithaca: Cornell University Press, 1976), figs. 408 and 409; Oliver Rand et al., *The Age of Breugel: Netherlandish Drawings in the Sixteenth Century* (Cambridge: Cambridge University Press, 1986)), p. 181; and Ehrhart, p. 4.

5. Fabius Planciades Fulgentius, *Fulgentius the Mythographer*, trans. Sebastian Evans, rev. by Charles W. Dunn (New York: Dutton, 1958), p. 64.

6. Sallust, the Platonist, *On the Gods and the World*, trans. [T. Taylor] (London, 1793), pp. 16–17, cf. Ficino, pp. 440, 452, 454, 402.

7. Hallett Smith, *Elizabethan Poetry: A Study in Conventions, Meaning, and Expression* (Cambridge: Harvard University Press, 1952), p. 6.

8. For the "realistic" explanation of these events, see Ehrhart, ch. 1.

9. See Helmut Nickel, "*The Judgment of Paris* by Lucas Cranach the Elder: Nature, Allegory, and Alchemy," *Metropolitan Museum Journal*, 16 (1981), 117–29.

10. *The Works of Edmund Spenser: A Variorum Edition*, ed. Greenlaw, et al., 10 vols. (Baltimore: Johns Hopkins University Press, 1932–57), III.viii.44; hereafter cited in text.

11. Thomas Heywood, *Troia Britanica* (1609), p. 176. Heywood describes Paris as possessing "True proportion of a perfect lover"; cf. *Chapman's Homer*, ed. Allardyce Nicoll (Princeton: Princeton University Press, 1967), III, 61, and Virgil, *Aen.* I, 117, Loeb Classical Library, trans. H. Rushton Fairclough, 2 vols. (London: Heinemann, 1916–18); Coluthus, *The Rape of Helen*, in *Oppian, Colluthus, Tryphiodorus*, trans. A. W. Mair (London: William Heinemann, 1928), p. 561; Guillaume de Lorris and Jean de Meun, *The Romance of the Rose*, trans. Charles Dahlberg (Princeton: Princeton University Press, 1971), p. 238, and Athenaeus, *The Deipnosophists*, trans. Charles Burton Gulick, 7 vols. (Cambridge: Harvard University Press, 1951–57), I, 81.

12. *Ovid's Heroicall Epistles*, trans. Wye Saltonstall (1637), p. 105.

13. *The Heroycall Epistles of the Learned Publius Ovidius Naso . . . with Aulus Sabinus Aunsweres*, trans. George Turbervile (1567), sig. M8; unless otherwise indicated, further citations from Ovid's *Heroides* will be from this edition of Turbervile's translation.

14. The Spenser Variorum does not actually affirm Tzetzes as Spenser's source, and Tzetzes himself credits the scholiastic tradition, citing Parthenius, for the name, "Corythus" (*Lycophronis Cassandram* [Oxford, 1697], p. 44); for discussion of Parthenius's *Erotica* in this connection, see T. C. W. Stinton, *Euripides and the Judgment of Paris* (London: Society for Promotion of Hellenic Studies, 1965), p. 40; and Howard Jacobson, *Ovid's Heroides* (Princeton: Princeton University Press, 1974), p. 179n.

15. Margaret R. Scherer, *The Legends of Troy in Art and Literature* (New York: Phaidon for the Metropolitan Museum, 1963), p. 194; cf. Julius Solinus, *The excellent and pleasant work of Julius Solinus Polyhistor*, trans. Arthur Golding (1587), sig. B3; and Giovanni Boccaccio, *Genealogie* (Paris, 1531), fol. 49.

16. Cf. *The Theogony, The Works of Hesiod, Callimachus, and Theognis*, trans. Rev. J. Banks (London, 1856), p. 49; *Aen.* III, 105.

17. See Frances Yates, *Astraea: The Imperial Theme in the Sixteenth Century* (London: Routledge & Kegan Paul, 1975), p. 50; Mihoko Suzuki, "'Unfity yokt together in one teeme': Vergil and Ovid in *The Faerie Queene*, III.ix," *English Literary Renaissance*, 17 (1987), 184; and Charles Bowie Millican, *Spenser and the Table Round: A Study in the Contemporaneous Background for Spenser's Use of Arthurian Legend* (Cambridge: Harvard University Press, 1932), pp. 149n, 155n. For the view that "Neither [England nor Faery Land] is more real than the other," see Judith Dundas, *The Spider and the Bee: The Artistry of Spenser's Faerie Queene* (Urbana: University of Illinois Press, 1985), p. 197.

18. Kathleen Williams, *Spenser's World of Glass: A Reading of The Faerie Queene* (Berkeley: University of California Press, 1966), p. 121.

19. For a differing view emphasizing contexts other than *Heroides* and "the alternate Helen myth," cf. Roche, *Kindly Flame*, esp. pp. 152–62.

20. See Natale Conti, *Mythologie* (Paris, 1627), p. 656.

21. The Spenser Variorum cites Upton (III, 566), but Upton's emphasis is on social and psychological irregularities in the lovers' conduct.

22. James A. Riddell and I are preparing our transcription of Ben Jonson's copious annotations to his copy of the 1617 Folio of *The Faerie Queene*. This volume, sold in 1884, is no. 177 in David McPherson, "Ben Jonson's Library and Marginalia; An Annotated Catalogue," *Studies in Philology*, 71 (1974), 91.

23. Mihoko Suzuki touches on some of the issues raised in this section, but differences in emphasis appear. For instance, in contrast to Suzuki's claim that Paridell and Hellenore, as opposed to Britomart and Spenser, "reduce and limit themselves in merely repeating literary tradition" (p. 185), I argue that they do not repeat, but reshape, literary tradition.

24. In "The reward of Whoredome by the fall of Helen," Helen confesses: "I vertue shund, I lothd a modest mynde, / I wayd not fame, my beauty made mee blinde" (T[homas] P[roctor], *A gorgious Gallery, of gallant Inventions* [1578], sig. L1).

25. See John Rupert Martin, *The Farnese Gallery* (Princeton: Princeton University Press, 1965), pp. 86–89, 114–15.

26. The theme of determinism in the Judgment of Paris story was restated forcefully in Spenser's time by Sir J[ohn] O[gle]: "*Venus* commanded, who could hir denie?" (*The Lamentation of Troy, for the death Hector* [1594], sig. C3); the author sees Spenser as "the only *Homer* living" (sig. B2).

27. Conti recalls that Paris was given to Archelas to be delivered to Priam's shepherds on Mount Ida (p. 651); see also Hyginus, *The Myths of Hyginus*, trans. and ed. Mary Amelia Grant (Lawrence: University of Kansas Press, 1960), p. 82.

28. Frances Yates recalls that Virgil's "Messianic Eclogue" had long been held apposite to parts of Isaiah and the Canticles (p. 50); Barclay's version of Mantuan's Sixth Eclogue associates Paris with Pan, Orpheus, and "joly Tyterus," and also with Saul, Moses, David, and Christ, in that all were shepherds (Alexander Barclay, *The Eclogues of Alexander Barclay*, ed. Beatrice White, EETS no. 175 [London: Oxford University Press, 1928], p. 198).

29. No reference to a golden apple appears in Homer, but see *The Theogony*, p. 13; and Lucius Apuleius, *The Golden Ass*, trans. W. Adlington, rev. S. Gaselee (London: William Heinemann, 1915), pp. 527, 531, 533; and *Claudian*, trans. Maurice Platnauer, Loeb Classical Library, 2 vols. (London: William Heinemann, 1922), II, 251.

30. George Peele, *The Dramatic Works of George Peele*, ed., R. Mark Benbow et al., 3 vols. (New Haven: Yale University Press, 1970), III, 77, hereafter cited in text.

31. Richard Barnfield, *Cynthia. With Certaine Sonnets, and the Legend of Cassandra* (1595), sig. B3.

32. Cf. *The Cleveland Museum of Art Bulletin*, 72 (April 1985), 190 for another Wtewael *Judgment of Paris* emphasizing rusticity of surroundings, but without the Marriage of Peleus and Thetis.

33. Sallust writes that Discord's "golden apple denotes the world" (p.16); although the apple in Coluthus is construed as "a love symbol" (p. 546) and the act of throwing it "a declaration of love," the figure develops the more physical, cosmic sense of the globe: see Plates 12, 14, and n. 34, below.

34. The globe held by Elizabeth I in HE's painting bears a family resemblance to the sphere held by Henry Howard in the anonymous portrait painted in 1594 (Roy Strong, *The English Icon: Elizabethan & Jacobean Portraiture* [London: Routledge & Kegan Paul, 1969], p. 208, fig. 165), and both seem to suggest the earthly globe such as that touched (and ruled?) by Elizabeth I in the Duke of Bedford portrait (p. 182, fig. 135).

35. But as the *Judgment* of the Argonaut Master indicates (Plate 14), the rural account of Ovid and Coluthus was also known, and the panels of Carracci, Wtewael, Rubens, and others show that, during the Renaissance, this version predominates; even so, see Ehrhart, pp. 30–34.

36. *Cynthia*, sig. B2ᵛ. Barnfield thinks of his "Affectionate Shepherd" (in *Cynthia*), written in Spenserian stanza, as the first imitation of *The Faerie Queene* (sig. A4ᵛ).

37. See Northrop Frye, "The Structure of Imagery in *The Faerie Queene*," in *Fables of Identity: Studies in Poetic Mythology* (New York: Harcourt, Brace, 1963), p. 70; Williams, p. 71; Humphrey Tonkin, *Spenser's Courteous Pastoral: Book Six of The Faerie Queene* (Oxford: Clarendon Press, 1972), p. 1; James Nohrnberg, *The Analogy of "The Faerie Queene"* (Princeton: Princeton University Press, 1976), chs. 1 and 5; and Susanne Woods, "Closure in *The Faerie Queene*," *Journal of English and Germanic Philology*, 76 (1977), 209.

38. See Coluthus, p. 551, and Stinton, Pls. IIIb and VIb and pp. 26–27.

39. T[homas] H[eywood], *Oenone and Paris* [1594], ed. Joseph Quincy Adams (Washington, D.C.: Folger Shakespeare Library, 1943), p. 16.

40. *Ovids Heroicall Epistles*, trans. John Sherburne (1639), p. 30.

41. Cf. Michael Drayton, *The Works of Michael Drayton*, ed. William Hebel (Oxford: Basil Blackwell, 1961), I, 93; here, Drayton's Rowland presents himself as more faithful and more betrayed than "*Oenon*."

42. See Jacobson, *Ovid's Heroides*, ch. 10, esp. pp. 181–83.

43. *The Heroides or Epistles of the Heroines*, trans. Henry T. Riley, 3 vols. (London, 1869), III, 49.

44. Vincenzo Cartari, *The Fountain of Ancient Fiction*, trans. Richard Linche (1599), sig. E3ᵛ.

45. The following discussion owes much to Ruth Samson Luborsky's essay, "The Illustrations to *The Shepheardes Calender*," *Spenser Studies* 2 (1981), pp. 3–53; hereafter cited in text.

46. *The kalender of Shepardes* [1518], sigs. I7, I8ᵛ.

47. The reader will notice the indebtedness of this section to Harry Berger, Jr., "The Aging Boy: Paradise and Parricide in Spenser's *Shepheardes Calender*," in *Poetic Traditions of the English Renaissance*, ed., Maynard Mack and George deForest Lord (New Haven: Yale University Press, 1982), pp. 25–46.

48. Richard Helgerson, *Self-Crowned Laureates: Spenser, Jonson, Milton and the Literary System* (Berkeley: University of California Press, 1983), p. 69.

49. One can read Perigot's complaint as if he were complaining about the pain his "younglings" are suffering, in which case the "mee" functions accusatively ("I pine me"); but this reading depends on an emphatic hiatus after the conjunc-

tion, albeit that Spenser's "and" follows a comma. The text suggests that, like his "younglings," Perigot has been victimized by Love. The two "meanings" are not mutually exclusive, and I intend only to draw attention to the tone linking Perigot's situation and complaint to Colin's lament. My argument is in strong concurrence with Patrick Cullen, who writes: "Colin's sestina treats seriously and elegaically the same themes the singing-contest treats comically and mock-tragically" (*Spenser, Marvell and Renaissance Pastoral* [Cambridge: Harvard University Press, 1970], p. 110).

50. H[eywood], *Oenone and Paris*, p. 23.

ANNE SHAVER

Rereading Mirabella

B OOK VI of *The Faerie Queene* begins with a contradiction. In the proem, the narrator says that present courtesy has decayed from its former perfection, but he also says that the present queen is the entire source of the virtue, and that in her court, "courtesies excell." He avoids the problem of explaining these two opposed assertions by setting the Book of Courtesy not in court but instead in two places antithetical to it, the lonely and nightmarish Forest Perilous of medieval romance and the deliberate pastoral retreat from centers of civilization rediscovered in the classics. In both settings, however, he explores versions of discourtesy which involve challenges to contemporary hierarchies of class or gender or both, thus illustrating the specific ways in which courtesy—those gestures of deference and *noblesse oblige* that smooth the rough edges of life in a hierarchic society—seems to him to have decayed in Elizabethan England.

Most studies of Book VI concentrate on the pastoral interlude in which Sir Calidore courteously tries to adapt his noble self to shepherdish ways in order to court the shepherdess Pastorella and in which, although he clumsily disperses Colin's "naked ladies lilly white," he is for a moment allowed to share the poet's vision. This final section of Book VI does end in resolution. Although the Blatant Beast cannot be permanently bound, Pastorella does turn out to be a true princess, relieving the noble Calidore of the embarrassing need to lose himself for love. Graceful gestures of humility toward his lady are becoming in a knight, but at the level of "polliticke vertues" hierarchies of both gender and class are essential to a gentleman's knowing who he is. Spenser reminds us of the true location of power in terms of gender:

> Ye gentle Ladies, in whose soueraine powre
>   Loue hath the glory of his kingdome left,
>   And th'hearts of men as your eternall dowre,
>   In yron chaines, of liberty bereft,

211

Deliuered hath into your hands by gift;
Be well aware, how ye the same doe vse,
That pride do not to tyranny you lift;
Least if men you of cruelty accuse,
He from you take that chiefedome, which ye doe abuse.
                                        (VI. viii. I)[1]

Courtly love is a game in which women have power accorded them by men. If they fail to play to their lovers' liking, all the men have to do is complain to Cupid, that jealous patriarch, who will restore order by stripping women of the dower that turns out not to be eternal after all.

This bald if paradoxical statement of the way things are between men and women does not occur in the pastoral section which comprises the last four cantos, but at the beginning of Canto viii, near the end of a series of imperfectly resolved encounters in the perilous forest, and in the middle of Mirabella's unresolvable story. I would like to begin a closer look at the relatively neglected first two-thirds of Book VI by re-examining Mirabella, the cruel beauty punished for all eternity because her refusal to return their love has caused the deaths of twenty-two suitors. Although the space occupied by her story, fifty-three stanzas spanning two cantos (vii and viii) suggests that she is important to the central concept of Book VI, most studies which mention her at all—and some do not—consign her without much analysis to the general category of enemies of courtesy.[2] At the 1988 meeting of the Modern Language Association, however, in a reexamination of Mirabella's crime, Sheila Cavanagh suggested that the reader is prevented from looking closely at this episode by narrative techniques that "deflect outrage" and "save male face." For example, Prince Arthur calls Cupid a "iust" god (VI.viii.23), and the narrator gives no details about the lady's motives before she is arraigned in Cupid's court. Cavanagh went on to say that Mirabella's low birth is seen as rendering her refusal to love all the more heinous, and that this, in combination with her being read as a Petrarchan cliché and her overt acceptance of her own punishment, creates a "layered" narrative which obscures responsibility for her torture.[3]

I would like to continue the process Cavanagh has begun and also take it a step in another direction, to examine Mirabella's punishment as well as her crime, comparing her not only with the other denizens of the Book VI forest, but with characters throughout the poem who have somehow avoided arousing the wrath of Cupid although they do challenge his lordship.

In being beautiful and refusing to love, low-born Mirabella does no more than several unpunished and largely sympathetic figures do. Her beauty cannot be the major issue, because even women who do accept their lovers cause trouble with their loveliness: Florimell, faithful to Marinell, is a case in point. Other beautiful women cause pain or at least discomfort through their initial reluctance to respond: Amoret, Pastorella, and even Britomart. While each of these heroines undergoes painful experiences, these are not presented unequivocally as punishments for misbehavior, and in any case they are not eternal. Refusal alone cannot be the crime, because Guyon blamelessly sublimates his sexuality in the service of Gloriana, while the young Prince Arthur not only refuses to love but openly scorns lovers, and is rewarded with the Faerie Queene. Finally, Belphoebe, just like Mirabella, attracts love through her beauty but refuses—without retribution—ever to love in return.

In some ways an even closer analogue to Mirabella can be found in the Squire of Dames, who is guity of a masculine variation of her behavior. If she is held responsible for twenty-two deaths from unrequited love, he has accomplished by his own count three hundred loveless seductions in one year. Like Mirabella, and unlike the others I have named, he is punished, though not by an implacable god. His particular lady has refused to grant him her favor until he can find three hundred more women who will refuse his services. Although she required that he do this within the same span of time—one year—he has been out three and so far has found only three women who have turned him down. He tells his story not to a seriously worried Arthur, as Mirabella does hers, but to a laughing Satyrane, and together they create a comic, cozily antifeminist boys' club atmosphere (III.vii.53–60). But if he were truly in love, or if his lady truly had power equivalent to Cupid's, his situation would be dire. Even if she granted him an indefinite extension, at the present rate it would take another 297 years to win her. An obvious difference here is tone, even genre. The Squire of Dames inhabits a comedy, and indeed so does the lady who has set his tasks, who is in effect refusing to love him and who is certainly not punished for it. For them, obviously, the whole thing is a game; and if the Squire's philandering ways have made him temporary prey to the lustful giant Argante, his rescue, unlike

Mirabella's, is an easy matter. Mirabella's much harsher punishment is just as absurdly impossible, but the game has turned deadly earnest and there is no redeeming comedy.

Another character whose story is closer in its serious tone to hers is the Redcrosse Knight, who enacts a variation of the refusal to love, this time in a potentially tragic mode, and who, like Mirabella, is harshly punished for it. His refusing to stay with Una because he doubts her chastity has uncovered his sexual vulnerability along with his moral arrogance, which backfires on him in the form of Orgoglio (whose "sib" Disdaine is Mirabella's torturer) and casts him into a dungeon of repentance. Prince Arthur's rescue of Redcrosse has none of the insouciant ease of Satyrane's rescue of the Squire of Dames; he labors long, almost losing his own squire to Duessa on the seven-headed beast, and brings Redcrosse out of prison very close to death. Even after rescue and rest, in the cave of Despair Redcrosse is again near death, this time by his own hand. But he does not, finally, die. Through the combined efforts of Una and the attributes who people the House of Holinesse, he is redeemed, reformed, and sent out to complete his task.

Like the ribald comedy acted out by the Squire of Dames, the genre here is different from the one that Mirabella inhabits. Although both are serious in tone, the story of Redcrosse is a religious allegory and a divine comedy, while that of Mirabella is at first glance a medieval romance. But her torturers, Disdaine and Scorne, are allegorical figures, and Disdaine is specifically called Orgoglio's sibling. Mirabella's story is a medieval romance invaded and altered by concerns new in Spenser's day, above all by concerns about her class and gender.

Joan Kelly-Gadol has pointed out the connection between those two attributes in the escalating anxiety brought on by social change in the Renaissance. If medieval courtly love was only a game, at least it was a game in which men shaped themselves to please women; Renaissance culture, on the other hand, was much more concerned with shaping women to please men. Sexual love, idealized in the secular literature of the Middle Ages, in the Renaissance must "lead to marriage and be confined to it," at least for women, whose chastity was directly connected with the desire "to limit and regulate membership in a hereditary aristocratic class," even as the real power of that class was being eroded by Tudor rule.[4] As once powerful feudal lords were forced to become courtiers and adopt feminine wiles—grace, attractiveness, flattery—in relation to the monarch, especially when that monarch was herself a woman, their perception of themselves as not-women needed reinforcement as it never had before, and women other than the queen who challenged gender hierarchy could no longer be humored. The growing permeability of class boundaries was upsetting those who felt their hereditary status being eroded by the newly moneyed merchants and professionals, but this was harder to control through law than were the rights of women, especially married women. Thus an unmarried, low-born woman claiming power over high-born men would be a trenchant representation of all that could endanger a conservative, masculine notion of a courteous society and a privileged self. This male anxiety, I believe, is reflected in the harsh absurdity of Mirabella's punishment, in the fact that, unlike the Squire of Dames, she cannot be laughed at and, unlike Redcrosse, she cannot be forgiven or redeemed.

Analogues for Mirabella in other Renaissance works in which the medieval purgatory of cruel beauties becomes not a purgatory but a perpetual hell suggest that anxieties about gender were widespread. Ariosto's Lidia is a very specific example as she explains her situation to Astolpho when he visits the underworld:

> Signor, Lidia sono io,
> del re di Lidia in grande altezza nata,
> qui dal guidicio altissimo di Dio
> al fumo eternamente condannata,
> per esser stat al fido amante mio,
> mentre io vissi, spiaccevole et in grata.
>
> (Canto 34.11)

['I am Lydia,' she began, 'daughter of the King of Lydia and born to eminence, but condemned to this eternal smoke by the supreme justice of God for having been obnoxious and spiteful to my faithful suitor while I lived' (Waldman trans., p. 413).]

It seems not to exonerate her that she was to have been a prize for this suitor's services to her father, or that, scorned, the same suitor ravaged her father's kingdom. What matters is that she had him in her power, exercised that power, and drove him to despair and death. His obsession is blamed entirely on her. She goes on to say that Hell is infinitely full of others like her, and the two she names are like her indeed. Daphne, who fled Apollo's uninvited lust, and Anarexetes, who is punished for the suicide of her unrequited lover, Iphis. Although these women are generally understood to be victims of aggressive men, here they are severely punished for their efforts to resist;

> Sta la cruda Anassarete piu al basso,
> ove e maggiore il fumo e piu martire.
> Resto converso al mondo il corpo in sasso,
> e l'anima qua giu venne a patire,
> poi che veder per lei l'afflitto e lasso
> suo amante appeso pote sofferire.
> Qui press e Dafne, ch'or s'avvede quanto
> errasse a fare Apollo correr tanto.
> (Canto 34.12)[5]

['Further down where the smoke is thicker and the torment worse, is cruel Anarexetes. Her body, on earth, was turned to stone and her soul came down here to suffer since she could endure to watch her poor afflicted lover hang himself for her. Near me is Daphne who now realizes her error in making Apollo run after her so' (Waldman trans., p. 412).]

Mirabella is also connected through language with a perpetually damned female in Book VI itself: the monster Echidna, mother of the Blatant Beast. Echidna is yet another of Spenser's variations on the theme of Homer's Scylla, "A faire young Mayden" in "her face and former parts," while "all her hinder parts did plaine expresse / A monstrous Dragon" so ugly that she frightened even the fiends in hell, and caused the gods to banish her

> Mongst rocks and caues, where she enrold doth lie
> In hideous horror and obscurity,
> Wasting the strength of her immortal age.
> (VI. vi. 11)

That Cupid's punishment of Mirabella, though couched in the finite terms "Till she had sau'd so many loues, as she did lose," is an eternal doom is just about to become apparent when the narrator tells us

So now she had bene wandring two whole yeares
   Throughout the world, in this vncomely case,
   Wasting her goodly hew in heauy teares,
   And her good dayes in dolorous disgrace . . .
                       (VI.vii.38)

Because they are so repulsive to the gods in power, each is doomed to "waste" her single most important attribute. Because she is ugly, Echidna must waste "the strength of her immortal age"; because she is rebellious, Mirabella must waste her youth and beauty.

When she first appears (VI.vi. 16) Mirabella looks like any other heroine of romance in need of rescue. She emerges briefly from the forest shadows when Serena and Timias glimpse her like a figure in a bad dream. She is in "mourning weed," and is being led by "a lewd fool." The narrator presents her as victim, not as transgressor, saying that she is "unmeetly" set upon a mangy jade, that shame has *befallen* her, and that later it will be told how she acquitted herself of this. Everything about the language here, except perhaps for the word "shame" which is deflected from modifying Mirabella by the no-fault word "befell," suggests wronged virtue and future deliverance of the sort expected in medieval romance.

This appearance occurs in the midst of other stories of rescuable and forgivable women for whom normal rules of behavior have been altered by courtesy: first Briana, then the unnamed battered lady rescued by Tristan, then Priscilla, and finally, both before and after Mirabella's very different story, Serena. Briana challenges normal gender hierarchy by choosing and pursuing a mate instead of waiting to be chosen and pursued. Her name, probably deriving from a Greek work for "strong",[6] suggests masculinity, as does her activity of seizing ladies and knights by force to make a cloak of their hair and beards in order to win Crudor, her reluctant beloved. In Spenser's rewriting of this activity, Sir Calidore fights Crudor, stops the evil custom, and marries the now-tamed couple to each other. At first glance it seems that Briana is rewarded for bad behavior by being given the man she so presumptuously sought, but along with that gift she is stripped of at least one of the sources of her unfeminine strength, the castle from which she launched her seneschal to collect the trophy beards and locks. In fact, like Britomart's restoring male rule to the land of the Amazons, Briana strips herself of pride and possessions, prostrating herself before Cal idore and giving him all her holdings, "land and fee," which he promptly turns over to the squire whose beard he had earlier saved. Thus Briana becomes Crudor's wife without dowry, entirely dependent on her man; her being forgiven hinges on her reassuming her rightful place in the hierarchy of gender.

Although the main focus of this episode is on gender, class also enters the picture when Calidore decimates not just Maleffort, Briana's armed seneschal, but all of the unarmed servants he encountered at her gate. Although Briana cries shame, he endures her as a scold, claiming that "it is no blame / To punish those, that doe deserue the same" (VI.i.26). On the other hand, he spares Sir Crudor's well-born life with this didacticism:

> Who will not mercie vnto others shew,
>   How can he mercy euer hope to haue?
>   To pay each with his owne is right and dew.
>   (VI.i.42)

In this reprise of Talus's rough justice in Book V, once again the sins of nobles are punished on the bodies of their lowborn followers.

The unnamed lady who appears next in the narrative is being as roughly led as Mirabella, in this case by a sadistic knight who is taking his disappointment in his own failure out on her. If that knight shows gender discourtesy by battering the lady he ought to protect, Tristan, to all appearances a young commoner dressed in Lincoln green, bends the rules of rank to fight him, rescue the lady, and escort her home. Although there is no blame suggested for this woman, the next to appear, Priscilla, has endangered herself and her reputation by slipping out of her father's house to meet her beloved in the forest. Calidore rescues both Priscilla and her wounded squire, restores the boy to his father, then takes Priscilla to hers, protecting her honor with a courteous lie which will enable her to be married to the higher-ranking man of her father's choice, though we are not given the end of her story. Finally, in the episode immediately preceding the first appearance of the beleaguered Mirabella, the wandering and therefore vulnerable Serena, along with Timias, undergoes rehabilitation with a hermit, who teaches them both the importance of appearances, blesses them and sends them on their way.

Up to this point the forest of Spenser's romance is not very different from its medieval precursors, in which women are sacrosanct, seldom blamed, and almost never punished. Moved, however, by a humanist belief in education somewhat at odds with a strong approval of birth rank and essential gender, Spenser adds the reclamation of these transgressing women to acceptable behavior.

Indeed most of these stories, along with those surrounding the villain Turpine, derive from the activities of Breus Sans Pité, the crudest and most arrogant enemy of courtesy in the Arthurian cycle—he also makes cloaks of beards, hates all knights errant, attacks unarmed men, and tortures women just to see them squirm.[7] What Spenser adds in his partial regendering of the story is a strong concern for honor connected with female sexual behavior: in medieval romance honor for men is a matter of good deeds and knightly skill, while the honor of women, though often connected with chastity, exists only in terms of their men. And he exhibits a new attitude toward class. It may be contrary to the medieval laws of arms that an undubbed boy fight a knight, but hierarchy is handled a little differently in Tristan's overthrow of the unnamed sadist. What relieves Calidore in judging the situation is not that he finds out that Lincoln-green clad Tristan is really a knight out of armor—which he is not—but that he is a prince in disguise. His class more than his chivalric rank within it gives him the right to engage another nobleman in combat.

That Spenser may be somewhat ambivalent on this subject is suggested by two subsequent episodes. At the beginning of the fourth canto, Calepine and Serena are rescued from Sir Turpine by a wild man, a naked creature without language whose essential nobility is contrasted to the supposedly civilized Turpine's brutality. Yet rank is important enough that Spenser is willing to undermine this contrast a little later by claiming that the wild man is nobly born, though he never provides the promised explanation (VI.v.1–2). Between these two views of the noble savage comes Calepine's rescue of a baby boy from a bear. As the child's origin is a mystery, Calepine offers him to the childless Matilde as

> This litle babe, of sweete and louely face,
> And spotlesse spirit, in which ye may enchace
> What euer formes ye list thereto apply,

Being now soft and fit them to embrace;
Whether ye list him traine in cheualry,
Or noursle vp in lore of learn'd Philosophy.

(VI.iv.35)

Thus Calepine, at least, espouses nurture as powerful enough to
create a son worthy of noble parents. Matilde, however, will not
have to debate this with her husband. Since what he wants and
has blamed her for the lack of is a son of his body to defend his
property against the giant he took it from by force, she "with her
husband under hand so wrought, / That when the infant vnto
him she brought, / She made him thinke it surely was his owne"
(VI.iv.38).

All this precedes the mysterious brief appearance of Mirabella
in Canto vi. What follows that appearance is Calidore's encounter with Turpine, who, like Breus, is an embodiment of the anti-
knight, and whose crimes against chivalry are finally punished
when Calidore hangs him by the heels from a tree. He will not
stay there long, though, because his faithful lady, Blandina, will
surely cut him down. Blandina is presented by the narrator as
guilefully courteous, but the first time we meet her she is doing
the courteous thing with no apparent ulterior motive. When
Turpine rudely refuses to share his horse with Calepine to ease
the wounded Serena across a river, Blandina offers her palfrey.
At that point, however, Calepine is so enraged by Turpine's
discourtesy that he would rather die than accept help from Turpine's woman, and he subsequently not only nearly drowns the
bleeding Serena, but ends up using her as a shield when Turpine
attacks him (VI.iii.32–33; 49). This episode is an astonishing
illustration of what can happen when men perceive women as
nothing more than extensions of themselves.

In her later dealings with Arthur, guileful or not, Blandina's
behavior is effective: she prevents Calidore's killing Turpine by
asking for his life in the time-honored courtly lady fashion, then
keeps peace at the dinner table with small talk. Her courtesy
works, but is suspect to the narrator apparently because she uses
it to get what she wants "Through tempering of her words &
lookes by wondrous skill. / Yet were her words and lookes but
false and fayned . . ." (vi.41–42). The narrator scorns her, but
does not punish her, and in fact leaves her with what she
desires—peace and her man. Thus even much-maligned Blandina can be counted among the rescued heroines of romance.

On the other hand, when Mirabella's story is actually told, not only is rescue impossible, but the very nature of her punishment prevents its completion, turning medieval romance into something as ironic and grotesque as a story by Kafka. The sentence Mirabella is accorded seems reasonable enough in the narrator's first account of the courtroom procedures: all she need do is wander "this worlds wyde wildernes" until she has saved twenty-two lovers (VI.vii.37). The painful absurdity becomes apparent in the second telling, when Mirabella, in her warning to Arthur, reveals that not only must she wander, she must do it "with these two lewd companions, and no more," as well as with the two leaking vessels through which will run an endless stream of contrition and tears (VI.viii.22–24). If the leaking bags are the visual symbol of her sentence's absurdity, other aspects of it are still more painfully frustrating. There is no mention of just how she is to save lovers, though she is credited with saving two. She certainly must not "save" them in the sense used in medieval romance or Petrarchan sonnets, because that would make her at best a two-timer, at worst a whore. And are these lovers she is to save to be her own or someone else's? Beyond the obscurity of all this, she is constantly in motion, pulled by the "mighty man" Disdaine, pushed and whipped by the "angry foole" Scorne. How can she stay in one place long enough to save anyone's lover? When she does pause to tell her story, her torturers turn on those who would set her free, so that Timias (who has already nearly died for love of Belphoebe, that other woman who refuses to love) and an untried young knight named Enias both find themselves bound by Disdaine and reviled by Scorne. Seeing Mirabella's plight, both young men prove themselves naive, old-fashioned readers, interpreting her as a normal lady in distress who wants only their heroic intervention to be set free from vulnerable monsters.

But even Prince Arthur, so successful in his intervention in earlier books, is helpless against these horrors. Fighting with the monstrous Disdaine, it is all he can do simply to contain for a moment this solider sibling of Orgoglio, the airbag he deflated so completely in Book I. If he could destroy Disdaine and Scorne with the help of the wild man who for a moment does seem to be making headway, he is prevented from doing so by Mirabella herself, who tells him first that her own life depends on Disdaine's, then that his does, and finally that rescue is impossible:

Nor heauens, nor men can me most wretched mayd
Deliuer from the doome of my desart,
The which the God of Loue hath on me layd,
And damned to endure this direfull smart,
For penaunce of my proud and hard rebellious hart.
                                        (VI.viii.19)

Thus the nature of Mirabella's punishment, along with her own acceptance of it, actually prevents her atonement and assures that her suffering will be eternal.

The harshness of this episode in a book heretofore so full of reconciliations, restored order, rescues, and courteously bent rules is startling, and suggests that Spenser himself found Mirabella's crime unforgivable. To go outside of Book VI, and return to earlier analogies, what makes her different from Redcrosse, the Squire of Dames, Prince Arthur, or Guyon? The most obvious answer is that she is a woman, and that it is the appropriate destiny of women to love men, and to put themselves in the hands of men. What makes her different from the women of Book VI, from Briana, the battered lady, Priscilla, Serena, or Blandina? However misguided and / or discourteous any of these women may be, they all love, or at least belong to, men. And none of them is designated, as Mirabella specifically is, as being "of meane parentage and kindred base" (vii.28).

When the poem returns to Mirabella, the episode of Arthur and Turpine having followed the first brief sighting of her, the first adjective applied to her, most strangely, is "free":

But turne we now backe to that Ladie free,
Whom late we left ryding vpon an Asse
Led by a Carle and foole, which by her side did passe.
                                        (VI.vii.27)

The description that follows is consistent only in its disapproval, for if it tells us that Mirabella was "of meane parentage and kindred base," it also says "She was a Ladie of great dignitie, / And lifted up to honorable place." It says that she scorned her many lovers because she believed that was the way to acquire even more of them, but it also says that she cared nothing for their suffering, for "She was borne free, not bound to any wight, / And so would euer liue and loue her owne delight" (28–30). She has boasted that she is "the Ladie of her libertie," and has god-like power to "saue or spill" the lovers pining for her. Because she owes her "honorable place" to the responses of men to her physical beauty rather than to her own birth, the implication is that she ought to be grateful to all of her admirers, and that she ought to choose one of them to be her "fere." The OED gives "equal" as the first meaning of "fere" in the late 16th century; the next is "husband or wife," and thus for Mirabella the word contains its own contradiction. Within Renaissance hierarchies of class and gender, a lowborn woman cannot be the equal of a nobly born man, and a wife cannot be the equal of her husband. Thus it would seem that her crime is legion; she claims power beyond her gender and beyond her class, and she also claims freedom from the strictures of romantic or marital commitment. When she is arraigned before Cupid, the second pun in her name becomes obvious. She is not only one who looks beautiful, Mira-bella, she is a "rebellious Mayd," Mi-rebel-la, reminiscent of that other unforgivable rebel, the democratic giant who "was admired much of fooles, women, and boys" (V.ii.30).

Further, Timias' involvement with both Mirabella and Belphoebe connects the presumptuous commoner with that independent foster-child of the goddess Diana, image of Elizabeth's private person. If, as it has often been suggested, evil or problematic queens such as Lucifera and Mercilla may be read as veiled comments on "the most excellent and glorious person of our sovereign the Queene" even though Gloriana is the only royal double designated by the poet, might not Mirabella be just such a response to the power and sexual independence, necessarily celebrated in Belphoebe, of Elizabeth's other "person," the "most vertuous and beautiful lady"? If her being "the Ladie of her libertie" is something which must be endured in a queen's private person, its destructive effect on Timias shows that it must not be allowed in the general run of women. This most vulnerable of young men is driven mad by Belphoebe's disdain and scorn; he recovers only to be bitten by the Blatant Beast, then finds himself bound and beaten by another version of Disdaine and Scorne. If there is any doubt that Timias is more valuable than Mirabella to those who matter in the world of Faerie Land, the scenes of Arthur's recognition of his lost-and-found squire dispels it. Arthur's emotions at these meetings are as passionate as any lover's, both at the first where he speaks, and the second where the poet narrates:

> My liefe, my life's desire,
> Why haue ye me alone thus long yleft?
> Tell me what worlds despight, or heauens yre
> Hath you thus long away from me bereft?
> (VI.v.23)

> But when approaching neare, he plainly found,
> It was his owne true groome, the gentle Squire,
> He thereat wext exceedingly astound,
> And him oft did embrace, and oft admire,
> Ne could with seeing satisfie his great desire.
> (VI.vii.27)

If this much-loved Timias, as is traditionally held, represents Ralegh and his difficulties with the queen, then his being in the company of Serena—since "Serena" was Ralegh's pet name for Elizabeth Throgmorton, the wife who cost him royal favor[8]—when he is bound and reviled by Disdaine and Scorne suggests still another connection between Elizabeth Tudor and the low-born Mirabella. It also suggests indirectly that in Spenser's view the queen's treatment of her courtier was deeply wrong.

Among the prominent female characters throughout the whole poem, Mirabella shares low parentage only with Lucifera, a queen whose right to rule is challenged; in both cases the characters' low birth—which not only disqualifies a person from ruling but according to the tenets of courtly love disqualifies a person from loving—may well be a smoke-screen for otherwise dangerous criticism of high-born Elizabeth. Certainly Lucifera's court in the House of Pride represents a failure of courtesy such as the narrator mourns in the proem to Book VI. Quite possibly the anxiety of being ruled by a woman exposed the constructs of class and gender as just that: constructs, not eternal essences.

Except for Mirabella's harsh punishment, the closest Spenser comes to imitating Ariosto's hell of proud beauties is in the list of women imprisoned under Lucifera's castle. The ones he names are all queens: Semiramis, Sthenoboea, and "High minded Cleopatra." Although they are also adulteresses and actively desiring women destroyed by lust and pride, the main charge against them is not that they were unchaste, but that they were "Proud wemen, vaine, forgetfull of their yoke" (I.v.50). This pride, though it manifests itself in lust rather than in a refusal to love, is fueled by the power of their rank and is an exercise of independence comparable to Mirabella's personal transgression. In the Renaissance, for a woman to claim the power actually to rule men, in love or politics, is to court the possibility of a violent punishment.

The story of Mirabella, however, is focused on love. If it refers to Elizabeth the "vertuous and beautiful lady," there is an additional puzzle in Mirabella's final words to Arthur, when he gives her one last chance to let him rescue her.

> Ah, nay Sir Knight (sayd she) it may not be
> But that I needes must by all meanes fulfill
> This penaunce, which enjoyned is to me
> Least unto me betide a greater ill . . .
>
> (VI. viii. 30)

What could be a "greater ill" than the Sisyphean impossibility of her present doom? Looking back at the actual courtroom scene where Mirabella receives her sentence, we see that through her tears she has prevented the god from making the judgement "as is by law ordayned / In cases like" (VI. vii. 36), and has received a lighter sentence than was customary. The customary one is not named, and of course death leaps to mind.

But in medieval courts of love the usual sentence in such cases is not to die, but to fall in love, often with someone unattainable or inappropriate. Such is the doom of the *Arcadia*'s Erona, whom an insulted Cupid makes marry and whimper like a puppy after self-seeking, cowardly, low-born Antiphilus; such is the case in a happier mode for *The Faerie Queene*'s Arthur. The implication is that Mirabella would rather endure her impossible quest than fall in love herself.

Spenser, for all his equating of courtesy with hierarchic if loving marriage, must realize that, for Queen Elizabeth, to marry at all would be to lose the self that can claim the power to rule England, and to love inappropriately could be to endanger the state. Mirabella may not be so much the bruised and punished enemy of courtesy as she is the strongest—because she suffers the most of all left alive—independent woman in Faerie Land, a whipping girl for untouchable royalty and one whose punishment is an attempt to beat back the dawning awareness that if one woman, even a queen, could with impunity—indeed, from political necessity—choose independence from male lordship in marriage, other hierarchies, such as a class structure based on noble birth, were also at risk.

Notes

1.   Edmund Spenser, *The Faerie Queene*, ed. Thomas P. Roche, Jr. ed (New Haven: Yale University Press, 1981). All quotations from the poem are taken from this edition.

2.   In Humphrey Tonkin's *Spenser's Courteous Pastoral* (Oxford University Press, 1972) and most other studies of Book VI, when Mirabella is mentioned at all—and often she is not—she is generally accepted either as C. S. Lewis defines her—a recognizable medieval type (*The Allegory of Love*, [Oxford University Press, 1936], 297, 352)—or as a rendering of "the vengeful, self-isolating lady of Petrarchan poetry" (Kenneth Gross, *Spenserian Poetics: Idolatry, Iconoclasm, Magic* [Ithaca, N.Y.: Cornell University Press, 1985], 213]. Tonkin, for example, offers her as one of the enemies of courtesy four times, undifferentiated from Turpine or the cannibals (158, 177, 181, 297). In *Spenser's World of Glass* (University of California Press, 1966) in one long paragraph (219–20) Kathleen Wiliams examines Mirabelle more extensively than most critics do, but easily concludes that her sin is great and her punishment necessary.

3.   Sheila Cavanagh, "'Faire of Face . . . though Meane her Lot': The Narrative of Sexual economies in Spenser and Chaucer." (MLA Session 767, 1988.)

4.   Joan Kelly-Gadol, "Did Women Have a Renaissance?" in *Becoming Visible: Women in European History*, eds. Renate Bridenthal and Claudia Koonz (Boston: Houghton Mifflin, 1977), 152, 157–59.

5.   Ludovico Ariosto, *Orlando Furioso*, Riccardo Ricciardi Editore, (Milano—Napoli, 1954), Canto 34.7–43. Quotations in English are from the translation by Guido Waldman (Oxford University Press, 1974).

6.   *The Faerie Queene*, Roche, ed., 1214.

7.   Sir Thomas Malory, *Works*, ed. Eugene Vinaver, 2nd edition, (Oxford University Press, 1971), 316, 379, 416–18.

8.   Edmund Spenser, *The Faerie Queene*, A. C. Hamilton, ed. (London and New York: Longman, 1977), 643.

WILLY MALEY

Spenser and Ireland:
A Select Bibliography

Introduction

*I*N RECENT years a number of crucial developments in the comprehension of Renaissance literature have altered significantly the complexion of Spenser studies. The drive towards interdisciplinary criticism has brought in from the margins of the literary canon an aspect of the poet's life hitherto confined to specialized monographs in scholarly journals, namely the question of his Irish experiences and the manner in which they impinge upon his writings. The impact of new ways of reading—one thinks here immediately of New Historicism and Cultural Materialism—has allowed for a broader contextual view of an author whose Englishness has always been compromised to a certain degree by his close involvement, for the entirety of his literary career, with England's first colony.

Coincidentally, fresh work in the field of early modern Irish history suggests a deeper implication in Irish affairs on the part of Spenser and some contemporaries than was thought previously. In light of the predictable exhaustion of other well-worked mines of Spenserian scholarship, these two rich veins of cross-cultural analysis signal a shift in emphasis which will no doubt be felt most strongly in the decade leading up to the 400th anniversary of the untimely death of "Colin Clout." The generation weaned on Gottfried's otherwise excellent edition of the *View* hungers for the full diet of bibliographical matter on Spenser's Irish milieu which was the *Variorum*'s singular deficiency.

In preparing this document, I was working with five basic types of material: contemporary descriptions of Ireland and the Irish; modern historiography of the period; secondary criticism of Spenser and Ireland; items relating specifically to Munster, the province with which the poet was most intimately associated;

227

and, finally, biographical information on patrons and acquaintances of Spenser active in Elizabeth's viceregal administration. Since no easily discernible lines of demarcation suggested themselves once the task of assembling the relevant data was accomplished, I have elected to present the *genre* alphabetically, by author, rather than thematically. I hope that the finished product appeals to a sufficient range of critical interests, and that the growing preoccupation with Spenser's Irish experiences will continue to stimulate a series of lively discussions in future years.

Anderson, Judith H. "The Antiquities of Fairyland and Ireland." *Journal of English and Germanic Philology*, 86 (1987), 199–214.

Arden, J. "Rug-Headed Irish Kerns and British Poets." *New Statesman* (July 13, 1979), 56–57.

Baker, David J. "'Some Quirk, Some Subtle Evasion': Legal Subversion in Spenser's *A View of the Present State of Ireland*." *Spenser Studies*, 6 (1986), 147–63.

Baumgartner, Virginia. *Irish Elements in Spenser's "Faerie Queene."* Columbia University, New York, unpublished Ph.D. thesis, 1972.

Beacon, Richard. *Solon his follie, or A Politique Discourse, touching the Reformation of common-weales conquered, declined or corrupted*, Oxford, 1594.

Bednarz, J. P. "Raleigh in Spenser's Historical Allegory." *Spenser Studies* 4 (1984), 49–70.

Berry, Henry F. "Sheriffs of the County Cork—Henry III to 1660." *Journal of the Royal Society of Antiquaries of Ireland*, 15 (1905), 39–52.

Bradbrook, Muriel C. "No Room at the Top: Spenser's Pursuit of Fame," in *Elizabethan Poetry*, ed. J. R. Brown, *Stratford-Upon-Avon Studies*, 2 (1960), London, pp. 91–109.

Bradshaw, Brendan. "Fr. Wolfe's Description of Limerick, 1574." *North Munster Antiquarian Journal*, 17 (1975), 47–53.

———. "The Elizabethans and the Irish." *Studies*, 66 (1977), 38–50.

———. "Sword, Word and Strategy in the Reformation in Ireland." *Historical Journal*, 21 (1978), 475–502.

———. "The Elizabethans and the Irish: A Muddled Model." *Studies*, 70 (1981), 233–44.

———. "Edmund Spenser on Justice and Mercy", *Historical Studies*, 16 (1987), 76–89.

————. "Robe and Sword in the Conquest of Ireland," in *Law and Government under the Tudors: Essays Presented to Sir Geoffrey Elton on His Retirement*, eds. C. Cross, D. Loades, and J. J. Scarisbrick. Cambridge: Cambridge University Press, 1988, pp. 139–62.

————. A. Hadfield, and W. T. Maley, eds. *Representing Ireland, 1534–1660*. Cambridge: Cambridge University Press, forthcoming.

Brady, Ciaran. "Faction and the origins of the Desmond Rebellion." *Irish Historical Studies*, 22 (1981), 289–312.

————. "Spenser's Irish Crisis: Humanism and Experience in the 1590s." *Past and Present*, 111 (1986), 17–49.

————. "Spenser's Irish Crisis: Reply to Canny." *Past and Present*, 120 (1988), 210–15.

————. "The Road to the *View*: On the Decline of Reform Thought in Tudor Ireland," in *Spenser and Ireland: An Interdisciplinary Perspective*, ed. P. Coughlan. Cork: Cork University Press, 1989, pp. 25–45.

Buck, P. M. "New Facts Concerning the Life of Edmund Spenser." *Modern Language Notes*, 19 (1904), 237–38.

Buckley, James. "Munster in A.D. 1597." *Journal of the Cork Historical and Archaeological Society*, 12 (1906), 53–68.

Buckley, W. E., ed. *Croftus, sive de Hibernia Liber*. London: Roxburgh Society, 1887.

Burridge, Ezekiel. *A Short View of the Present State of Ireland in the year 1700*, Dublin or London, 1708.

Butler, R., ed. "A Treatice of Ireland by John Dymmok, *c.* 1599." *Tracts relating to Ireland*. 2 vols. Irish Archaeological Society, Dublin, 2 (1843), pp. 5–11.

Byrne, M. J., trans. *Ireland under Elizabeth: by Don Philip O'Sullivan Baer*. 2nd ed. New York: Catholic University Press, 1970.

Canny, Nicholas P. *The Formation of the Old English Elite in Ireland*. Dublin: National University of Ireland, 1975.

————. *The Elizabethan Conquest of Ireland: A Pattern Established, 1565–76*. Hassocks, Sussex: The Harvester Press, 1976.

————. "Rowland White's 'Discors Touching Ireland', *c.* 1569." *Irish Historical Studies*, 20 (1977), 439–63.

————. "Rowland White's 'The Dysorders of the Irisshery', 1571." *Studia Hibernica*, 19 (1979), 147–60.

————. "Edmund Spenser and the Development of an Anglo-Irish Identity." *The Yearbook of English Studies: Colonial and Imperial Themes*, 13 (1983), 1–19.

————. "Protestants, Planters and Apartheid in Early Modern Ireland." *Irish Historical Studies*, 25 (1986), 105–115.

————. "Identity Formation in Ireland: The Emergence of the Anglo-Irish," in *Colonial Identity in the Atlantic World, 1500–1800*, eds. N. Canny and A. Pagden. Princeton, New Jersey: Princeton University Press, 1987, pp. 159–212.

————. " 'Spenser's Irish Crisis': A Comment." *Past and Present*, 120 (1988), 201–209.

————. "Introduction: Spenser and the Reform of Ireland," in *Spenser and Ireland: An Interdisciplinary Perspective*, ed. P. Coughlan. Cork: Cork University Press, 1989, pp. 9–24.

Carpenter, F. I. "Desiderata in the Study of Spenser." *Studies in Philology*, 19 (1922), 238–43.

————. "Spenser in Ireland." *Modern Philology*, 19 (1922), 405–419.

————. *A Reference Guide to Edmund Spenser*. Chicago: Chicago University Press, 1923.

Cavanagh, S. T. " 'Such Was Irena's Countenance': Ireland in Spenser's Prose and Poetry." *Texas Studies in Language and Literature*, 28 (1986), 24–50.

Churchyard, Thomas. *A Scourge for Rebels*. London, 1584.

————. *A Wished Reformation of a Wicked Rebellion*. London, 1598.

————. *The Fortunate Farewel to the Earle of Essex*. London, 1599.

Coleman, J. "The Poet Spenser's Wife." *Journal of the Cork Historical and Archaeological Society*, 2nd ser., 1 (1895), 131–33.

Cooper, L. T. "Spenser's *Veue of the Present State of Ireland*: An Introduction with Notes on the First 55 Pages in Grosart's Edition." Cornell University, unpublished M. A. thesis, 1913.

Coughlan, Patricia. " 'Some Secret Scourge which shall by her come unto England': Ireland and Incivility in Spenser," in *Spenser and Ireland: An Interdisciplinary Perspective*, ed. P. Coughlan. Cork: Cork University Press, 1989, pp. 46–74.

Covington, F. F. "Another View of Spenser's Linguistics." *Studies in Philology*, 19 (1922), 244–48.

————. *Spenser in Ireland*. Yale University, unpublished Ph.D. thesis, 1924.

————. "Spenser's Use of Irish History in the Veue of the Present State of Ireland." *University of Texas Bulletin, 2411: Studies in English*, 4 (1924), 5–38.

Crino, A. M. "La Relazione Barducci-Ubaldini Sull'Impresa D'Irlanda (1579–1581)." *English Miscellany*, 19 (1968), 339–67.

Crowley, S. "Some of Spenser's Doneraile Neighbours." *The North Cork Writers Journal*, 1 (1985), 71–75.

Davies, John. *A Discovery of the True Causes why Ireland was never entirely Subdued, nor brought under Obedience of the Crowne of ENGLAND, untill the Beginning of his Majesties happie Raigne.* London, 1612.

De Breffney, B. "An Elizabethan Political Painting." *Irish Arts Review*, 1 (1984), 39–41.

Derricke, John. *The Image of Irelande.* London, 1581.

Devereux, Robert. *Lawes and orders of Warre, established for the good conduct of the service in Ireland.* London, 1599.

"Dialogue between Peregryne and Sylvanus, *c.* 1598." London: Public Record Office. State Papers, Ireland, 63/203/119, ff. 283–357.

Dickins, Bruce M. "The Irish Broadside and Queen Elizabeth's Types." *Transactions of the Cambridge Bibliographical Society*, 1 (1949), 48–60.

Draper, J. W. "Spenser's Linguistics in The Present State of Ireland', *Modern Philology*, 17 (1919), 111–26.

————. "More Light on Spenser's Linguistics." *Modern Language Notes*, 41 (1926), 127–28.

Duncan-Jones, K., and J. Van Dorsten. *Miscellaneous Prose of Sir Philip Sidney.* Oxford: Clarendon, 1973.

Dunlop, Robert. "The Plantation of Munster, 1584–1589." *English Historical Review*, 3 (1888), 250–69.

————. "Sixteenth-Century Maps of Ireland." *English Historical Review*, 20 (1905), 309–337.

————. "An Unpublished Survey of the Plantation of Munster in 1622." *Royal Society of Antiquaries of Ireland*, 54 (1924), 128–46.

Eccles, Mark. "Barnabe Googe in England, Spain, and Ireland." *English Literary Renaissance*, 15 (1985), 353–70.

"Edmund Spenser." *Journal of the Cork Historical and Archaeological Society*, 3 (1894), 89–100.

Falkiner, C. L. *Illustrations of Irish History and Topography, Mainly of the Seventeenth Century.* London, 1904.

————. "Barnaby Rich's 'Remembrance of the State of Ireland, 1612', with Notices of Other Manuscript Reports, by the same Writer, on Ireland under James the First." *Proceedings of the Royal Irish Academy*, 26 (1906), 125–42.

————. "William Farmer's 'Chronicles of Ireland' from 1594 to 1613." *English Historical Review*, 22 & 30 (1907), 104–130 & 527–52.

————. "Spenser in Ireland," in *Essays Relating to Ireland: Biographical, Historical, and Topographical*. London, 1909, pp. 3–31.

Falls, Cyril. *Elizabeth's Irish Wars*. 2nd ed. New York: Cornell University Press, 1970.

Fogarty, Anne. "The Colonization of Language: Narrative Strategies in *A View of the Present State of Ireland* and *The Faerie Queene*, Book VI," in *Spenser and Ireland: An Interdisciplinary Perspective*, ed. P. Coughlan. Cork: Cork University Press, 1989, pp. 75–108.

Gilbert, J. T. *History of the Irish Confederation and the War in Ireland, 1641–1643*. 7 vols. Dublin, 1882–1891.

Gottfried, R. B. *A Vewe of the Presente State of Ireland*. Yale University, unpublished Ph.D. thesis, 1935.

————. "Spenser's Ireland Dialogue." *Times Literary Supplement*, 35 (February 8, 1936), 116.

————. "Spenser and Stanyhurst." *Times Literary Supplement*, 35 (October 31, 1936), 887.

————. "The Date of Spenser's *View*." *Modern Language Notes*, 52 (1937), 176–80.

————. "Spenser as an Historian in Prose." *Transactions of the Wisconsin Academy of Sciences, Arts, and Letters*, 30 (1937), 317–29.

————. "Spenser's *View* and Essex." *PMLA*, 52 (1937), 645–51.

————. "The Debt of Fynes Moryson to Spenser's *View*." *Philological Quarterly*, 17 (1938), 297–307.

————. "Irish Geography in Spenser's *View*." *English Literary History*, 6 (1939), 114–37.

————. ed. *A Historie of Ireland (1571) by Edmund Campion*. New York: Scholars' Facsimiles and Reprints, 1940.

————. "The Early Development of the Section on Ireland in Camden's *Britannia*." *English Literary History*, 10 (1943), 17–30.

————. ed. *The Works of Edmund Spenser: A Variorum Edition*, 11 vols. Baltimore: Johns Hopkins University Press, 1932–1949, 9, *The Prose Works*, 1949.

Graham, Rigby. *Edmund Spenser's Kilcolman*. Leicester: Brewhouse Private Press, 1975.

Gray, M. M. "The Influence of Spenser's Irish Experience on The Faerie Queene." *Review of English Studies*, 6 (1930), 413–28.

Greenblatt, Stephen J. "To Fashion a Gentleman: Spenser and the Destruction of the Bower of Bliss," in *Renaissance Self-Fashioning: From More to Shakespeare*. Chicago: University of Chicago Press, 1980, pp. 157–92.

Greenlaw, E. A. "Spenser and the Earl of Leicester." *PMLA*, 25 (1910), 535–61.

———. "Spenser and British Imperialism." *Modern Philology*, 9 (1912), 1–24.

———. Review of Pauline Henley, *Spenser in Ireland*. *Modern Language Notes*, 45 (1930), 320–323.

Grennan, Eamonn. "Language and Politics: A Note on Some Metaphors in Spenser's *A View of the Present State of Ireland*." *Spenser Studies*, 3 (1982), 99–110.

Gross, Kenneth. "Mythmaking in Hibernia (*A View of the Present State of Ireland*)," in *Spenserian Poetics: Idolatry, Iconoclasm, and Magic*. Ithaca, N.Y. and London: Cornell University Press, 1985, pp. 78–109.

Guiney, L. I. "Sir Walter Raleigh of Youghal in the County of Cork." *Atlantic Monthly*, 66 (1890), 779–86.

Hadfield, Andrew. *The English View of Ireland c. 1540–c. 1600, with special reference to the Works of Edmund Spenser*. New University of Ulster at Coleraine, unpublished Ph.D. thesis, 1988.

———. "The Spectre of Positivism?: Sixteenth-Century Irish Historiography." *Text and Context*, 3 (1988), 10–16.

———. "Spenser's *A View of the Present State of Ireland*: Some Notes Towards a Materialist Analysis of Discourse," in *Anglo-Irish and Irish Literature: Aspects of Language and Culture*. 2 vols., eds. B. Bramsback and M. Croghan. Stockholm: Uppsala, 1988, 2, pp. 265–72.

Hadsor, Richard. "Discourse of Ireland." *Ulster Journal of Archaeology*, 2 (1854), 245–53.

Harington, John. "A Short View of the State of Ireland in 1605." Ed. by W. D. Macray, *Anecdota Bodleiana*, 1, Oxford, 1879.

Heffner, Ray. "Spenser's Acquisition of Kilcolman." *Modern Language Notes*, 46 (1931), 493–98.

———. "Essex and Book Five of *The Faerie Queene*." *English Literary History*, 3 (1936), 67–82.

————. Review of W. L. Renwick's edition of *A View of the Present State of Ireland* (London, 1934). *Modern Language Notes*, 52 (1937), 1, 57–58.

————. "Spenser's View of Ireland: Some Observations." *Modern Language Quarterly*, 3 (1942), 507–15.

Henley, Pauline. *Spenser in Ireland* Cork: Cork University Press, 1928.

————. "Spenser's 'Stony Aubrian'." *Times Literary Supplement*, 35 (November 28, 1936), 996.

Hennessey, J. P. "Sir Walter Raleigh in Ireland." *Nineteenth Century*, 10 (1881), 660–82.

————. *Sir Walter Raleigh in Ireland*. London, 1883.

Henry, L. W. "Contemporary sources for Essex's Lieutenancy in Ireland, 1599." *Irish Historical Studies*, 11 (1958), 8–17.

Hill, Christopher. "Seventeenth-century English Radicals and Ireland," in *Radicals, Rebels and Establishments*, ed. Patrick J. Corish. *Historical Studies*, 15 (1985), Belfast, pp. 33–49.

Hinton, Edward M. *Ireland Through Tudor Eyes*. Philadelphia: University of Pennsylvania Press, 1935.

————. ed. "Rych's *Anothomy of Ireland*, with an account of the author." *PMLA*, 55 (1940), 74–101.

Hogan, E., ed. *The Description of Ireland, and the state thereof as it is at this present in anno 1598*. Dublin, 1878.

————. ed. "Haynes' 'Observations of the State of Ireland in 1600.'" *Irish Ecclesiastical Record*, 8 (1887), 1112–1122; 9 (1888), 54–66, 160–74.

————. "The Blessed Edmund Campion's *History of Ireland* and its Critics," *The Irish Ecclesiastical Record*, 12 (1891), 629–41, 725–35.

Hogan, James. "Shane O'Neill comes to the Court of Elizabeth," in *Feil-scribhinn Torna: Essays and studies Presented to Professor Tadhg ua Donnchadha on the Occasion of His Seventieth Birthday*, ed. S. Pender. Cork: Cork University Press, 1947, pp. 154–70.

————. and N. M. O'Farrell, eds. *The Walsingham Letter-book or Register of Ireland, May, 1578 to December, 1579*. Dublin: Irish Manuscripts Commission, 1959.

Hore, Henry F., ed. "The Description and Present State of Ulster, 20 Dec. 1586, by Marshal Henry Bagenal." *Ulster Journal of Archaeology*, 2 (1854), 137–60.

————. ed "Sir Henry Sidney's Memoir of his Government of Ireland, 1583." *Ulster Journal of Archaeology*, 3 (1856), 33–52, 85–109, 336–57; 5 (1857), 299–323; 8 (1860), 179–95.

————. "Woods and Fastnesses in Ancient Ireland." *Ulster Journal of Archaeology*, 6 (1858), 145–61.

————. and J. Graves. *The Social State of the Southern and Eastern Counties of Ireland in the Sixteenth Century*. Dublin, 1870.

Hughes, C., ed. *Shakespeare's Europe: Unpublished Chapters of Fynes Moryson's Itinerary*. London, 1903.

Hulbert, Viola B. "Spenser's Relation to Certain Documents on Ireland." *Modern Philology*, 34 (1937), 345–53.

Hull, V. "Edmund Spenser's Mona-Shul." *PMLA*, 56 (1941), 578–79.

Jardine, Lisa. "Mastering the Uncouth: Gabriel Harvey, Edmund Spenser and the English experience in Ireland," in New Perspectives in Renaissance Thought: *Essays in Honour of Charles B. Schmitt*, eds. J. Henry and S. Hutton. London: Duckworth, 1990, pp. 68–82.

Jenkins, Raymond. "Spenser and the Clerkship in Munster." *PMLA*, 47 (1932), 109–121.

————. "Spenser's Hand." *Times Literary Supplement*, 31 (7 January, 1932), 12.

————. "Spenser at Smerwick." *Times Literary Supplement*, 32 (May 11, 1933), 331.

————. "Newes out of Munster, a document in Spenser's Hand." *Studies in Philology*, 32 (1935), 125–30.

————. "Spenser with Lord Grey in Ireland." *PMLA*, 52 (1937), 338–53.

————. "Spenser: The Uncertain Years 1584–1589." *PMLA*, 53 (1938), 350–62.

————. "Spenser and Ireland," in *That Soveraine Light: Essays in Honor of Edmund Spenser 1552–1952*, eds. W. R. Meuller and D. C. Allen. Baltimore: Johns Hopkins University Press, 1952, pp. 51–62.

Jones, H. S. V. "Spenser's Defense of Lord Grey." *University of Illinois Studies in Language and Literature*, 5 (1919), 7–75.

————. "A View of the Present State Of Ireland," in *A Spenser Handbook*. New York: Cornell University Press, 1930, pp. 377–87.

Jones, W. "Doneraile and Vicinity." *Journal of the Cork Historical and Archaeological Society*, 7 (1901), 238–42.

Joyce, P. W. "Spenser's Irish Rivers," in *The Wonders of Ireland*, Dublin, 1911, pp. 72–114.

Judson, Alexander C. *Spenser in Southern Ireland*. Bloomington, Ind.: Indiana University Press, 1933.

———. "Two Spenser Leases." *Modern Language Quarterly*, 50 (1944), 143–147.

———. *The Works of Edmund Spenser: A Variorum Edition*, 9 vols. Baltimore, 1932–49, 11, *The Life of Edmund Spenser*, 1945.

———. "Spenser and the Munster Officials", *Studies in Philology*, 44 (1947), 157–73.

Keightley, T. "Irish Rivers Named in *The Faerie Queene.*" *Notes and Queries*, 4 (August 28, 1869), 169–70.

Kliger, S. "Spenser's Irish Tract and Tribal Democracy." *South Atlantic Quarterly*, 49 (1950), 490–97.

Koller, K. "Spenser and Raleigh." *English Literary History*, 1 (1934), 37–60.

Lennon, Colm. *Richard Stanyhurst: The Dubliner, 1547–1618*. Dublin: Irish Academic Press, 1981.

Lewis, C. S. "Spenser's Irish Experiences and *The Faerie Queene.*" *Review of English Studies*, 7 (1931), 83–85.

Lupton, Julia. "Home-making in Ireland: Virgil's Eclogue I and Book VI of *The Faerie Queene*," *Spenser Studies*, 8 (1987), 119–45.

Laysaght, S. "Kilcolman Castle." *The Antiquary*, 5 (1882), 153–56.

McCabe, Richard A. "The Fate of Irena: Spenser and Political Violence," in *Spenser and Ireland: An Interdisciplinary Perpsective*, ed. P. Coughlan. Cork: Cork University Press, 1989, pp. 109–125.

MacCaffrey, W. T. *Queen Elizabeth and the Making of Policy, 1572–1588*. Princeton, N.J.: Princeton University Press, 1981.

MacCarthy-Morrogh, Michael. *The Munster Plantation: English Migration to Southern Ireland, 1583–1641*. Oxford: Clarendon Press, 1986.

McClintock, H. F. "A Sixteenth Century Dutch 'Account of Ireland'." *Journal of the Royal Society of Antiquaries of Ireland*, 9 (1939), 223–25.

McCracken, E. "The Woodlands of Ireland circa 1600." *Irish Historical Studies*, 11 (1959), 271–96.

McGuire, James K. *Spenser's View of Ireland and Sixteenth Century Gaelic Civilization*. Fordham University, unpublished Ph.D. thesis, 1958.

McLane, Paul E. "Was Spenser in Ireland in Early November 1579?" *Notes and Queries*, 204 (1959), 99–101.

McLean, George E. *Spenser's Territorial History: Book V of the Faerie Queene and A View of the Present State of Ireland.* The University of Arizona, unpublished Ph.D. thesis, 1986.

Mac Lir, M. "Spenser as High Sheriff of Cork County." *Journal of the Cork Historical and Archaeological Society*, 7 (1901), 249–50.

McNeill, C., ed. "Lord Chancellor Gerrard's 'Notes on Ireland' (1577–8)." *Analecta Hibernica*, 2 (1931), 93–291.

Macray, W. D., ed. *A Short View of the State of Ireland Written in 1605, by J. Harington. Anacdota Bodleiana*, 1, Oxford, 1879.

Magill, Andrew J. *Spenser and Ireland: A Synthesis and Revaluation of Twentieth Century Scholarship.* University of Texas at Austin, unpublished Ph.D. thesis, 1967.

Maley, W. T. *Edmund Spenser and Cultural Identity in Early Modern Ireland.* University of Cambridge, unpublished Ph.D. thesis, 1989.

————. *A Spenser Chronology.* London: Macmillan, forthcoming.

————. ed. *The Supplication of the blood of the English, most lamentably murdered in Ireland, Cryeng out of the yearth for revenge. c. 1598. Analecta Hibernica*, forthcoming.

Marjarum, E. W. "Wordsworth's View of the State of Ireland." *PMLA*, 55 (1940), 608–11.

Martin, W. C. *Edmund Spenser, "A View of the Present State of Ireland": An Annotated Edition.* Cornell University, unpublished Ph.D. thesis, 1925.

————. "The Date and Purpose of Spenser's *Veue*." *PMLA*, 47 (1932), 137–43.

Maxwell, Constantia. *Irish History from Contemporary Sources (1509–1610).* London, 1923.

————. "Edmund Spenser: The Poet in Exile (1580–1598)," *The Stranger in Ireland: From the Reign of Elizabeth to the Great Famine.* London: Jonathan Cape, 1954, pp. 20–37.

"Memorials of Edmund Spenser, the Poet, and his Descendants in the County Cork, from the Public Records of Ireland." *Journal of the Cork Historical and Archaelogical Society*, 14 (1908), 39–43.

Meyer, Sam. *An Interpretation of Edmund Spenser's 'Colin Clout.'* Cork: Cork University Press, 1969.

Michie, Sara. *Celtic Myth and Spenserian Romance.* University of Virginia, unpublished Ph.D. thesis, 1935.

Miller, L., and E. Power, eds. *Holinshed's Irish Chronicle.* North America: Academic Press, 1979.

Moore, C. "Spenser's Knowledge of the Neighbourhood of Mitchelstown." *Journal of the Cork Historical and Archaeological Society,* 10 (1904), 31–33.

————. "The Bregoge." *Journal of the Cork Historical and Archaeological Society,* 19 (1913), 40–42.

Moore, Marianne. "Spenser's Ireland," in *The Complete Poems of Marianne Moore.* New York, 1981, pp. 112–13.

Morgan, Hiram. "The Colonial Venture of Sir Thomas Smith in Ulster, 1571–5." *Historical Journal,* 28 (1985), 261–78.

Morley, Henry, ed. *Ireland under Elizabeth and James I, described by Edmund Spenser, by Sir John Davies . . . and by Fynes Moryson.* London, 1890.

Morton, Grenfell. *Elizabethan Ireland.* London: Longman, 1971.

Moryson, Fynes. *An Itinerary.* London, 1617.

M. R. S. A. "Sir Walter Raleigh's House at Youghal." *Journal of the Cork Historical and Archaeological Society,* 1 (1892), 129–30.

O'Brien, George, ed. *Advertisements for Ireland: Being a Description of the State of Ireland in the reign of James I.* Dublin: The Royal Society of Antiquaries of Ireland, 1923.

O'Connor, P. J. "The Munster Plantation Era: Rebellion, Survey and Land Transfer in North County Kerry." *Journal of the Kerry Archaeological and Historical Society,* 15 (1982), 15–36.

O'Donovan, J., ed. *Annals of the Kingdom of Ireland, by the Four Masters, from the earliest period to the year 1616.* 6 vols. Dublin, 1851.

————. "Errors of Edmund Spenser: Irish Surnames." *Ulster Journal of Archaeology,* 6 (1858), 135–44.

O'Grady, S., ed. *Pacata Hibernia, by T. Stafford, London 1633.* 2 vols. London, 1896.

O'Laidhin, T., ed. *Sidney State Papers, 1565–70.* Dublin: Irish Manuscripts Commission, 1962.

O'Mahoney, J., ed. *The History of Ireland, by Geoffrey Keating.* New York, 1886.

Ong, W. J. "Spenser's View and the Tradition of the 'Wild' Irish." *Modern Language Quarterly,* 3 (1942), 561–71.

O'Rahilly, T. A. "Identification of the Hitherto Unknown River 'Aubrian', of Spenser Fame." *Journal of the Cork Historical and Archaeological Society,* 22 (1916), 49–56.

O'Sullivan, M. D. "Barnabe Googe: Provost-Marshal of Connaught, 1582–1585." *Journal of the Galway Archaeological and Historical Society,* 18 (1938), 1–39.

Pafford, J. H. P., ed. *Lodowick Bryskett: Literary Works.* Farnborough, Hants: Gregg Internationl, 1972.

"Pedigree of the Poet Spencer's Family." *Journal of the Cork Historical and Archaeological Society,* 12 (1906), facing page 197.

Pinkerton, W. "Barnaby Googe." *Notes and Queries,* 3 (1883), 141–43, 181–84, 301–302, 361–62.

Plomer, H. R. "Edmund Spenser's Handwriting." *Modern Philology,* 21 (1923), 201–207.

————. and T. P. Cross, eds. *The Life and Correspondence of Lodowick Bryskett.* Chicago: University of Chicago Press, 1927.

Pollen, J. H. "The Irish Expedition of 1579." *The Month,* 101 (1903), 69–85.

The Present State of Ireland Together with Some Remarks upon the Ancient State Thereof. London, 1673.

Quinn, D. B. "'A Discourse of Ireland' (*Circa* 1599): A Sidelight on English Colonial Policy." *Proceedings of the Royal Irish Academy,* 47 (1942), 151–66.

————. "Sir Thomas Smith (1513–1577) and the Beginnings of English Colonial Theory." *Proceedings of the American Philosophical Society,* 89 (1945), 543–60.

————. "Edward Walshe's 'Conjectures' Concerning the State of Ireland." *Irish Historical Studies,* 5 (1947), 303–322.

————. *The Elizabethans and the Irish.* Ithaca, N.Y.: Cornell University Press, 1966.

————. "The Munster Plantation: Problems and Opportunities." *Journal of the Cork Historical and Archaeological Society,* 71 (1966), 19–40.

Renwick, W. L. "Spenser's Galathea and Naera." *Times Literary Supplement,* 28 (March 14, 1929), 206–207.

————. ed. *A View of the Present State of Ireland, by Edmund Spenser,* London: Scholartis Press, 1934.

————. ed. *A View of the Present State of Ireland, by Edmund Spenser.* Oxford: Clarendon Press, 1970.

Rich, Barnaby. *A Right Exelent and pleasaunt Dialogue, betwene Mercury and an English Souldier: Contayning his Supplication to Mars: Bewtified with sundry worthy Histories, rare inventions and politike devises.* London, 1574.

———— *Allarme to England, foreshewing what perilles are procured, where the people live without regarde of Martiall lawe*. London, 1578.

————. "A lookynge [-Glase] for hyr Ma^{ti} wherein to veue Ireland, *c.* 1599." London: *Public Record Office*. State Papers, Ireland, 63/205/72, ff. 169–179.

————. *A Short Survey of Ireland*. London, 1609.

————. *A New Description of Ireland*. London, 1610.

The Irish Hubbub or, The English Hue and Crie. London, 1617.

Scott, H. S., ed. *The Journal of Sir Roger Wilbraham, Solicitor-General in Ireland and Master of Requests, for the years 1593–1616*. London: Royal Historical Society, 1902.

Sheehan, Anthony J. "The Overthrow of the Plantation of Munster in October 1598." *The Irish Sword*, 15 (1982), 11–22.

Shepherd, Simon. *Spenser*. New York and London: Harvester Wheatsheaf, 1989.

Smith, A., ed. *A Brife Description of Ireland. Made in this yeere, 1589, by Robert Payne, Tracts Relating to Ireland, Irish Archaeological Society*, 1 (1841), Dublin, pp. 1–14.

Smith, Roland M. "Spenser's Irish River Stories." *PMLA*, 50 (1935), 4, 1047–1056.

————. "Una and Duessa", *PMLA*, 50 (1935), 917–19.

————. "Spenser's Tale of the Two Sons of Milesio." *Modern Language Quarterly*, 3 (1942), 547–57.

————. "The Irish Background of Spenser's *View*." *Journal of English and Germanic Philology*, 42 (1943), 499–515.

————. "More Irish Words in Spenser." *Modern Language Notes*, 59 (1944), 472–77.

————. "Spenser, Holinshed, and the *Leabhar Gabhala*." *Journal of English and Germanic Philology*, 43 (1944), 390–401.

————. "Spenser's 'Stony Aubrian'." *Modern Language Notes*, 59 (1944), 1–5.

————. "A further note on Una and Duessa." *PMLA*, 61 (1946), 592–96.

————. "Irish Names in *The Faerie Queene*." *Modern Language Notes*, 61 (1946), 27–38.

————. Review of R. B. Gottfried's edition of *The Prose Works of Edmund Spenser* (Baltimore: Johns Hopkins University Press, 1949). *Journal of English and Germanic Philology*, 49 (1950), 405–416.

————. "Origines Arthurianae: The Two Crosses of Spenser's Red Cross Knight." *Journal of English and Germanic Philology*, 54 (1955), 670–83.

————. "Spenser's Scholarly Script and 'Right Writing'," in *Studies in Honor of T. W. Baldwin*, ed. D. C. Allen. Urbana, Ill.: University of Illinois Press, 1958, pp. 66–111.

Snyder, Edward D. "The Wild Irish: A Study of Some English Satires Against the Irish, Scots, and Welsh." *Modern Philology* 17 (1920), 687–725.

"Spenser in Ireland: Review of Pauline Henley, *Spenser in Ireland* (Cork: Cork University Press, 1928)." *Times Literary Supplement*, 27 (7 June, 1928), 422.

Spenser, Edmund. *A View of the State of Ireland as it was in the reign of Queen Elizabeth. Written by way of a Dialogue between Eudoxus and Ireneus: To which is prefix'd the Author's Life, and an Index added to the Work.* Dublin, 1763.

————. *A View of the Present State of Ireland*, in *Ancient Irish Histories*, ed. J. Ware. 2 vols., Dublin, 1809, 1, pp. 1–266.

————. *A View of the Present State of Ireland*, in *Ireland under Elizabeth and James I, described by Edmund Spenser, by Sir John Davies . . . and by Fynes Moryson*, ed. H. Morley. London, 1890.

————. *A View of the Present State of Ireland*, ed. W. L. Renwick. London: Scholartis Press, 1934.

————. *A View of the Present State of Ireland*, Oxford, 1970.

Steinberg, Clarence. "Atin, Pyrochles, Cymochles: On Irish Emblems in *The Faerie Queene*." *Neuphilologische Mitteilungen*, 72 (1971), 749–61.

A View of the present state of Ireland, with an account of the origin and progress of the disturbances in that Country. By an Observer. 2nd ed. London, 1797.

A View of the Present State of Affairs in the Kingdom of Ireland; in three discourses, viz. 1. A list [by T. Prior] *of the Absentees of Ireland. 2. The Present State of Ireland Consider'd. 3. A modest proposal for preventing the children of Ireland from being a burden to their parents or the country. By Dr Swift.* London, 1730.

Walsh, Peter. *A Prospect of the State of Ireland, from the year of the world 1750, to the year of Christ 1652.* London, 1682.

"War-Cries of Irish Septs." *Ulster Journal of Archaeology*, 3 (1856), 203–212.

Ware, James, ed. *Two Histories of Ireland.* Dublin, 1633.

Watanabe-O'Kelly, Helen. "Edmund Spenser and Ireland: A Defence." *Poetry Nation Review*, 6 (1980), 16–19.

Welply, W. H. "Spenser in Ireland." *Times Literary Supplement*, 32 (18 May, 1933), 348.

————, "Edmund Spenser's Brother-in-law, John Travers." *Notes and Queries*, 179 (1940), 70–78, 92–97, 112–15.

White, J. G. *Historical and Topographical Notes on Buttevant, Castletownroche, Doneraile, Mallow, and Places in Their Vicinity*. 4 vols., Cork, 1905–1916.

Wilson, F. P. "Spenser and Ireland." *Review of English Studies*, 2 (1926), 456–57.

Wood, H., ed. *The Chronicle of Ireland, 1584–1608, by J. Perrot.* Dublin: Irish Manuscripts Commission, 1933.

Yeats, W. B. "Edmund Spenser," In *Essays and Introductions*, London, 1961, pp. 356–83.

University of Strathclyde

FORUM

Arthur's Deliverance of Rome?
(Yet Again)

[The Forum Section of *Spenser Studies* VIII reproduces (335–347) A. Kent Hieatt's paper (summarized) on the projected continuation of *The Faerie Queene*, and Thomas P. Roche, Jr.'s response to it, at the 1988 International Congress on Medieval Studies, Kalamazoo. Space was lacking for Hieatt's later rejoinder, which now appears below in amended form.]

*H*OW GRATIFYING that Tom Roche and I chose the same path at the parting of the way and stepped off arm-in-arm: we agree that at some point Spenser thought of crowning his Arthur's career with a heroic poem on the deliverance of Rome.

But we straggle apart at the next intersection. Roche says: the real engine driving Spenser here is not Malory, who did not and could not make much of Arthur's achievement, because, living before the Reformation, Malory could not see the achievement as the defeat of the Antichrist. The driving force for Spenser was the allegorical meaning of the conquest of Jerusalem in *Gerusalemme liberata*: the defeat of the Antichrist so as to attain the Heavenly Jerusalem;[1] and for protestant Spenser the Antichrist was Roman Catholicism, not Islam.

Note that Roche says "Malory" here, and forgets Hardyng. In exactly the same pre-Reformation situation that Roche emphasizes in the case of Malory, Hardyng *did* make a great deal of Arthur's achievement. What the scores of inventors of British history say, from Geoffrey of Monmouth in the twelfth century up to Hardyng, and on into the sixteenth-century chronicles (and Spenser knew a printed version of Geoffrey as well as he did of Hardyng, and knew several sixteenth-century chronicles), is that Arthur's final and greatest achievement was the defeat of the Romans in battle, after which he was betrayed by Mordred and lost all in the internecine strife of his passing. Hardyng's only difference from the others is to complete the defeat of the Romans by Arthur's actual conquest of Rome. Of course this

243

remains Arthur's greatest achievement. One way of assessing the weight that the "British historians" assigned to this invented accomplishment is to say that they were anxious above all to give Britain an imperial past measuring up to the actual ones of their early Roman conquerors and of Charlemagne's exemplary revanche upon Rome. When they date Arthur's coronation in Rome, they place it about 250 years before Charlemagne's actual coronation there in 800. Malory got from somewhere the added touch that, like Charlemagne, Arthur was crowned there on Christmas Day.

The reason that Malory alone, unlike all the other inventors of British history, could not, as Roche says, make much of Arthur's defeat of the Romans has nothing to do with Malory's lack of Protestant fervor (which I never tried to dower him with, in spite of all the paganism that he imputes to the enemies of the British, as in all other medieval heroic accounts on a Christian base). *Like* us Spenserians, Malory wanted to be encyclopedic, and to include not only British history but also all the romance material and decay of the Round Table which were really his chief interests—Lancelot, the Grail, and all that. *Unlike* every other author of British history, including the twelfth-, fifteenth-, and sixteenth-century ones that Spenser had read, he left the affair of the Romans dangling in mid-air and put off Mordred's final betrayal and Arthur's consequent abandonment of a project across the Channel (warring on Lancelot in this case) so as to devote most of his book to romance and the descending arc of that decay.

It seems to me wrong-headed to play down Spenser's share of the imperial side of "British history" and to play up his participation in Protestant fervor against papistry. Surely Spenser was animated by both—the Renaissance dream of the imperial nation-state, and Protestant activism, shared by Sidney, Leicester, Walsingham, and Essex. The automatic rejection of the sweet fruition of an earthly crown as the motivation for anything important whatsoever runs into trouble here.

Now for the second of our partings of the way. Did the whole idea of a heroic sequel to *The Faerie Queene* evaporate with the death of Leicester in 1588, as Roche suggests, because there was no longer an unmarried candidate for Elizabeth's hand? Is the allusion to Arthur's death the quietus of both Leicester and any previously contemplated continuation of *The Faerie Queen*?

But *Leicester himself* was married! *If an unmarried candidate was literally the* sine qua non, *then the whole idea of a heroic sequel would have become infeasible, not first in 1588, when Leicester died, but beginning in 1576, when Leicester got married.* In the literal sense Roche intends, that is, Spenser would have been deprived of the possibility of celebrating not only Essex but also Leicester as Arthur, spouse of Elizabeth the Faery Queene, long before Leicester died and possibly before Spenser had got very far with the idea that eventuated in *Faerie Queene* I–III in 1590, let alone a post-twelve book continuation. Leicester had secretly married Lettice (Knollys) Devereux, Countess of Essex, almost as soon as her husband died in 1576—admittedly something Spenser would have been unlikely to know. In 1578 her father Sir Francis Knollys, an important figure, compelled Leicester to repeat the ceremony before highly placed witnesses, who were, however, still pledged to secrecy. But not strictly enough. Simier learned the secret and told Elizabeth in 1579. She imprisoned Leicester briefly but was dissuaded from putting him in the Tower, or worse. He was released, and regained influence. Thereafter there was no reason to keep the marriage secret. The gaff was blown. The Knollys faction had every reason to spread the word. Leicester is on record as having bestowed an elaborate New Year's gift on his step-son (who was of course Essex, thus cozily related, in addition to his other family-ties mentioned by Roche). (And see the *DNB* article on Leicester for more such public acts relating to his marriage.)

It's true that later on, as Roche says, Spenser knew that the married Essex could not literally have espoused Elizabeth as the Faery Queen; but as early as 1579 the upwardly mobile twenty-five-year-old who was subtly self-fashioning himself into Our New Poet, and who recognized that his patron Leicester was still a royal favorite, would have accurately perceived that Leicester was barred from marrying Elizabeth in exactly the same way as Essex was later on.

So that Leicester's death in 1588 would have entailed no dramatic disappointment of Spenser's hopes for a sequel to *The Faerie Queene*. Some kind of initial disappointment far earlier seems likely indeed. (I agree with Roche that some initial plan probably got aborted.) If, however, the disappointment had entailed the rejection of the idea of a sequel, then Spenser would not have raised this idea in his 1590 letter.

Incidentally, Roche's notion of a threnody for Leicester's death in the prolepsis of Arthur's death in I. vii.36 is beautiful but strikes me as not cohering with what Roche and I now seem to agree on: the mention in II.x.49, published at the same time, of Arthur's subsequent climactic accomplishment. Spenser is more likely imagining that it was not until *after* Arthur's full victory (perhaps just after) that he died. So did the traditional British Arthur, after his partial victory. After all, Arthur's other self, Artegall, is also to die early, by treachery, and to be survived by his mate. It is an attractive mythic pattern that Britain's antique heroes should have achieved the goal only momentarily but would return as the Tudors after an aeon, so as to attain it sempiternally.

So far, however, Roche's (and my) main problem here has been only stated, not solved. How could the Arthur of a sequel to *The Faerie Queene* be said to marry the Faery Queen when both Leicester and Essex, the only two contemporary figures who would have suited in terms of projected allegory and patronage, were married to others?

Symbolic flexibility is an interesting feature of eulogy. When, for instance, Shakespeare needed to say that the childless Elizabeth I was the parent of her successor James I, who continued the line as she had continued it from her father, he clothed the facts suitably: "as when / The bird of wonder dies, the maiden phoenix, / Her ashes new create another heir / . . . Who from the sacred ashes of her honor / Shall star-like rise . . ." (*Henry VIII* V.iv.40–46). Spenser could easily have formulated a politic Arthur institutionally mated to the Faery Queen without benefit of clergy—heroic love in suprasensual friendship—as for instance in the form proposed[2] to cover the mention of Essex in connection with the "Brydale day" in *Prothalamion* 157–61 (Accession Day, Elizabeth as the virgin bride of England, Arthur as England, etc., summarized in *Variorum* VIII, 503). There are perhaps simpler ways to achieve the same end. The poet who explained Ralegh's enduring love-match with Elizabeth Throgmorton as an enduring amorous devotion to the queen (*Faerie Queene* IV.vii.35–viii.18), and who in *Astrophel* confused Stella with Sidney's wife, Frances Walsingham, could have managed it all with one hand tied behind his back.

That in 1590 Spenser was thinking of Essex as the right Arthur for Roman conquest in a sequel seems to me to cohere with the dedicatory sonnet to him in *Faerie Queene* I–III (*Variorum* III,

192). Uniquely in that collection of sonnets Essex is said to possess magnificence: "Magnificke Lord, whose vertues execllent. . . ." Compare the "Letter of the Authors" first published in the same volume: "So in the person of prince Arthure I sette forth magnificence in particular, which virtue . . . is the perfection of all the rest. . . ." Another feature of the sonnet to Essex, which is unique among the dedicatory ones, is that Spenser promises him, *later*, more significant celebration, "when my Muse, whose fethers nothing flitt / Doe yet but flagg, and lowly learne to fly / With bolder wing shall dare aloft to sty / To the last praises of this Faery Queene, / Then shall it make more famous memory / Of thine Heroicke parts. . . ." How much later? I think Spenser means the kind of poetry that he would have attempted in his sequel, a kind which he describes in *Faerie Queene* I.xi.vi.

Surprisingly there is evidence that Spenser was still thinking this way in 1596, although he may have been doing no more than whistling in the dark or trying to keep Essex happy. It is as though he could not give up the idea of the loftier Ariostan and (much more) Tassonian kind of "politic" poem, with armies locked in battle over the fates of nations, as described in the stanza in 1590. It is only with such an epic that he, and English letters, could have cut a figure on the European scene. In *Prothalamion* of 1596 he directly addresses Essex (who with others had temporarily captured Cadiz) and the tone is much the same, down to a supposititious, only symbolic bridal day: "through thy prowesse and victorious armes, / Thy country may be freed from forraine harmes: / And great *Elisaes* glorious name may ring / Through al the world, fil'd with thy wide Alarmes, / Which some braue muse may sing / To ages following, / Upon the Brydale day, which is not long: / Sweete *Themmes* runne softly, till I end my Song." Spenser leaves in suspense whether it is his own song in the refrain which, before long, that brave muse may sing.

What really happened before long was that the poet and the Arthur whom I am promoting here and Gloriana were all dead. What I attempted in my original article—the promotion, in Shakespeare's *Cymbeline*, of the *Kimbeline* of lines immediately following "Till *Arthur* all that reckoning defrayed" to an adversarial, anti-imperialistic, Jacobean relationship to Spenser's imperialistic Elizabethan Arthur—is both corrected and complemented (without their realizing it) by Patricia Parker's

"Romance and Empire: Anachronistic *Cymbeline*"[3] and an article by Emrys Jones cited there.[4]

Let me not be curmudgeonly. As to Roche's send-off, I have rapped my own head for not seeing earlier the main point discussed here. Carrie Harper and the *Variorum* editors should have picked up Marie Walther's point, but *de mortuis*. New annotations in Bert Hamilton's and Tom Roche's fine editions zero in on later work and could not be expected to have picked up this.

(Having said that, maybe I can afford one Parthian shot. I've always had trouble with Frye's assignment of private virtues to I–III [only for individuals] and political ones to IV–VI [at least one other participant]. Holiness [I] teaches me to love God with all my heart and to love my neighbor [two other participants] as myself. Most of Spenser's temperance [II] also requires parties of the second part. Chastity [III] includes one person's unchanging love for another participant. Real *Polliticke* virtue (cf. the Letter), on the other hand, is the virtue of "a good gouernor," or of Arthur "after that hee came to be king.")

A. Kent Hieatt
University of Western Ontario

NOTES

1. On the allegory in *GL* the following is penetrating: David Quint, "Political Allegory in the *Gerusalemme Liberata*," *RenQ*, 43 (Spring 1990), 1–29.
2. Dan S. Norton, "Queen Elizabeth's 'Brydal Day'." *MLQ*, 5 (1944), 149–54.
3. In *Unfolded Tales: Essays on Renaissance Romance*, ed. George M. Logan and Gordon Teskey (Ithaca: Cornell University Press, 1989), pp. 189–207.
4. "Stuart Cymbeline," *Essays in Criticism*, 11 (1958), 84–89.

GLEANINGS

The Illustrations to
The Shepheardes Calender: II

"Perhaps the mystery is a little *too* plain," said Dupin . . . "A little too self-evident."

Edgar Allan Poe, "The Purloined Letter"

THE MOST obvious element, the self-evident one, in each of the twelve illustrations to *The Shepheardes Calender* is the inset of the zodiac figure in a wreath of clouds. Although the only mystery concerning them noticed by modern scholars has been the discrepancy between figure and text in "November,"[1] the question for the contemporary reader must have been what they were doing there at all. As identificatory signs for exclusive use in calendars they would have seemed completely out of place in illustrations to a book of new poetry.

Because identificatory images never jumped genres, their presence represents a break with the conventions for book illustrations.[2] Broadly speaking, we may distinguish three kinds of illustrations for the Tudor period: the specific, the general, and the identificatory. The specific kind depicts part of the text, as we see in the major portions of the *Calender*'s cuts. The general kind, ordinarily on the title-page, functions to sort texts: a ship may be used to indicate a text on navigation, or travel, or personal adventure but it will not appear, for instance, in a romance; a plant may indicate a gardening book or it may be a decoration, but it will not indicate a text on navigation. The identificatory kind does more than sort, it is unique to the genre or book and does not appear elsewhere.[3]

The zodiac figure in a wreath of clouds was, until its incorporation in the illustrations to Spenser's *Calender*, an identificatory image for the traditional calendar where it appears in series of the Labors of the Months and in certain representations of Zodiac Man (Plates 1 and 2).[4]

In an important way, the Tudor conventions represent the antithesis of what is normal for us. Today we are used to spotting

SEPTEMBRE.

The laſt quar ter the.b.daſ at.ri.of the clocke befoze none,tem, perate with mild and cold windes. The newe Mone the.rii.daye, at.ii.of the clocke.rrr.minutes in the mozning,bery ſeaſonable weather. The.i. quarter the.rir.daye,at.b.a clocke after noone temperate.The ful mone the.rrbii.day, at.bii. of the clocke.rrii.minu.after none, raine wyth thunder,and lightning.

OCTOBER.

The laſt quar ter the.4.day at.bi.of the clock after none,rain e could. The new mone the.ri.day at.iii.of the clock rrrbi.min.after none,rainy wether. The firſt quarter,the.rir.day,at.r.a clocke befoze none, much winde,mired with raine.The full mone the.rrbii.day, at.iiii.a clock,and.rrrii.min.in the mozning,hail,clondes and extreme ceulde.

Nouem-

NOVEMBRE.

The laſt quar ter the.iii.da at.b.a clock in the mozninge,raine, with much turba tiô in thair. The new mone the.r. day,at.iiii.of the clucke.ii.min.in the mozning berye temperate foz the time of the yeare.The firſt quarter the.rbiii.daye, at.bii.a clocke in mozning,rain and cold. The ful mone the.rrb daye,at.b.of the clocke.rii.min. after none,foz the ſeaſon moderate and winedy.

DECEMBRE.

The laſt quar ter the.ii.dai at.ri.of the clock befoze none,rain The newe mons the.ir.daye,at.8. a clocke.rrri.min. after none,colde e rainy. The.i.quarter the.i3 day,at.b.a clock in the mozning,bery teperate as the time ſerueth.The ful mone the.25.daye at.b.a clocke .iii.min.in the mozninge,berye cold,with haile,and darke weather.The laſte quarter the laſt day, at.biii.a clocke at nighte, windy and could.

PLATE 21. Labors of the Months, in William Cunningham, *Almanack*. John Day, 1558.

visual quotations; they form, at this writing in 1990, a necessary part of the paintings of, as examples, Jasper Johns and Rauschenberg and, earlier, of Picasso and Braque. The works of these artists cannot be compared aesthetically with the simple cuts of the *Calender*, but they share one feature. The immediate visual impact of their work is: look at me, I'm new.

The newness matters for our assessment of the young Spenser. No ordinary printer of the time, on his or her own, would have abrogated the contemporary conventions. And Hugh Singleton, the printer of the *Calender*, was less than ordinary—he was floundering. This means that the different designers of the cuts must have received directions to include the particular zodiac figure from someone other than the printer. For the author to have given such directions for illustrations was not uncommon in this period: John Blagrave, John Foxe, Sir John Harington, Conrad Heresbach and, consummately, John Shute, were all involved in, specifically directed, or made the illustrations in their books.[5]

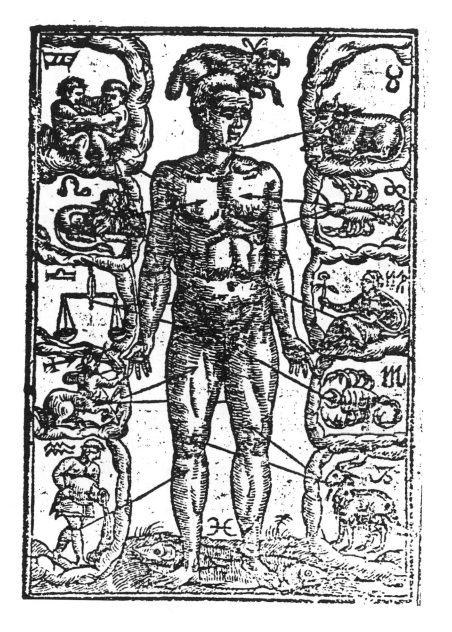

PLATE 22. Zodiac Man in Edward Pond, *Almanack.* for E. White, the assigne of J. Roberts, 1603.

Had the *Calender*'s cuts lived up in execution to the innovations they embody, both the newness and the direction would probably have been noted before now. Had the circumstances been otherwise, had the unknown patron who subsidized the design and making of these blocks given money enough to hire better artists, had the production been consistent, I think the finished illustrations would have substantiated artistically the experiments they incorporate. As it is, when we put the more notable readings in my previous essay together with the assessment given here about the figure of the zodiac in a wreath of clouds, a case for authorial direction is indicated.

Ruth Samson Luborsky[6]
Philadelphia, Pennsylvania

NOTES

1. Discussed in my previous essay on the illustrations in *Spenser Studies*, II, p. 53, n.70.
2. The rules of the game for book illustrations were, of course, uncodified. I've worked them out slowly by observing the players and their results—the printers and their books—during the years spent in documenting later Tudor book illustrations. That documentation will appear in *A Guide to English Illustrated Books: 1536–1603*, by Ruth Samson Luborsky and Elizabeth M. Ingram, forthcoming from Scolar Press. The *Guide* includes 5,060 different images in approximately 1,800 books.
3. Two examples: Identificatory images for Family of Love books include a medallion, an emblem of a heart, and an image of Charitas (Hendrik Niclas, *Comœdia*, 1574. STC 18550). Various versions of schoolboys in an apple tree appear only in William Lily's "Grammar" printed from 1574 through 1599 (STC 15617, 15621.5, 15624).
4. The zodiac figure in a wreath of clouds appears in seven of the nine different series of Labors of the Months in books printed between 1536 and 1603. Twenty-nine individual copies remains today; of these, only eighteen complete examples survive, the rest being fragments. These figures do not reflect the actual number of almanacs with illustrations of the Labors that were printed because the yearly almanac was by definition ephemeral. Three examples of the complete series that most probably first appeared in almanacs exist today in books printed to last—Bibles and psalters.
    Of the 146 illustrated almanacs, 108 contain images of Zodia Man. In at least two of these versions, one signed by the initials C. I., the conventional zodiac figures supposedly controlling the various parts of his body are depicted in a wreath of clouds (Plate 22). (A fragment of an almanac issued by Hugh Singleton in 1552 contains part of an image of Zodiac Man but it does not show zodiac figures in a wreath of clouds [STC 427.7]) ("Zodiac Man" is preferred here to "Anatomical Man.")

5.   In the preliminaries to his book *The mathematicall jewell*, 1585 (STC 3119), John Blagrave writes: "I was forced to cut al the prints my self to my great paines and let of time." The mentions of the illustrations in the text of John Foxe's *Actes and Monuments*, 1563 (STC 11222) reveal collaboration with the printer, John Day, and/or direction by Foxe. Sir John Harington, through his servant Thomas Combe, was involved in the cuts to *The Metamorphosis of Ajax*, 1596 (STC 12779) and *An anatomie of the metamorphosed Ajax*, 1596 (STC 12771.5). In the third part (Book) of his *Foure bookes of husbandry*, 1577 (STC 13196). Conrad Heresbach refers the reader to a picture of a plant "whereof I have here set before you" (R4ᵛ). John Shute, most probably, was responsible for the design and perhaps the making of the four engravings and one woodcut in his *The first and chief groundes of architecture*, 1563 (STC 22464).

6.   The research was supported in part by a grant from the National Endowment for the Humanities, RC-20823-84.

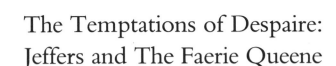

The Temptations of Despaire:
Jeffers and The Faerie Queene

Visitors to Tor House, Robinson Jeffer's home in Carmel, California, are shown the room where Jeffers died in 1962. There docents read his poem, "The Bed by the Window," which begins, "I chose the bed downstairs by the sea-window for a good death-bed / When we built the house . . ." The poem continues, "I often regard it [Death], / With neither dislike nor desire; rather with both, so equalled / That they kill each other and a crystalline interest / Remains alone . . ." On an exposed beam above that bed Jeffers painted, some seventy years ago, lines from Edmund Spenser's poetic allegory, *The Faerie Queene*:

> Sleepe after toyle, port after stormie seas,
> Ease after warre, death after life does greatly please.

Docents and scholars generally see in the inscription Jeffers's stoic acceptance of death. Jeffers's poem, "The Bed by the Window," which appeared in 1932, is often similarly interpreted. But a reading, in context, of the Spenser passage, reveals a deeper ambiguity in Jeffers's attitude towards death.

The lines from Spenser appear in Book I, Canto ix, Stanza 40 of *The Faerie Queene*. In Canto ix, the Redcrosse Knight, accompanied by the Lady Una, encounters Despaire, who attempts to convince him to kill himself. They meet in a cave. At their feet lies the fresh corpse of a fallen knight, a victim of suicide. As part of his discourse, Despaire, in stanza 40, speaks temptingly of death, saying:

> What if some litle paine the passage have,
> That makes fraile flesh to feare the bitter wave?
> Is not short paine well borne, that brings long ease,
> And layes the soule to sleepe in quiet grave?

Despaire concludes with the two lines that appear over Jeffers's bed, "Sleepe after toyle, port after stormie seas, / . . ." etc. The

Redcrosse Knight has met his most formidable foe and is seduced by the argument. Finally Despaire gives Redcrosse the means to kill himself: ". . . Swords, ropes, poison, fire, / . . . But when as none of them he saw him take, / He to him raught a dagger sharpe and keene, / And gave it him in hand . . ." The Redcrosse Knight raises his hand to kill himself. At that moment, Una stays his hand:

> Out of his hand she snatcht the cursed knife,
> And threw it to the ground, enraged rife,
> And to him said, "Fie, fie, faint harted knight,
> What meanest thou by this reprochfull strife?
> . . . . .
> Come, come away, fraile, feeble, fleshly wight,
>   Ne let vaine words bewitch they manly hart,
>   Ne divelish thoughts dismay thy constant spright.
> . . . . .
> Arise, Sir knight arise, and leave this cursed place
>
>   (stanzas 52–53)

Thus, through Una's intervention, the Redcrosse Knight, having overcome the deadliest and most treacherous of his foes, leaves the abode of Despaire and turns his back on suicide.

Certainly Jeffers knew, in context, the lines inscribed above his bed. That his wife bore the same name as Spenser's Lady Una must have given the lines a special significance.

Elsewhere Jeffers recognized the seductiveness of suicide. In his later poem, "The Deer Lay Down Their Bones," written after his wife's death, Jeffers deals explicitly with this attraction. In this poem, the poet finds a sanctuary of death, a place where fatally wounded deer go to die. He is tempted to end his life there.

> But that's a foolish thing to confess and a little cowardly.
>   We know that life
> Is on the whole quite equally good and bad, mostly gray
>   neutral, and can be endured
> To the dim end, no matter what magic of grass, water and
>   precipice, and pain of wounds,
> Makes death look dear.

The poet wonders why he should ". . . wait ten years more or less, / Before I crawl out on a ledge of rock and die snapping, like a wolf / Who has lost his mate?" And then he recalls, "I am bound by my own thirty-year-old decision: who drinks the wine / Should take the dregs . . ." The "thirty-year-old decision," in this context, must have been a conscious choice to renounce suicide. The specific time references in "The Deer Lay Down Their Bones" would indicate that the decision was reached in the early 1920s, a period of personal turmoil and of immense change in Jeffers's poetic style. Jeffers's inscription, on the beam above his chosen death bed, of Despaire's argument for suicide, dates roughly from this period.

Suicide was not uncommon in the social and intellectual milieu Jeffers encountered after his move to Carmel in 1914. Among the California bohemians who frequented Carmel and who killed themselves were Jack London and Carrie Sterling, the wife of the San Francisco poet, George Sterling. Sterling became Jeffers's good friend and one of his earliest and greatest admirers; and in 1926 Sterling, too, committed suicide. As quoted in S. S. Albert's *A Bibliography of the Works of Robinson Jeffers*, the poet describes a dream he had during the night before he learned of Sterling's death. In the dream Jeffers found himself with Sterling in "the interior of an ancient church, a solid place of damp stone about which the earth had crept up." Jeffers writes, "Sterling and I were there in the stone twilight . . . and I said though it was pleasant we mustn't stay, it was time to return out-doors. But he [Sterling] preferred to stay, and I returned alone . . ." The setting of the dream resembles the cave of Despaire in *The Faerie Queene*. As the Redcrosse Knight resisted the temptation of suicide, so Jeffers did not follow his friend into death.

Yet Jeffers was attracted to suicide. The docents of Tor House do well to stress the importance of the lines so carefully painted on the beam above the poet's bed. However, they are no simple expression of the peace that comes after death. Taken within the context of *The Faerie Queene*, the words of Despaire proclaim the debt the poet owed to his wife, Una. They were, as well, a warning for Jeffers against the seductive charm of suicide.

Alex A. Vardanis
University of Vermont

Index

Contents of Previous Volumes

VOLUME III (1982)

VOLUME V (1984)

VOLUME VI (1985)